Kawasaki & 440 Twins Owners Workshop Manual

by Mansur Darlington
with an additional chapter on the 1977 to 1981 models
by Pete Shoemark

Models covered

KZ400. 398cc. UK and US 1974 to 1976	KZ400 H. 398cc. US 1979
KZ400 S. 398cc. US 1975 to 1977	Z400 G. 398cc. UK 1979 to 1980
KZ400 D. 398cc. US 1975 to 1977	KZ440 A. 443cc. US 1980 to 1981
Z400 D. 398cc. UK 1976 to 1979	Z440 A. 443cc. UK 1981
KZ400 B. 398cc. US 1978 to 1979	KZ440 B. 443cc. US 1980 to 1981
Z400 B. 398cc. UK 1978 to 1980	Z440 C. 443cc. UK 1980 to 1981
KZ400 C. 398cc. US 1978	KZ440 D. 443cc. US 1980 to 1981

ISBN 0 85696 711 4

© Haynes Publishing 1997

ABCDE
FGHIJ

2

All rights reserved. No part of this book may be reproduced or transmitted in
any form or by any means, electronic or mechanical, including photocopying,
recording or by any information storage or retrieval system, without permission
in writing from the copyright holder.

Printed in the USA   *(281 - 10W10)*

Haynes Publishing Group
Sparkford Nr Yeovil
Somerset BA22 7JJ England

Haynes Publications, Inc
861 Lawrence Drive
Newbury Park
California 91320 USA

Acknowledgements

The author wishes to thank Kawasaki Motors (UK) Limited for the technical assistance given so freely whilst this manual was being prepared, and for permission to reproduce their drawings. The model used for the photographic sequences was supplied by Davick Motique of Long Eaton Nottinghamshire, who also provided the new parts and gaskets used in the rebuild. The machine shown on the cover was provided by courtesy of Simi Valley Kawasaki Inc, Simi Valley, California. Brian Horsfall assisted with the dismantling and rebuilding of the machine and also devised various ingenious methods for overcoming the lack of service tools. Les Brazier arranged and took all the photographs. The author would also like to thank Jeff Clew for his guidance and editorship.

We would also like to thank the Avon Rubber Company who kindly supplied the illustrations and advice about tyre fitting.

About this manual

The author of this manual has the conviction that the only way in which a meaningful and easy to follow text can be written is to first do the work himself, under conditions similar to those found in the average home. As a result, the hands seen in the photographs are sometimes the hands of the author together with another engineer who assisted. The machine photographed was a used model that had covered three thousand miles, so that the conditions encountered would be similar to those found by the average rider.

Unless specially mentioned, and therefore considered essential, Kawasaki service tools have not been used. There is invariably some alternative means of slackening or removing some vital component when service tools are not available and the risk of damage has to be avoided at all costs.

Each of the six Chapters is divided into numbered Sections. Within the Sections are numbered paragraphs. In consequence, cross reference throughout this manual is both straightforward and logical. When a reference is made 'See Section 1.6' it means see Section 1, paragraph 6 in the same Chapter. If another Chapter were meant, the text would read 'See Chapter 4, Section 1.6'. All the photographs are captioned with a Section paragraph number to which they refer and are always relevant to the Chapter text adjacent.

Figure numbers (usually line illustrations) appear in numerical order, within a given Chapter. Figure 1.1 there refers to the first figure in Chapter 1.

Left-hand and right-hand descriptions of parts of the machine or the machine itself, refer to the right and left side of the machine, with the rider seated in the normal riding position.

Motorcycle manufacturers continually make changes to specifications and recommendations, and these, when notified, are incorporated into our manuals at the earliest opportunity.

We take great pride in the accuracy of information given in this manual, but motorcycle manufacturers make alterations and design changes during the production run of a particular motorcycle of which they do not inform us. No liability can be accepted by the authors or publishers for loss, damage or injury caused by any errors in, or omissions from, the information given.

Introduction to the Kawasaki KZ400 Twins

The Kawasaki name first figured in commerce during 1878 when a dockyard was started in Tokyo. Early in this century Kawasaki diversified their interest to cover the manufacture of rail locomotives and rolling stock together with various other heavy industrial products. Today, the production capabilities include aircraft, rolling stock, commercial vehicles, airport ground support equipment and of course motorcycles. It was not until the late 1950's that Kawasaki commenced building motorcycles which at that time were becoming universally popular in Japan.

From building small two-stroke commuter-type motorcycles and mopeds, Kawasaki have risen to capture an important slice of the motorcycle market both in Japan and abroad.

The KZ400 machines covered in this manual are the first of this company's line to cater for the motorcyclist who requires the sophistication of the 'Super Bike' but neither the cost nor the cubic capacity.

Recently introduced, no major modifications have yet been made to the machines in the range which include models with disc or drum front brakes and with electrically assisted starting or the traditional kick-start.

Contents

Note: General descriptions and specifications are given in each Chapter immediately after the list of contents. Fault diagnosis is given at the end of the Chapter.

1975 Kawasaki (K) Z400 D

Ordering spare parts

When ordering spare parts for your machine it is advisable to deal directly with an accredited Kawasaki dealer who should be able to supply you with parts from stock.

Always quote the engine and frame numbers in full, particularly if you have an older machine. The frame number is stamped on the steering head of the frame. The engine number is stamped on the crankcase adjacent to the crankcase oil dipstick. Quote the full model number of the machine and, where necessary, the colour scheme.

Use only parts of genuine Kawasaki supply. Pattern parts are

available, some of which originate in the country of the machine's manufacture. These parts do not necessarily make a satisfactory replacement although they are cheaper initially.

Some of the more expendable parts such as spark plugs, bulbs, tyres, oils and greases etc, can be obtained from accessory shops and motor factors, who have convenient opening hours, charge lower prices and can often be found not far from home. It is also possible to obtain parts on a Mail Order basis from a number of specialists who advertise regularly in the motor cycle magazines.

Frame number location

Engine number location

Routine maintenance

Periodic routine maintenance is a continuous process that commences immediately the machine is used and continues until the machine is no longer fit for service. It must be carried out at specified mileage recordings or on a calendar basis if the machine is not used regularly, whichever is the soonest. Maintenance should be regarded as an insurance policy, to help keep the machine in the peak of condition and to enusre long, trouble-free service. It has the additional benefit of giving early warning of any faults that may develop and will act at a safety check, to the obvious advantage of both rider and machine alike.

The various maintenance tasks are described, under their respective mileage and calendar headings. Accompanying diagrams are provided, where necessary. It should be remembered that the interval between the various maintenance tasks serves only as a guide. As the machine gets older, is driven hard or is used under particularly adverse conditions, it is advisable to reduce the period between each check.

Some of the tasks are described in detail, where they are not mentioned fully as a routine maintenance item in the text. If a specific item is mentioned but not described in detail, it will be covered fully in the appropriate chapter. No special tools are required for the normal routine maintenance tasks. The tools contained on the tool kit supplied with every new machine will suffice, but if they are not available, the tools found in the average household will make an adequate substitute.

Weekly or every 200 miles

Check the oil level of the engine/gearbox unit. A sight glass is fitted in the lower edge of the primary drive case. The oil must be visible at this window, the correct level being halfway between the top and the bottom of the glass.

Check the tyre pressures. Always check the tyres when they are cool, using a pressure gauge of known accuracy.

Check the level of the electrolyte in the battery. Use only distilled water to top up, unless there has been a spillage of acid. **Do not** overfill.

Give the whole machine a close visual inspection for loose nuts and bolts and fittings and frayed control cables etc. Make sure the lights, horn, traffic indicators and speedometer function correctly. Remember that the efficient working of most of these components is a statutory requirement. Check, and if necessary adjust both brakes.

Check hydraulic fluid level (where disc brake is fitted).

Monthly or every 500 miles

Complete each of the checks listed in the weekly/200 mile service, then attend to the following items:

Adjust the final drive chain and lubricate.

Check the tightness of the cylinder head bolts, the exhaust pipe clamps and the carburettor tops.

Three monthly or 2,000 miles

Complete each of the checks listed in the monthly/500 mile service, then attend to the following items:

Change the engine oil.

Check the clutch operation and adjust if necessary.

Check the carburettor settings and adjust if necessary.

Check the camshaft chain play and adjust if necessary.

Check the contact-breaker setting and adjust if necessary.

Remove the spark plugs, clean and adjust the points gap. If the electrodes are badly eroded or the insulators badly fouled, both plugs should be renewed.

Check the valve clearances with the engine **COLD** and adjust as necessary.

Remove the air filter element. The element should be cleaned using an air hose, or if only lightly soiled by gently brushing. If the element is damp or oily it must be replaced.

Remove and clean the petrol tap filter gauze and the filter bowl. Check that the fuel pipes are free from sediment and are not split or perished.

Remove and clean the final drive chain. Check the chain for wear when completely free from old grease or oil. Lubricate the chain thoroughly before replacement. Check the condition of the gearbox and rear wheel sprockets.

Work round the machine checking and tightening any loose nuts or bolts.

Carry out general lubrication of any exposed cycle parts.

Six monthly or every 4,000 miles

Complete all checks listed in the three monthly/2,000 mile service, then attend to the following items:

Renew the oil filter element.

Check the steering head for play and adjust if necessary.

Check the wheel spokes for tightness and the rim for alignment.

Check the front fork oil level and top-up if necessary.

Check the brake linings or pads for wear.

Yearly or every 6,000 miles

Complete all the checks under the previous headings then carry out the following additional tasks:

Change the air cleaner element.

Change the front fork oil.

Change the brake fluid.

Check the swinging arm bushes for wear and renew, if worn.

Where a yearly roadworthiness test is required by law (as is the case in the UK where an MoT test is required) it is useful to perform the once yearly service immediately before the test and ensure that the machine is in the best possible condition.

2 Yearly or every 12,000 miles

In addition to the complete service advised for the yearly service the following items should be attended to:
Remove the wheels and regrease the wheel bearings.
Regrease the speedometer gear housing.
Regrease the brake camshaft(s).
Repack the steering head bearings with grease.
Note: No specific mention has been made of tyre wear since it assumed the rider will maintain a regular check. Apart from the statutory requirements relating to the minimum depth of tread permissable, a tyre that has cracked or damaged sidewalls should also be renewed immediately, in the interests of safety.

Check oil content regularly and top up when necessary

Don't omit to check level of fluid in master cylinder

Drum brakes have visual indication of brake lining wear

Chain can be lubricated in position with special chain lubricant

Summary of routine maintenance, adjustments and capacities

Spark plugs	NGK B-8ES
Spark plug gap	0.028 in. - 0.032 in. (0.7 - 0.8 mm)
Contact breaker gap	0.012 in - 0.016 in. (0.3 - 0.4 mm)
Valve clearances - inlet and exhaust (cold engine):	
KZ400 D, D3 up to engine no. 062317 (1974, 1975, early 1976) and KZ400 S (1975)	0.0032 - 0.0051 in (0.08 - 0.13 mm)
KZ400 D3 from engine no. 062318 on, D4 (late 1976, 1977) and KZ400 S2, S3 (1976, 1977)	0.0039 - 0.0059 in (0.10 - 0.15 mm)
Tyre pressures:	
Front	27 psi (1.9 kg/cm^2)
Rear	28 psi (2.0 kg/cm^2)
For continuous high speed travel increase the pressure by 3 - 6 psi.	
Fuel tank capacity	3.08 Imp. galls. 3.7 US galls. (14 litres)
Fuel tank reserve capacity	5.25 Imp. pints 3.2 US quarts (3 litres)
Engine oil capacity	5.25 Imp. pints 3.2 US quarts (3 litres) SAE 20W/50
Front fork oil capacity (per leg):	
KZ400 and KZ400 D	155 – 165 cc
KZ400 S	161 – 166 cc
Front fork oil level	13.4 – 14.2 in (340 – 360 mm)
Fork oil type	SAE/5W20

Dimensions

	KZ400	KZ400 Special
Overall length	81.51 in. (2080 mm)	81.9 in. (2075 mm)
Overall width	31.9 in. (810 mm)	31.1 in. (775 mm)
Overall height	44.1 in. (1,120 mm)	41.3 in. (1050 mm)
Wheel base	53.31 in. (1360 mm)	53.5 in. (1370 mm)
Weight	375 lbs (170 kg)	366 lbs (166 kg)

Recommended lubricants

Component	Castrol product
Engine/gearbox unit	Castrol GTX
Telescopic forks	Castrol Fork Oil
Hydraulic front brake master cylinder	Castrol Girling Universal Brake and Clutch Fluid
Control cables	Castrol Everyman Oil
Grease nipples and wheel bearings	Castrol LM Grease
Chain	Castrol Chain Lubricant

Chapter 1 Engine, clutch and gearbox

Contents

Specifications

Engine

Type	Vertical parallel twin cylinder, overhead camshaft.
Bore	64 mm (2.60 in.)
Stroke	62 mm (2.44 in.)
Cubic capacity	398 cc (24.3 cu in)
Comp. ratio	9 : 1
Max. bhp	35 @ 8,500 rpm
Max. torque	3.17 kg-m @ 7,500 rpm (21.3 ft/lbs)

Piston

Oversizes ...	0.5 mm and 1.0 mm (0.020 inch - 0.040 inch)
Ring end gap ...	0.2 mm - 0.4 mm (0.0078 inch - 0.015 inch)

Standard ring groove clearance:

Top ...	0.0016 in - 0.0018 in (0.040 mm - 0.045 mm)
Second ...	0.0010 in - 0.0011 in (0.025 mm - 0.030 mm)
Oil ...	0.0010 in - 0.0011 in (0.025 mm - 0.030 mm)
Cylinder bore clearance ...	0.0013 in - 0.0021 in (0.034 mm - 0.054 mm)

Valves and springs

Valve seat angle ...	45°

Valve stem diameter:

Inlet ...	0.2742 in - 0.2748 in (6.965 mm - 6.980 mm)
Exhaust ...	0.2738 in - 0.2744 in (6.955 mm - 6.970 mm)
Valve stem wear limit ...	0.27 in - 0.26 in (6.96 mm and 6.85 mm)

Valve stem clearance:

Inlet ...	0.0008 in - 0.002 in (0.02 mm - 0.05 mm)
Exhaust ...	0.0011 in - 0.0023 in (0.03 mm - 0.06 mm)

Valve spring free length:

Inner ...	1.41 inch (32.4 mm)
Outer ...	1.47 inch (37.3 mm)

Service limit:

Inner ...	1.22 inch (31.0 mm)
Outer ...	1.47 inch (36.0 mm)

Valve clearances - inlet and exhaust (cold engine):

KZ400 D, D3 up to engine no. 062317 (1974, 1975, early 1976) and KZ400 S (1975) ...	0.0032 - 0.0051 in (0.08 - 0.13 mm)
KZ400 D3 from engine no. 062318 on, D4 (late 1976, 1977) and KZ400 S2, S3 (1976, 1977) ...	0.0039 - 0.0059 in (0.10 - 0.15 mm)

Camshaft

Camshaft journal/cylinder head cover clearance ...	0.0012 inch - 0.0034 inch (0.033 mm - 0.087 mm)
Service limit ...	0.007 inch (0.18 mm)
Camshaft journal diameter ...	1.100 in - 1.101 in (27.955 mm - 27.97 mm)
Service limit ...	1.098 in (27.91 mm)

Valve timing

	Open	Close	Duration
Inlet ...	26° BTDC	74° ABDC	280° Total
Exhaust ...	68.5° BBDC	31.5° ATDC	280° Total

Crankshaft

Main bearing clearance ...	0.0014 in - 0.003 in (0.036 mm - 0.078 mm)
Wear limit ...	0.0043 in (0.11 mm)
Crankshaft journal diameter ...	1.416 in - 1.4173 in (35.984 mm - 36.0 mm)
Wear limit ...	1.414 in (35.94 mm)
Big-end clearance ...	0.0016 in - 0.0027 in (0.041 - 0.071 mm)
Wear limit ...	0.003937 in (0.1 mm)
Big-end journal diameter ...	1.416 in - 1.4173 in (35.984 mm - 36.00 mm)
Wear limit ...	1.414 in (35.94 mm)
Con-rod side clearance ...	0.006 in - 0.0098 in (0.15 mm - 0.25 mm)
Wear limit ...	0.0177 in (0.45 mm)
Gudgeon pin diameter ...	0.59 in - 0.5905 in (14.994 mm - 15.0 mm)
Wear limit ...	0.5889 in (14.96 mm)
Small end I.D. ...	0.5906 in - 0.5911 in (15.003 - 15.014 mm)
Wear limit ...	0.5925 in (15.05 mm)

Clutch

No of plates:

Plain ...	Five (5)
Inserted ...	Six (6)
No of springs ...	Four (4)
Friction plate thickness ...	0.1141 in - 0.12204 in (2.9 mm - 3.1 mm)
Wear limit ...	0.0984 in (2.5 mm)
Clutch spring free length ...	1.3307 in (33.8 mm)
Wear limit ...	1.2716 in (32.3 mm)

Oil pump

Outer rotor/inner rotor clearance ...	0.0009 in - 0.0045 in (0.025 mm - 0.115 mm)
Wear limit ...	0.0082 in (0.21 mm)
Rotor side play ...	0.0011 in - 0.0035 in (0.03 mm - 0.09 mm)
Wear limit ...	0.0059 in (0.15 mm)
Outer rotor/pump body clearance ...	0.0039 in - 0.0059 in (0.10 mm - 0.015 mm)
Wear limit ...	0.0098 in (0.25 mm)

Gearbox

Type	5-speed constant mesh.
Gear ratios	
1st	2.571 : 1 (36/14)
2nd	1.684 : 1 (32/19)
3rd	1.273 : 1 (28/22)
4th	1.040 : 1 (26/25)
5th	0.889 : 1 (24/27)
Primary reduction ratio	2.435 : 1 (56/23)
Final reduction ratio	3.000 : 1 (45/15)
Overall drive ratio	6.493 : 1 (5th gear)

Main torque wrench settings

Cam box nuts	18 - 22 ft/lbs	(2.5 - 3.0 kg -m)
Cylinder head bolts 8 mm	18 - 22 ft/lbs	(2.5 - 3.0 kg - m)
Cylinder head bolts 6 mm	95 - 113 in/lbs	(1.1 - 1.3 kg - m)
Crankcase bolts 8 mm	18 - 22 ft/lbs	(2.5 - 3.0 kg - m)
Crankcase bolts 6 mm	69 - 87 in/lbs	(0.8 - 1.0 kg - m)
Crankshaft bearing cup bolts	18 - 22 ft/lbs	(2.5 - 3.0 kg - m)
Big-end cap bolts	24 - 27 ft/lbs	(3.3 - 3.7 kg - m)

1 General description

The engine fitted to the Kawasaki KZ400 series is a single overhead camshaft vertical parallel twin. The 360° webbed crankshaft which runs on four shell main bearings is balanced by two rotating weights one of which lies forwards of the crankshaft and one aft. The weights are timed and driven by a chain, driven from a sprocket lying between the two centre bearings and next to the camshaft drive sprocket. The camshaft drive chain passes through a tunnel between the cylinders and so to the camshaft which is mounted on the cylinder head. All engine castings are manufactured from aluminium alloy, the barrels being fitted with dry steel liners. The crankcases, which house the crankshaft and gearbox components, separate in the horizontal plane to facilitate easy dismantling and reassembly. Wet sump lubrication is supplied by a gear driven vane-type oil pump, the oil passing through a wire gauze trap and paper filter element under pressure to all working surfaces of the engine.

The multi-plate clutch is fitted to the right-hand side of the engine, primary drive being through a triplex Hy-Vo chain. A five speed constant mesh gearbox then transmits power through a roller chain to the rear wheel. Depending on the model, starting is effected by kickstart or an electric starter motor. Where starter motors are utilized a kickstart lever is also fitted, for emergency use. Electrical power is generated by a crankshaft driven alternator, via a rectifier to the 12v battery. Ignition is supplied by a single coil and contact breaker.

2 Operations with engine/gearbox in frame

It is not necessary to remove the engine unit from the frame in order to dismantle the following items:
1 Right and left crankcase covers and final drive sprocket cover.
2 Clutch assembly and gear selector components (external).
3 Oil pump and filter.
4 Alternator and starter motor (where fitted).
5 Cylinder head and cylinder head cover.
6 Cylinder block, pistons and rings.

3 Operations with engine/gearbox unit removed from frame

As previously described the crankshaft and gearbox assemblies are housed within a common casing. Any work carried out on either of these two major assemblies will necessitate removal of the engine from the frame so that the crankcases can be separated.

4 Removing the engine/gearbox unit

1 Place the machine on its centre stand making sure that it is standing firmly. Although by no means essential it is useful to raise the machine a number of feet above floor level by placing it on a long bench or horizontal ramp. This will enable most of the work to be carried out in an upright position, which is eminently more comfortable than crouching or kneeling in a puddle of sump oil.
2 Place a suitable receptacle below the crankcase and drain off the engine oil. The sump plug lies just forward of the oil filter housing. The oil will drain at a higher rate if the engine has been warmed up previously, thereby heating and thinning the oil. Approximately 5½ pints (3 litres) should drain out. Undo the oil filter chamber bolt and remove the chamber and filter.
3 Disconnect the battery by unbolting the positive lead (red). The battery is located beneath the dualseat, which will hinge up to the right to give access.
4 Turn the fuel tap to the 'stop' position and remove the fuel lines from either the tap unions or the carburettor float chamber unions. In both cases the pipes are held by small spring clips.
5 Unhook the rubber strap which holds the rear of the fuel tank in place. The tank can now be slid back, to disengage the front mounting rubbers, and lifted from position.
6 Unscrew the two nuts which clamp each exhaust pipe retaining flange to the cylinder head. Slide the clamps back and remove the split clamps which fit into the exhaust pipe. The rear of each exhaust system is held to the frame by the pillion footrest bolt. When removing these bolts make sure the exhaust pipe/silencer is securely held otherwise it may fall free suddenly and become damaged.
7 Unscrew the knurled ring in the front of the cylinder head and pull the tachometer drive cable from position.
8 Pull off the right-hand side cover which will give access to the main electrical components. Disconnect both electrical harness plugs from the sockets below the regulator. Prise the rubber boot off the starter solenoid and disconnect the main starter lead.
9 Loosen the screw clips at either end of the main breather pipe and pull the pipe from position at both unions.
10 Pull off the spark plug caps and disconnect the spade terminals on the ignition coil. Undo the two bolts which hold the ignition coil bracket to the frame.
11 Pull the left-hand side cover from position and remove the air cleaner box mounting bolts on both sides. Loosen the two screw clips which hold the air cleaner hoses to the carburettor mouths, and pull the hoses from position. Loosen the carburettor stub screw clips. Push the carburettors down at the rear so that they clear the air cleaner hoses; this will automatically pull the carburettors from the inlet mounting stubs. The carburettor

4.6a Remove the two clamp bolts and . . .

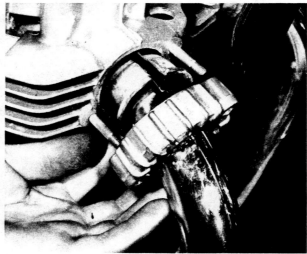

4.6b . . . pull out the split collets

4.6c Remove rear footrests and silencer bolts

4.7 Unscrew knurled tachometer union ring

4.8a Disconnect both multi-point sockets and . . .

4.8b . . .disconnect the starter lead on solenoid

4.9 Breather hose held by screw clips

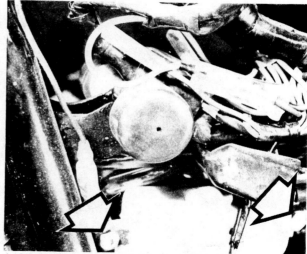
4.10 Coil mounted on bracket by two bolts

4.11a Loosen all four carburettor hose clips

4.11b Unscrew the two air box bolts (where fitted)

4.11c Pull carburettors down at rear to release

4.12 Remove right-hand footrest and stand spring

4.13a Clutch cable nipple secured by split pin

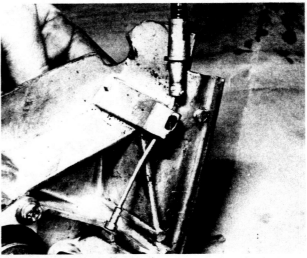

4.13b Pull outer cable from anchor

4.14a Disconnect drive chain at spring link

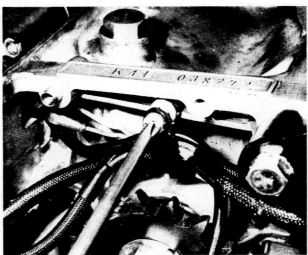

4.14b Wiring clip held by a single screw

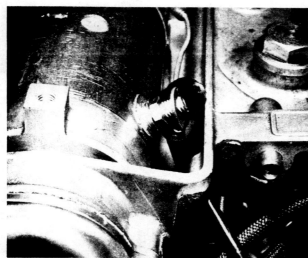

4.14c Remove starter motor lead from terminal

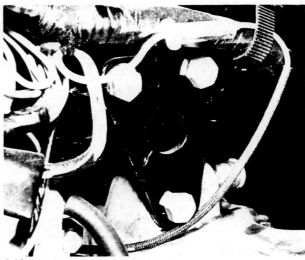

4.16a Head steady bracket held by three bolts and . . .

4.16b . . . breather cover retained by four bolts

4.19a Top rear bolt holds earth wire and stop lamp bracket

4.19b Engine removal requires great care

assembly can now be slid to the right, still attached to the throttle cables. In order to avoid damage during engine removal it is wise to remove the carburettors from the machine in order that they may be stored in a safe place. To remove the throttle cables, loosen both adjuster screw locknuts and screw one adjuster right in. Loosen the other adjuster and screw it right out so that the cable can slide across through the slit in the mounting bracket. Disconnect the cable nipple from the cable drum. Repeat this operation with the other cable. Tape the two cables to the top frame tube.

12 Remove the gear change lever and the kickstart lever. Both are retained on their splined shafts by pinch bolts which must be removed completely to allow the levers to be pulled off. Undo the left-hand footrest bolt and remove the footrest and side stand spring.

13 Remove the four crosshead screws which hold the final drive sprocket cover in place. Pull the cover from position. The clutch cable must be disconnected before the cover can be removed completely. Screw in the adjuster on the clutch lever at the handlebar lever, and pull the outer cable from position. This will allow enough slack at the clutch operating arm to permit the nipple to be prised free. Note the split pin which retains the nipple in place, this must be removed first. Take care not to misplace the tensioner spring which lies between the cable anchor in the cover and the operating arm.

14 With the final drive chain link positioned on one of the sprockets, carefully prise off the spring link and disconnect and remove the final drive chain. Loosen the wiring harness clamp which is located just above the gearbox sprocket and disconnect the various wires and cables.

15 Remove the two bolts which hold the starter motor cover and prise the cover from position. Remove the starter lead from the terminal and disconnect the neutral warning light lead at its snap connector.

16 Remove the three bolts and nuts which retain the cylinder head steady plate to the frame top tube and the breather cover. Remove the breather cover, which is retained by four bolts and washers.

17 Loosen the stop lamp swtich adjuster nut and pull the switch from position in the bracket. Disconnect the operating spring from the eye in the rear brake lever.

18 Remove the nuts from the three engine mounting bolts and remove each bolt in turn. If necessary, lift the engine slightly to free a tight bolt. Remove the front engine mounting plates which are held by one common bolt and two individual bolts. Two spacers are fitted between the frame and the crankcase on the two rear mounting bolts. Note their relative positions.

19 Before the engine is removed from the frame check that all wiring leads are disconnected and will not get trapped or chafed. The engine is very heavy, and maneouvering for removal requires care and patience. It is therefore advised that two stalwart assistants are on hand for this operation, one assistant being briefed to aid in the lifting and the other to give directions and help steady the cycle parts.

5 Dismantling the engine/gearbox unit: general

1 Before commencing work on the engine unit, the external surfaces should be cleaned thoroughly. A motorcycle has very little protection from road grit and other foreign matter which sooner or later will find its way into the dismantled engine if this simple precaution is not carried out.

2 One of the proprietary cleaning compounds such as Gunk or Jizer can be used to good effect, especially if the compound is first allowed to penetrate the film of grease and oil before it is washed away. In the USA Gumout degreaser is an alternative.

3 It is essential when washing down to make sure that water does not enter the carburettors or the electrics particularly now that these parts are more vulnerable.

4 Collect together an adequate set of tools in addition to those of the tool roll carried under the seat.

5 If the engine has not been previously dismantled, an impact

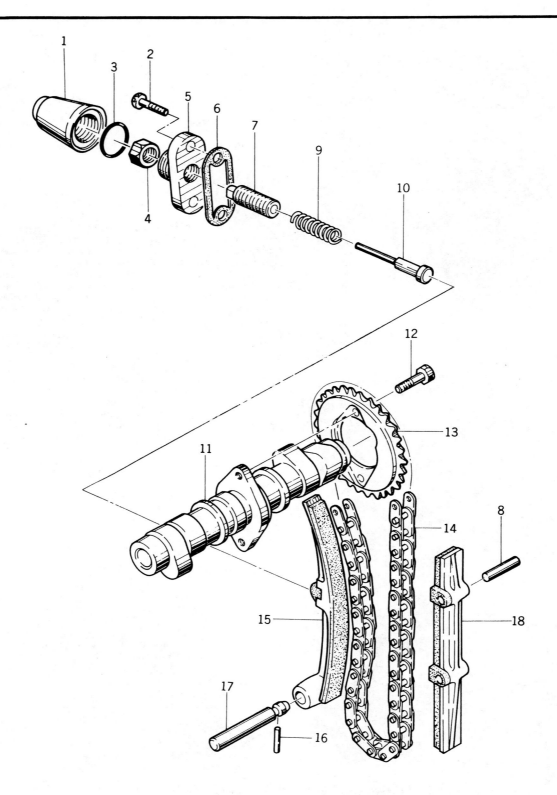

Fig. 1.1 Camshaft, chain and tensioner

1 Chain tensioner cap
2 Screw - 2 off
3 'O' ring
4 Lock nut
5 Chain tensioner body
6 Gasket

7 Pushrod guide
8 Anchor pin - 2 off
9 Chain tensioner spring
10 Adjuster pushrod
11 Camshaft

12 Sprocket holding
   bolt - 2 off
13 Camshaft sprocket
14 Camshaft drive chain
15 Camshaft chain guide

16 Locking pin
17 Chain tensioner
   pivot shaft
18 Chain tensioner
   tensioner blade

6.3a Remove the contact-breaker cover . . .

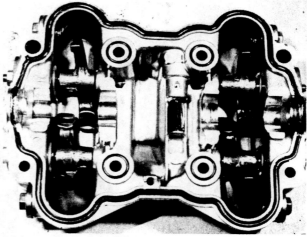

6.3d . . . note the four 'O' rings

6.3b . . . to give access to 17 mm hexagon for crankshaft rotation

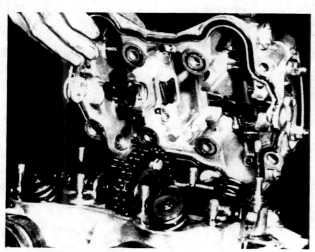

6.3c Lift off the cylinder head cover . . .

screwdriver will prove essential. This will safeguard the heads of the crosshead screws used for engine assembly. These are invariably machine-tightening during manufacture. **Caution** - Use great care as the screws and cases are easily damaged. Use a crosshead type screwdriver and NOT one of the Phillips type, which will slip out of the screws.

6 Avoid force in any of the operations. There is generally a good reason why an item is sticking, probably due to the use of the wrong procedure or sequence of operations.

7 Dismantling will be made easier if a simple engine stand is constructed that will correspond with the engine mounting points. This arrangement will permit the complete unit to be clamped rigidly to the workbench, leaving both hands free for dismantling.

6 Dismantling the engine/gearbox: removing the cylinder head cover and cylinder head

1 Loosen the eight cylinder head cover retaining bolts in an even and criss-cross sequence. With the bolts removed the cylinder head cover can be gently prised off its dowel pins. It is probable, particularly if the engine has not previously been dismantled, that the cylinder head cover will be difficult to remove. This is due to the glue-type sealing compound applied to the rubber ring which constitutes the oil tight joint between the cylinder head cover and the cylinder head. Note that this rubber ring is only fitted to the 1974 and 1975 models. During removal, the sealing ring may stay in its retaining groove in either the head or the cover. The camshaft end plugs must stay in whichever component the sealing ring remains. Note the location of the four oil way 'O' rings and remove them.

2 Unscrew the camshaft chain tensioner cap and remove it, together with the 'O' ring. The chain tensioner is retained by two crosshead screws which, when removed, will allow the tensioner assembly to be pulled out as a complete unit.

3 Remove the contact breaker cover. This will give access to a special hexagon machined on the end of the contact breaker cam. Loosen and remove the two bolts which locate the camshaft sprocket to the camshaft. A 17 mm spanner fitted to the contact breaker cam hexagon will allow the engine to be rotated to facilitate this operation. Pull the camshaft out of the sprocket until the sprocket can be disengaged from the chain. The camshaft and sprocket can now be removed completely. Take care during this operation not to drop the camshaft chain down between the two cylinders; as soon as the camshaft and sprocket have been removed a screwdriver or rod should be slipped under the chain and allowed to rest in the camshaft bearing halves.

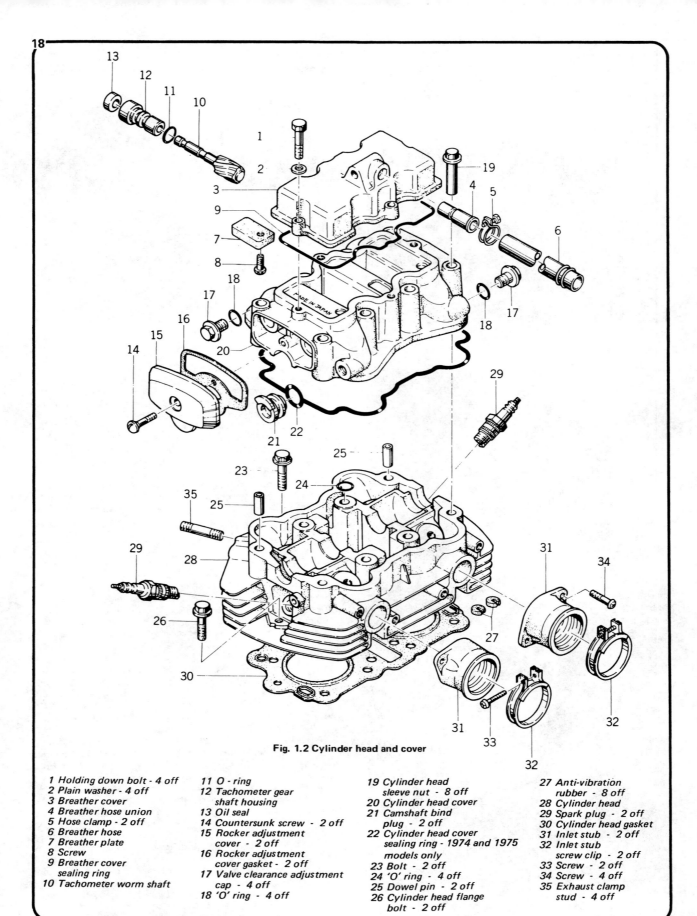

Fig. 1.2 Cylinder head and cover

1 Holding down bolt - 4 off
2 Plain washer - 4 off
3 Breather cover
4 Breather hose union
5 Hose clamp - 2 off
6 Breather hose
7 Breather plate
8 Screw
9 Breather cover
  sealing ring
10 Tachometer worm shaft

11 O - ring
12 Tachometer gear
  shaft housing
13 Oil seal
14 Countersunk screw - 2 off
15 Rocker adjustment
  cover - 2 off
16 Rocker adjustment
  cover gasket - 2 off
17 Valve clearance adjustment
  cap - 4 off
18 'O' ring - 4 off

19 Cylinder head
  sleeve nut - 8 off
20 Cylinder head cover
21 Camshaft bind
  plug - 2 off
22 Cylinder head cover
  sealing ring - 1974 and 1975
  models only
23 Bolt - 2 off
24 'O' ring - 4 off
25 Dowel pin - 2 off
26 Cylinder head flange
  bolt - 2 off

27 Anti-vibration
  rubber - 8 off
28 Cylinder head
29 Spark plug - 2 off
30 Cylinder head gasket
31 Inlet stub - 2 off
32 Inlet stub
  screw clip - 2 off
33 Screw - 2 off
34 Screw - 4 off
35 Exhaust clamp
  stud - 4 off

6.4a Camshaft sprocket is retained by two bolts

6.4d Place dowel through chain to prevent it falling

6.4b Pull camshaft out with chain OFF sprocket

6.4c Remember to loosen cylinder flange bolts

Dropping the chain during dismantling is not of great importance if the engine is being stripped completely but it will cause considerable problems if only a top-end overhaul is anticipated. The chain is very difficult to retrieve.

4   Remove the two remaining cylinder head holding down bolts, one of which lies adjacent to each spark plug hole. The cylinder head is now ready for lifting. A soft-nosed mallet may be used with care to knock the cylinder head off its dowels. Lift the cylinder head up until the cam chain becomes taut, slip another screwdriver between the cylinder head and block and between the two runs of cam chain. The top screwdriver can now be removed, and the cylinder head lifted clear. Remove the cylinder head gasket and the two 'square' 'O' rings.

7   Dismantling the engine/gearbox: removing the cylinder block, pistons and rings

1   Rotate the crankshaft until both pistons are at TDC. With the use of a soft-nosed mallet free the cylinder block and work it gently up the holding down studs. Once again, if the engine has not been dismantled since leaving the factory, the cylinder block may effectively be 'glued' to the crankcase mouth due to the type of sealing compound applied to the base gasket. If difficulty is encountered refer to the accompanying photograph where it will be seen that the two 6 mm cylinder head holding down bolts can be utilised to push the block from position. Place a short steel rod in each bolt hole allowing the rods to bear on small pieces of steel, to protect the crankcase edges. Insert the two bolts and screw them down evenly about ¼ (quarter) of a turn each, until the block begins to lift. Great care must be taken during this operation to ensure that the crankcase edges are adequately protected and that the pressure from the rods is evenly distributed.

2   Slide the cylinder block up and off the pistons taking care to support each piston as the cylinder block becomes free. If a top end overhaul only is being carried out, place a clean rag in each crankcase mouth before the lower edge of each cylinder frees the rings. This will preclude any small particles of broken ring falling into the crankcase. Invert the cylinder block and, where fitted, remove the two large 'O' rings, one of which fits over each protruding cylinder sleeve.

3   Prise the outer gudgeon pin circlip of each piston from position. The gudgeon pins are a light push fit in piston bosses so can be removed with ease. If any difficulty is encountered, apply to the offending piston crown a rag over which boiling water has just been poured. This will give the necessary temporary

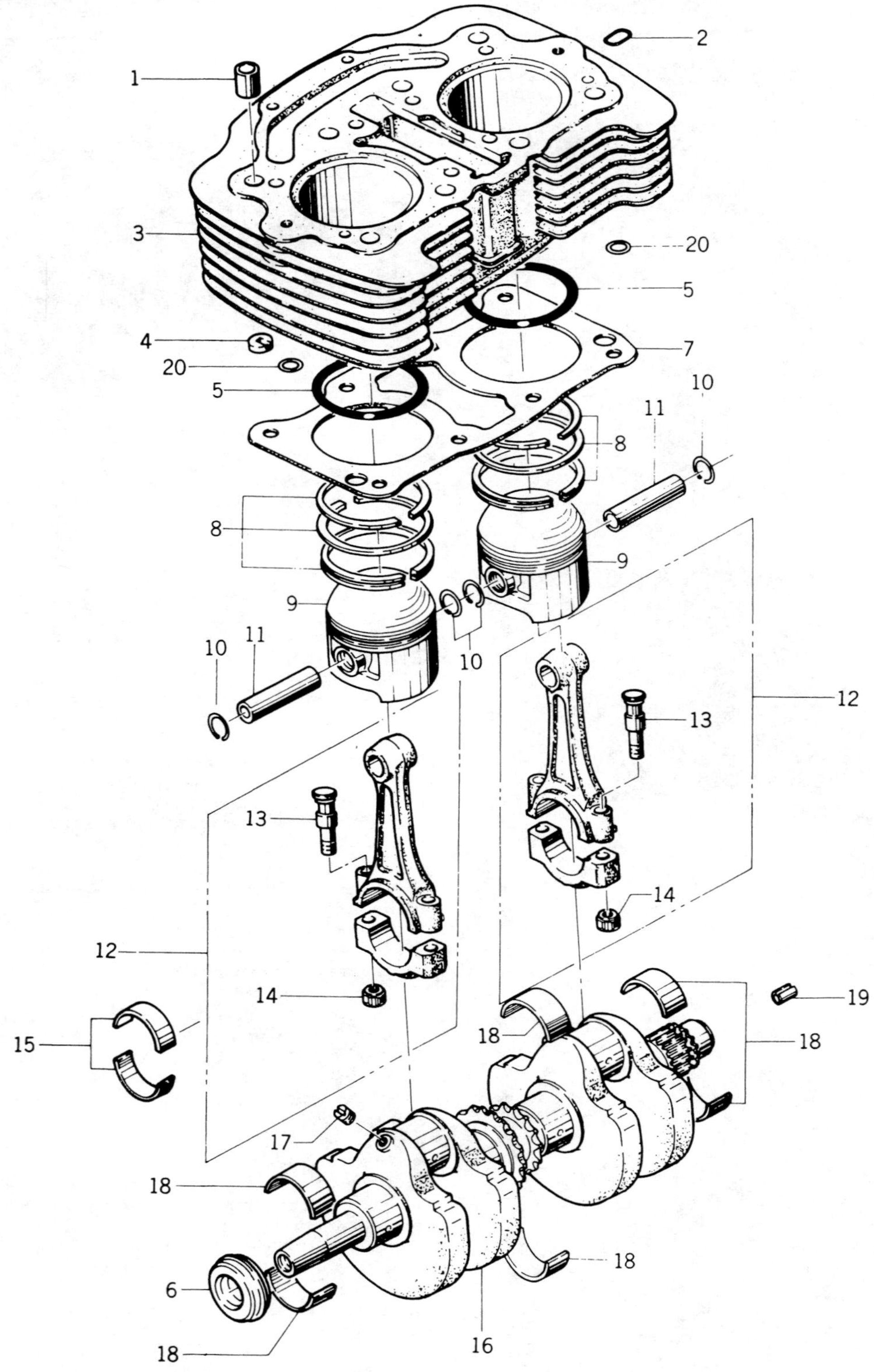

Fig. 1.3 Cylinder block, pistons and crankshaft

1 Dowel pin - 2 off
2 Oil feed 'O' ring - 2 off
3 Cylinder block
4 Anti-vibration
  rubber - 12 off
5 Cylinder sleeve
  'O' ring - 2 off (where fitted)

6 Alternator side oil seal
7 Cylinder base gasket
8 Piston ring set - 2 off
9 Piston - 2 off
10 Gudgeon pin
   circlip - 4 off
11 Gudgeon pin - 2 off

12 Connecting rod
   - complete - 2 off
13 Bearing cap bolt - 4 off
14 Bearing cap nut - 4 off
15 Big-end bearing
   shell - 4 off
16 Crankshaft assembly

17 Sludge trap plug
   - 2 off
18 Main bearing
   shell - 8 off
19 Dowel pin
20 Oil feed 'O' ring

7.1 If cylinders are tight they can be pushed free

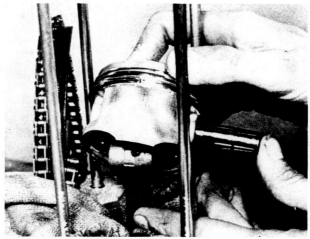

7.3b Push out gudgeon pin to release piston

7.2 Slide cylinder block up evenly and squarely

7.3a Prise out and DISCARD old circlips

expansion to the piston bosses to allow the gudgeon pin to be pushed out. Before removing each piston, scribe the cylinder identification inside the piston skirt. A mark R or L will ensure that the piston is replaced in the correct bore, on reassembly. It is unnecessary to mark the back and front of the piston because this is denoted by an arrow mark cast in the piston crown.

4   Each piston is fitted with two compression rings and an oil control ring. It is wise to leave the rings in place on the pistons until the time comes for their examination or renewal in order to avoid confusing their correct order.

5   In the tunnel of the cylinder block will be found the camshaft chain guide. Slide out the lower retaining pin and remove the guide from the top.

8   Dismantling the engine/gearbox: removing the left-hand crankcase cover, starter motor and alternator

1   Unscrew the oil pressure indicator switch as it protrudes and may become damaged.

2   Remove the eight (8) alternator cover screws, and pull the cover from position, together with the gasket.

3   The starter motor is held in its housing by two bolts passing through lugs in the motor end plate and into the crankcase. Once the bolts have been removed the motor can be gently eased backwards and up out of the housing. The drive sprocket is fully floating on the splines of the starter motor armature and will remain in mesh with the drive chain as the motor is eased out of position. **Warning**: do not hit the starter motor on the splined shaft as this may damage the reduction gear in the motor.

4   Remove the starter motor chain and drive sprocket.

5   To remove the alternator rotor retaining bolt it is necessary to stop the engine from rotating. This is best achieved by placing a close fitting metal bar through one or both small end eyes and allowing the bar to bear down on small wooden blocks placed across the crankcase mouth. On no account must the bar be allowed to bear directly onto the gasket face. Having stopped the engine from rotating remove the rotor retaining bolt. Note that this bolt must be removed in a clockwise direction as it has a left-hand thread.

6   Removal of the rotor bolt will give access to an internal thread in the rotor boss. This thread facilitates the use of Kawasaki extractor tool No. 57001-254 which should be used to remove the rotor. If this puller is not available a legged sprocket puller should **not** be used as a substitute. Although it is possible to fit such a device it is likely to damage the alternator rotor. If it is impossible to remove the rotor and a major overhaul of the

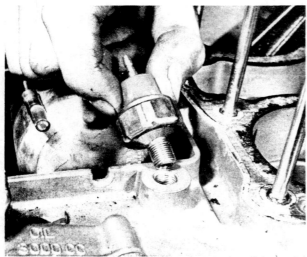
8.1 Unscrew the oil pressure warning switch

8.3a Ease starter motor from position . . .

8.3b . . . leaving chain and sprocket in position

8.5 Alternator centre bolt has LEFT-HAND thread

9.1 Final drive sprocket can be held as shown with CARE

10.1a Contact breaker plate held by three screws but . . .

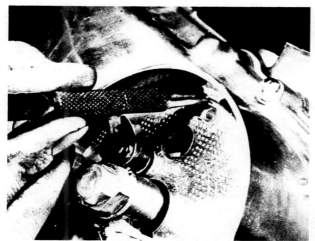

10.1b . . . Punch mark plate position before removal of screws

11.3a Remove clutch plates, noting their position

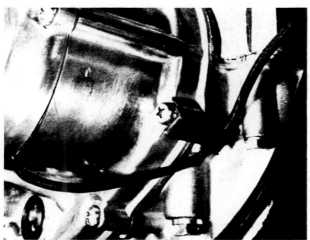

10.1c Low tension lead held by smalll clip

10.2 ATU held by a single bolt

engine is anticipated the rotor may be removed later on after the cases have been separated. If, when the lower portion of the crankcase has been lifted off, small wooden wedges are very carefully driven between the rear of the rotor and the crankcase wall, the rotor should drive off. This method require considerable care and should only be indulged in as a last resort.

7 With the rotor removed from the shaft, the starter driven sprocket can be slid off the shaft.

9 Dismantling the engine/gearbox: removing the gearbox final drive sprocket

1 Knock down the tab washer that locks the final drive sprocket nut and undo the nut. In order to undo the nut the sprocket must be prevented from rotating. This is best accomplished by locking the crankshaft as previously described and placing the gearbox in 5th (top) gear. The centre nut may now be undone with ease. Remove the sprocket and the distance collar.

10 Dismantling the engine/gearbox: removing the contact breaker plate and the automatic timing unit

1 Remove the contact breaker cover plate if this has not already been done. The contact breaker plate is retained by three screws through sloppy holes, which allow a small amount of timing adjustment. Before loosening the screws and removing the plate, mark the plate and the top screw boss with a punch to allow easy and accurate timing on replacement. Ensure that the two punch marks are placed accurately adjacent to each other. Remove the contact breaker plate and pull the wiring grommet from position in the casing. The low tension lead may now be freed from the wiring clip which is held by the primary drive casing front screw.

2 The automatic timing unit is retained by a single bolt in the end of the crankshaft. With a 17 mm spanner holding the crankshaft rotation bolt, the ATU bolt can be easily loosened and the unit pulled from place.

11 Dismantling the engine/gearbox: removing the primary drive cover and dismantling the clutch

1 The primary drive cover is retained by twelve (12) crosshead

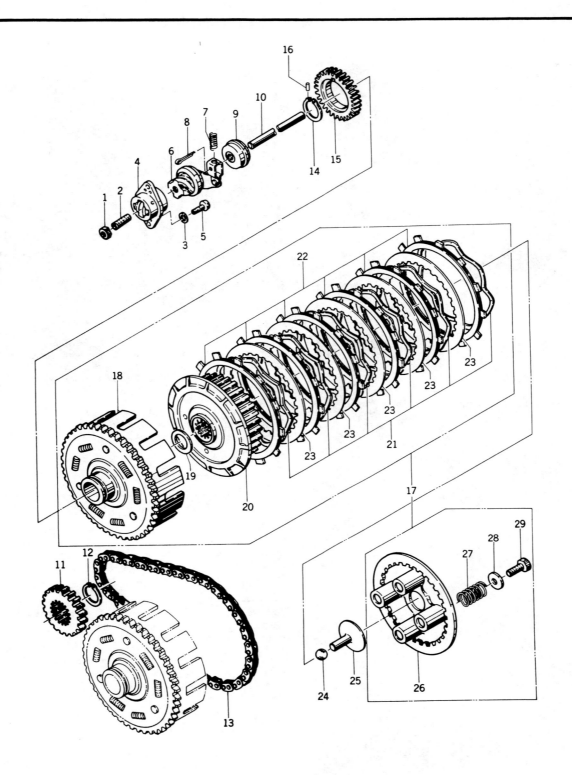

Fig. 1.4 Clutch assembly

1 Lock nut	8 Split pin	16 Gear drive pin	23 Plain clutch
2 Adjuster screw	9 Oil seal	17 Clutch assembly - complete	plate - 5 off
3 Plain washer - 2 off	10 Clutch pushrod	18 Clutch outer drum	24 Steel ball - 3/8''
4 Clutch lifter body	11 Primary drive	19 Thrust washer	25 Clutch operation thrust piece
5 Screw - 2 off	12 Circlip	20 Clutch centre boss	26 Pressure plate
6 Clutch lifter	13 Primary drive chain	21 Disengagement ring - 6 off	27 Clutch spring - 4 off
quick-screw	14 Circlip	22 Friction clutch	28 Plain washer - 4 off
7 Return spring	15 Oil pump drive gear	plate - 6 off	29 Bolt - 4 off

11.3b Pull out 'mushroom' head push rod

12.1 Oil pump located on two dowel pins

11.4 Clutch centre is held by circlips

screws. Remove the screws followed by the casing and the gasket.

2   Unscrew the four clutch bolts and remove them together with the springs and washers. Remove the clutch pressure plate.

3   Lift out the clutch plates and expander rings making sure they remain in their correct relative positions. Pull out the mushroom head clutch pushrod and the main length of the clutch pushrod from the left-hand side. Note that 3/8" steel ball lies between the two pushrods.

4   Remove the circlip and washer from the clutch shaft and pull the clutch centre boss off the shaft. The clutch outer drum is held in the same way.

5   Remove the circlip that retains the primary drive pinion on the splined crankshaft. The clutch outer drum and the primary drive pinion can now be simultaneously eased off their respective shafts together with the triplex Hy-Vo primary drive chain. The oil pump drive pinion is retained on the rear of the clutch drum by a circlip. Note the drive peg, which is a push fit in the boss and is easily misplaced.

12 Dismantling the engine/gearbox: removing the oil pump

1   Remove the four (4) oil pump retaining screws and pull the oil pump assembly off the dowel pins, away from the crankcase wall. Note the position of the three oil way 'O' rings.

2   If the internal components of the oil pump require inspection due to a suspect pump, remove the circlip and washer from the inner end of the drive shaft and carefully prise the two halves of the pump body apart. Removal of the inner rotor will allow the drive pin to be slid from position and the oil pump shaft, together with the drive gear, to be removed.

13 Dismantling the engine/gearbox: removing the gearchange mechanism

1   Remove the gearchange shaft holding plate, which is retained by two screws. Disengage the change pawl from the pins in the end of the change drum and pull the gearchange shaft and main gearchange arm out of the casing.

2   Remove the single screw from the end of the gearchange drum and lift off the end cap. Pull out the six (6) gearchange pins.

3   The gearchange drum stopper plate can now be removed. The plate is held by two (2) countersunk screws. Care should be

11.5 Remove primary drive assembly as a unit

13.1 Gearchange arm held by plate and screws

13.2a Remove single screw and cover plate to . . .

13.2b . . . give access to the change pins

14.1a Detach holding plate and circlip to . . .

14.1b . . . release the kickstart shaft collar

taken when undoing these slotted screws as they are punch-locked to ensure that they remain tight.

14 Dismantling the engine/gearbox: removing the kickstart return spring and shaft locator collar

1   Remove the circlip which holds the nylon spring guide and pull the guide from place inside the spring. With a pair of pliers, lift the spring outer end from position in the crankcase anchor hole, and allow the tension to be released slowly in an anti-clockwise direction. Remove the spring.

2   Remove the kickstart shaft locator circlip and the kickstart shaft boss retainer plate. The plate is held by two countersunk screws.

3   No further dismantling of the kickstart assembly can be accomplished until after the crankcases are separated.

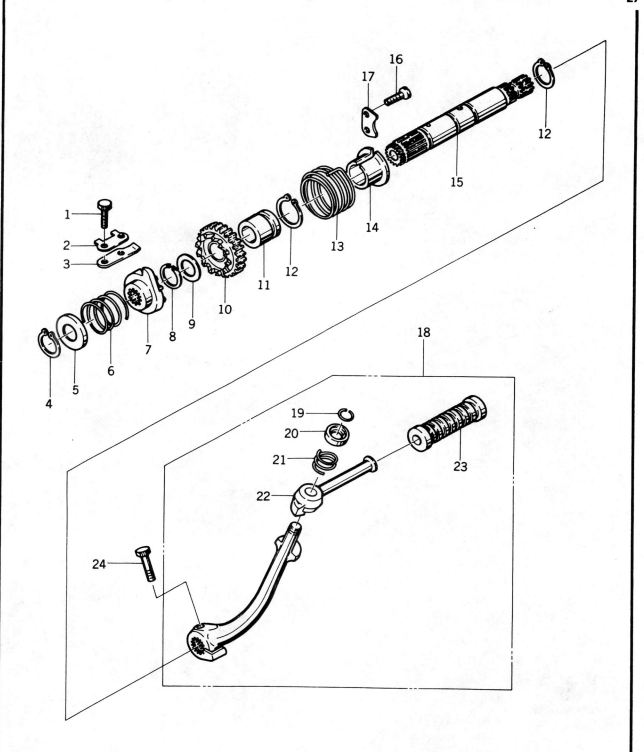

Fig. 1.5 Kickstart mechanism

1 Bolt - 2 off
2 Tab washer
3 Ratchet pawl stop
4 Circlip
5 Spring cap
6 Ratchet spring

7 Ratchet pawl
8 Circlip
9 Thrust washer
10 Ratchet wheel
11 Kickstart location collar
12 Circlip - 2 off

13 Kickstart return spring
14 Spring guide
15 Kickstart shaft
16 Screw - 2 off
17 Location collar plate
18 Kickstart lever - complete

19 Circlip
20 Plain washer
21 Spring
22 Kickstart lever crank
23 Rubber
24 Pinch bolt

16.2 Remove change drum stopper before . . .

16.4 . . .separating the crankcase

17.1a Remove the layshaft followed by . . .

17.1b . . . the mainshaft

17.1c Study the gear assemblies before dismantling

17.2 Pull out rod to free gear selectors

17.3a Cam stopper plate retained by circlip

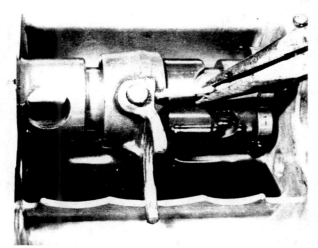

17.3b Selector fork guide pin held by spring pin

17.3c Pull guide pin out to release fork

15 Dismantling the engine/gearbox: removing the oil filter chamber cover and gauze trap cover

1   The oil filter chamber cover and the paper filter element may have been removed during engine oil drainage at the commencement of dismantling. The chamber cover is retained by a single centre bolt and sealed by a large 'O' ring. With the chamber removed, the element will lift out.
2   Lying next to the oil filter cover is the oil gauze trap cover, which is retained by five (5) crosshead screws. Remove the cover, together with the gasket and gauze.

16 Dismantling the engine/gearbox: separating the crankcase halves

1   Place the engine with the crankcase mouths facing upwards.
2   Remove the change drum stopper housing bolt, detent spring and plunger. Note the sealing 'O' ring. Remove the six (6) upper crankcase half retaining screws. The screws are located towards the rear of the engine.
3   Invert the engine so that it rests securely on the rear edge of the crankcase, and the cylinder block holding down studs. Loosen and remove the fourteen (14) crankcase retaining screws in an even and criss-cross sequence.
4   The lower crankcase half is now ready for lifting from position. A soft-nosed mallet may be used to separate the cases. It should be noted that a number of indentations have been provided at various points around the crankcase joint. A large screwdriver may be placed in these indentations and used as a lever to facilitate separation. On no account should levers of any description be placed between the mating faces of the two crankcase halves. The aluminium faces are easily damaged and this treatment will inevitably end in oil leakage at a later date.

17 Dismantling the engine/gearbox: removing the gearbox components and kickstart assembly

1   Lift out the mainshaft and layshaft together, complete with their bearings and gear clusters. Remove the bearing half clips which lie in grooves in the bearing seatings.
2   Pull out the selector fork slide rod towards the primary drive side and remove the two selector forks.
3   Pull the gearchange drum out of its bearing as far to the primary drive side as possible. Prise off the circlip on the drum end and remove the drum stopper cam plate. Remove the small peg from the drum end.
4   Remove the split pin that retains the selector fork guide pin and pull the pin out of the fork. The selector fork can now be slid from the gearchange drum which will now be free for removal.
5   Knock down the ears of the kickstart pawl guide plate bolts and remove the two bolts. Pull the kickstart shaft boss from position in the crankcase. The kickstart shaft together with the pawl and ratchet wheel can now be pulled up and out of the crankcase.

18 Dismantling the engine/gearbox: removing the crankshaft assembly and crankshaft balance weights

1   Remove the four bolts that retain the main bearing centre cap and also the two crosshead screws which pass through the cap and hold the balance weight chain guide. Tap the centre cap from position.
2   Mark all four balancer weight bearing blocks with a centre punch so that the blocks can be replaced in their original relative positions, on reassembly. Remove the eight (8) bearing block holding bolts and the balancer weight assemblies off their

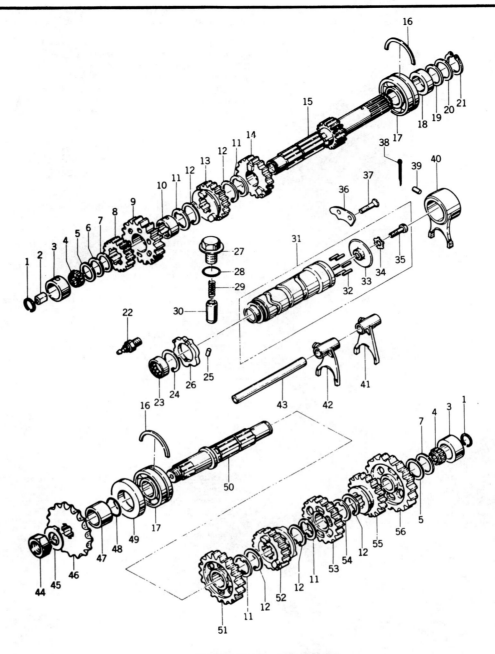

Fig. 1.6. Gearbox components

1	Circlip - 2 off	13	Mainshaft 3rd gear pinion - 22T	26	Stopper plate		selector fork
2	Plug	14	Mainshaft 4 th gear pinion - 25T	27	Stopper plunger housing	41	1st gear selector fork
3	Needle bearing outer race - 2 off	15	Mainshaft/1st gear pinion - 14T	28	'O' ring	42	2nd and 3rd gear selector fork
4	Needle roller bearing - 2 off	16	Bearing halfclip - 2 off	29	Detent spring	43	Selector fork rod
5	Steel thrust washer - 2 off	17	Journal ball bearing - 2 off	30	Stopper plunger	44	Sprocket nut
6	Phosphor-bronze thrust washer	18	Distance collar	31	Gear change drum	45	Tab washer
7	Steel thrust washer - 2 off	19	Shim - u.r.	32	Change drum pin - 6 off	46	Final drive sprocket
8	Mainshaft 2nd gear pinion - 19T	20	Shim - u.r.	33	Pin retainer plate	47	Distance collar
9	Mainshaft top gear pinion - 27T	21	Circlip	34	Lock washer	48	'O' ring
10	Mainshaft top gear bush	22	Neutral gear indicator switch	35	Screw	49	Oil seal
11	Thrust washer - 4 off	23	Needle roller bearing	36	Change drum locator plate	50	Layshaft
12	Circlip - 5 off	24	Circlip	37	Countersunk screw - 2 off	51	Layshaft 2nd gear pinion
		25	Drive pin	38	Split pin	52	Layshaft top gear pinion
				39	Location pin	53	Layshaft 3rd gear pinion
				40	4th gear and top gear	54	Thrust washer
						55	Layshaft 4th gear pinion
						56	Layshaft 1st gear pinion

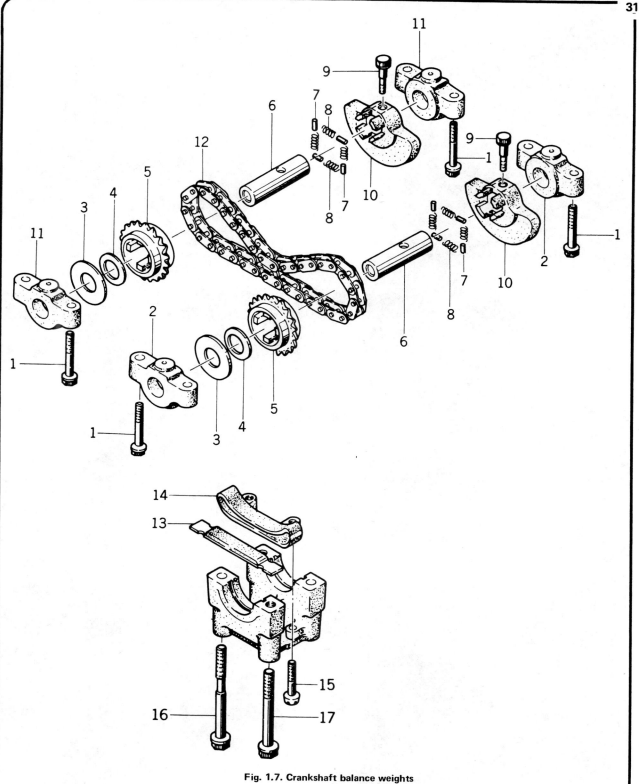

Fig. 1.7. Crankshaft balance weights

1	Bearing block holding down bolts - 8 off	4	Thrust washer - 2 off
2	Balance weight bearing block - 2 off	5	Balance weight sprocket
3	Thrust washer - 2 off	6	Balance shaft - 2 off
		7	Plunger pin - 8 off
		8	Balance weight spring - 8 off

9	Balance weight bolt - 2 off	13	Chain guide
10	Balance weight - 2 off	14	Chain tensioner
11	Balance weight bearing block - 2 off	15	Screw - 2 off
12	Chain	16	Bolt - 2 off
		17	Bolt - 2 off

18.1a Remove screws and bolts on main bearing cap . . .

18.1b . . . to allow removal of the cap and . . .

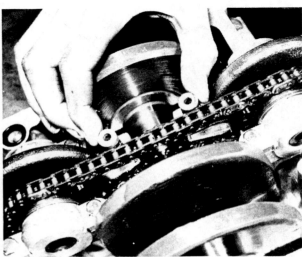

18.1c . . . the balance chain guide piece

18.2a When removing the balance weights . . .

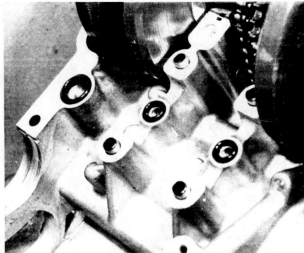

18.2b . . . note the position of the five 'O' rings

18.4a Lift out the crankshaft assembly complete

18.4b Crankcase, general view

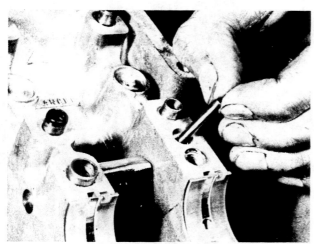

18.5a Dowel pin in bearing cap fitting surface . . .

18.5b . . .secures chain guide pivot pin

respective dowel pins. In order to ensure that each set of balance weights and balance blocks remain in correct relationship with each other, pass a length of wire through each balance weight shaft centre and tie the wire around the weight.

3   Remove the four 'O' rings from position in the oilways.

4   The crankshaft assembly together with the camshaft chain can now be lifted out of position on its bearing halves. Do not remove the bearing shells at this stage.

5   Pull the locking pin from position in the left-hand centre main bearing support and knock the chain tensioner pivot rod out towards the primary drive side of the engine. This will allow the chain tensioner blade to be removed.

19 Dismantling engine/gearbox: removing the gearbox bearings and dismantling the gear clusters

1   Two types of gearbox bearing are utilised. The input end of the mainshaft and the output end of the layshaft run on large diameter journal ball bearings. The other ends of both shafts, being under less load are run on smaller, caged needle roller bearings. The journal ball bearings are an interference fit on their respective shafts and may be carefully tapped from position. If the bearings are excessively tight a special bearing puller may be required. This tool is listed as Kawasaki service tool No. 57001-158.

2   The gearbox shaft needle roller bearings are retained on the shafts by spring 'C' clips. Removal of the clips will allow the cages to be pulled from position.

3   The inner end of the gearchange drum runs on a caged needle roller bearing lying in a blind hole in the gearbox wall. In the unlikely event that this bearing is worn, it can be hooked from position with a small screwdriver or the tang of a file. Do not remove this bearing unless it is worn as it is unlikely that damage can be avoided during removal, necessitating replacement by a new component in any event.

4   It should not be necessary to dismantle the gear cluster unless damage has occurred to any of the pinions or a fault has become apparent in a gearbox shaft.

5   The accompanying illustrations show how the clusters are arranged on their shafts. It is imperative that the gear clusters, including the thrust washers and circlips are assembled in **EXACTLY** the correct sequence otherwise constant gear selection problems will arise.

6   In order to eliminate the risk of incorrect reassembly make a rough sketch as the pinions are removed. Also strip and rebuild as soon as possible to reduce any confusion which might occur at a later date.

20 Examination and renovation: general

1   Before examining the component parts of the dismantled engine/gear unit for wear, it is essential that they should be cleaned thoroughly. Use a paraffin/petrol mix to remove all traces of oil and sludge which may have accumulated within the engine.

2   Examine the crankcase castings for cracks or other signs of damage. If a crack is discovered, it will require professional attention or in an extreme case, renewal of the casting.

3   Examine carefully each part to determine the extent of wear. If in doubt, check with the tolerance figures whenever they are quoted in the text. The following sections will indicate what type of wear can be expected and in many cases, the acceptable limits.

4   Use clean, lint-free rags for cleaning and drying the various components, otherwise there is risk of small particles obstructing the internal oilways.

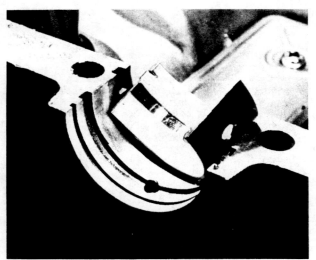

21.4a Bearing shells are located by tongues

21.4b Marks on back of shells indicate fitting sizes

21.5a Big-end shells fit in similar manner to mains

21.5b Marks on big-end caps ensure correct replacement

24.2 Balance weight assemblies can be dismantled for inspection

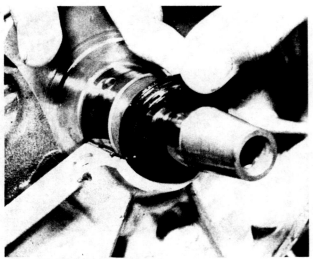

25.1a Oil seals on crankshaft ends . . .

21 Examination and renovation: main bearings and big-end bearings

1   The Kawasaki KZ400 series are fitted with shell type bearings on the crankshaft and the big-end assemblies.
2   Bearing shells are relatively inexpensive and it is prudent to renew the entire set of main bearing shells when the engine is dismantled completely, especially in view of the amount of work which will be necessary at a latter date if any of the bearings fail. Always renew the four (4) sets of main bearings together.
3   Wear is usually evident in the form of scuffing or score marks in the bearing surface. It is not possible to polish these marks out in view of the very soft nature of the bearing surface and the increased clearance that will result. If wear of this nature is detected, the crankshaft must be checked for ovality as described in the following section.
4   Failure of the big-end bearings is invariably accompanied by a pronounced knock within the crankcase. The knock will become progressively worse and vibration will also be experienced. It is essential that bearing failure is attended to without delay because if the engine is used in this condition there is a risk of breaking a connecting rod or even the crankshaft, causing more extensive damage.
5   Before the big-end bearings can be examined the bearing caps must be removed from each connecting rod. Each cap is retained by two high tensile bolts. Before removal, mark each cap in relation to its connecting rod so that it may be replaced correctly. As with the main bearings, wear will be evident as scuffing or scoring and the bearing shells must be replaced as two (2) complete sets.
6   Replacement bearing shells for either the big-end or main bearings are supplied on a selected fit basis (ie; bearings are selected for correct tolerance to fit the original journal diameter), and it is essential that the parts to be used for renewal are of identical size. The bearing size is stamped on the rear face of each shell. The marking will almost invariably be STD (standard size) but it is wise to make certain.

22 Examination and renovation: crankshaft assembly

1   If wear has necessitated the renewal of the big-end and/or main bearing shells, the crankshaft should be checked with a micrometer to verify whether ovality has occured. If the reading on any one journal varies by more than 0.002 inch (0.06 mm) the crankshaft should be renewed.
2   Mount the crankshaft by supporting both ends on V blocks or between centres on a lathe and check the run-out at the centre main bearing surfaces by means of a dial gauge. The run-out will be half that of the gauge reading indicated. The correct run-out as standard is under 0.0008 inch (0.02 mm) and if it exceeds 0.002 inch (0.05 mm) the crankshaft should be renewed.
3   The clearance between any set of bearings and their respective journal may be checked by the use of plastigauge (press gauge). Plastigauge is a graduated strip of plastic material that can be compressed between two mating surfaces. The resulting width of the material when measured with a micrometer will give the amount of clearance. For example if the clearance in the big-end bearing was to be measured, plastigauge should be used in the following manner.

    Cut a strip of plastigauge to the width across the bearing to be measured. Place the plastigauge strip across the bearing journal so that it is parallel with the crankshaft. Place the connecting rod complete with its half shell on the journal and then carefully replace the bearing cap complete with half shell onto the connecting rod bolts. Replace and tighten the retaining nuts to the correct torque and then loosen and remove the nuts and the bearing cap. Without bending or pressing the plastigauge strip, place it at its thickest point between a micrometer and read off the measurement. This will indicate the precise clearance. The original size and wear limit of the crankshaft journals and the standard and service limit clearance between all the bearings is given in the specifications at the beginning of this Chapter.
4   The crankshaft has drilled oil passages which allow oil to be fed under pressure to the working surfaces. It will be noted that a screw plug is fitted on each web of the crankshaft, directly adjacent to the big-end journals. Removal of these plugs will allow the oilways to be cleaned out with a petro-degradable substance such as 'Gunk' and then to be blown clear with a high pressure air line to remove all foreign matter. It will be necessary to use a 'punch' screwdriver to remove these two (2) blanking plugs as they are by necessity extremely tight. On replacement, the threads of each plug should be lightly coated with a non-permanent locking fluid to ensure perfect security.
5   When refitting the connecting rods and shell bearings, note that under no circumstances should the shells be adjusted with a shim, 'scraped in' or the fit 'corrected' by filing the connecting rod and bearing cap or by applying emery cloth to the bearing surface. Treatment such as this will end in disaster; if the bearing fit is not good, the parts concerned have not been assembled correctly. This advise also applies to the main bearing shells. Use new big-end bolts too - the originals may have stretched and weakened.
6   Oil the bearing surfaces before reassembly takes place and make sure the tags of the bearing shells are located correctly. After the initial tightening of the connecting rod nuts, check that each connecting rod revolves freely, then tighten to a torque setting of 24 - 27 ft/lbs (3.3 - 3.7 kg/m). Check again that the bearing is quite free.

23 Connecting rods: examination and renovation

1   It is unlikely that either of the connecting rods will bend during normal usage, unless an unusual occurrence such as a dropped valve has caused the engine to lock. Carelessness when removing a tight gudgeon pin can also give a rise to a similar problem. It is not advisable to straighten a bent connecting rod; renewal is the only satisfactory solution.
2   The small end eye of the connecting rod is unbushed and it will be necessary to renew the connecting rod if the gudgeon pin becomes a slack fit. Always check that the oil hole in the small end eye is not blocked since if the oil supply is cut off, the bearing surfaces will wear very rapidly.

24 Examination and renovation: the balance weights and drive chain

1   When checking the balance weight assemblies it is best to check each set independently to avoid accidental interchange of the component parts.
2   Separate the balance weight assembly into its component parts. The bearing blocks will pull off the shaft either side of the sprocket and weight. Note and record the number of shims and their original positions. Tap the sprocket from place with a soft-nosed mallet. The springs and pins in the cush drive spider can now be prised carefully from position.
3   Measure each shaft and its corresponding bearing diameter with a micrometer or vernier gauge. The correct sizes are as follows:

	Standard	Service limit
Balancer shaft	0.7861" - 0.7866"	0.7846"
	(19.967 - 19.980 mm)	(19.93 mm)
Bearing block I.D.	0.7876" - 0.7885"	0.7905"
	(20.007 - 20.028 mm)	(20.08 mm)

4   Measure the free length of each cush spring. Replace any spring that is shorter than the service limit.

Standard	Service limit
Cush spring 0.386'' - 0.410''	0.354''
(9.8 - 10.4 mm)	(9.0 mm)

5   Check the balancer weight chain for wear. This is most easily accomplished as follows:

Hold the chain at one end over a fixed anchor and pull it taut with a force of about 11 lbs (5 kg) using a spring balance. Using a vernier gauge or steel rule measure a 20-link length from the centres of the link pins. The measurement should read as follows:

Standard	Service limit
Chain length 6.3''	6.4''
(160 mm)	(162.4 mm)

6   Replace the components in the reverse order of dismantling. The sprocket must be replaced with its punch marked face away from the balance weight, but the punch mark pointing towards the balance weight as a whole. This is to ensure that the sprocket will be correctly timed for balance weight timing on replacement.
7   Replace the bearing blocks with the machined faces towards the balance weight. The small diameter shim on the sprocket side should be replaced before the remainder of the shims.

25 Oil seals: examination and replacement

1   An oil seal is fitted to the right-hand end of the crankshaft assembly, to prevent oil from entering the contact breaker. There is also an oil seal fitted behind the gearbox final drive sprocket. If either seal is damaged or has shown a tendency to leak, it must be renewed.
2   Oil seals also tend to lose their effectiveness if they harden with age. It is difficult to give any firm recommendations in this respect except to say that if there is any doubt about the condition of a seal, renew it as a precaution.

26 Examination and renovation: cylinder block

1   The usual indication of badly worn cylinder bores and pistons is excessive smoking from the exhausts, high crankcase compression which causes oil leaks, and piston slap, a metallic rattle that occurs when there is little or no load on the engine. If the top of the cylinder bore is examined carefully, it will be found that there is a ridge at the front and back the depth of which will indicate the amount of wear which has taken place. This ridge marks the limit of travel of the top piston ring.
2   Since there is a difference in cylinder wear in different directions, side to side and back to front measurements should be made. Take measurements at three different points down the length of the cylinder bore, starting just below the top piston ring ridge, then about 2½ inch (60 mm) below the top of the bore and the last measurements about 1 inch (25 mm) from the bottom of the cylinder bore. The cylinder measurement as standard and the service limit are as follows:

Standard	Service limit
Cylinder bore 2.510'' - 2.5198''	2.5228''
(63.984 - 64.004 mm)	(64.08 mm)

If any of the cylinder bore inside diameter measurement exceed the service limit the cylinder must be bored out to take the next size of piston. If there is a difference of more than 0.002'' (0.05 mm) between any two measurements the cylinder should, in any case, be rebored.
3   Oversize pistons are available in two sizes 0.020'' (1.0 mm) and 0.040'' (2.0 mm). If a cylinder bore requires boring to more than 2.5582'' (64.98 mm) the cylinder block must be renewed.
4   Check that the surface of the cylinder bore is free from score marks or other damage that may have resulted from an earlier

engine seizure or a displaced gudgeon pin. A rebore will be necessary to remove any deep scores, irrespective of the amount of bore wear that has taken place, otherwise a compression leak will occur.
5   Make sure the external cooling fins of the cylinder block are not clogged with oil or road dirt which will prevent the free flow of air and cause the engine to overheat.
6   If removed for any reason, the cylinder block and cylinder head holding down studs are removed from the crankcase, they should be smeared with Loctite before they are reinserted. This is essential if risk of oil seepage is to be avoided, as some of the studs pierce the oil galleries.

Fig. 1.8. Freeing gummed rings

27 Examination and renovation: pistons and piston rings

1   Attention to the pistons and piston rings can be over looked if a rebore is necessary, since new components will be fitted.
2   If a rebore is not necessary, examine each piston carefully. Reject pistons that are scored or badly discoloured as the result of exhaust gases by-passing the rings.
3   Remove all carbon from the piston crowns, using a blunt scraper, which will not damage the surface of the piston. Clean away carbon deposits from the valve cutaways and finish off with metal polish so that a smooth, shining surface is achieved. Carbon will not adhere so readily to a polished surface.
4   Small high spots on the back and front areas of the piston can be carefully eased back with a fine swiss file. Dipping the file in methylated spirts or rubbing its teeth with chalk will prevent the file clogging and eventually scoring the piston. Only very small quantities of material should be removed, and never enough to interfere with the correct tolerances. Never use emery paper or cloth to clean the piston skirt; the fine particles of emery are inclined to embed themselves in the soft aluminium and consequently accelerate the rate of wear between bore and piston.
5   Measure the outside diameter of the piston about 0.2'' (5.0 mm) up from the skirt at right angles to the spine of the gudgeon pin. If the measurement is under the service limit the piston should be renewed.

Standard	Service limit
Piston diameter 2.5173'' - 2.5181''	2.5118''
(63.94 - 63.96 mm)	

The above measurement only applies to a standard piston. If an over size piston is being checked, the service limit is the original size of the piston minus 0.006'' (0.15 mm).
6   Check that the gudgeon pin bosses are not worn or the circlip grooves damaged. Check that the piston ring grooves are not enlarged. Side float should not exceed 0.008'' (0.22 mm) for the top ring, and 0.0075'' (0.20 mm) for the second ring and oil scraper ring.

25.1b . . . located in grooves next to bearing shells

28.2a Use valve spring compressor to remove collets and ...

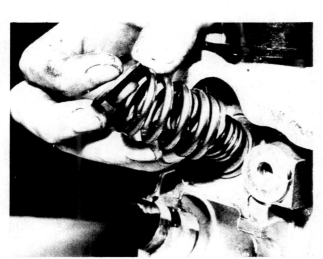

28.2b . . . allow removal of spring cap and springs

7 Piston ring wear can be measured by inserting the rings in the bore from the top and pushing them down with the base of the piston so that they are square with the bore and close to the bottom of the bore where the cylinder wear is least. Place a feeler gauge between the ring end. If the clearance exceeds the service limit the ring should be renewed.

	Standard	Service limit
End gap	0.008″ - 0.016″	0.027″
	(0.2 - 0.4 mm)	(0.7 mm)

8 Check that there is no build up of carbon either in the ring grooves or the inner surfaces of the rings. Any carbon deposits should be carefully scraped away. A short length of old piston ring fitted with a handle and sharpened at one end to a chisel point is ideal for scraping out encrusted piston ring grooves.
9 All pistons have their size stamped on the piston crown, original pistons being stamped standard (STD) and oversize pistons having the amount of oversize indicated.

28 Examination and renovation: cylinder head and valves

1 It is best to remove all carbon deposits from the combustion chambers before removing the valves for inspection and grinding-in. Use a blunt end chisel or scraper so that the surfaces are not damaged. Finish off with a metal polish to achieve a smooth, shining surface. If a mirror finish is required a high speed felt mop and polishing soap may be used. A chuck attached to a flexible drive will facilitate the polishing operation.
2 A valve spring compression tool must be used to compress each set of valve springs in turn, thereby allowing the split collets to be removed from the valve cap and the valve springs and caps to be freed. Keep each set of parts separate and mark each valve so that it can be replaced in the correct combustion chamber. There is no danger of inadvertently replacing an inlet valve in an exhaust position, or vice-versa, as the valve heads are of different sizes. The normal method of marking valves for later identification is by centre punching them on the valve head. This method is not recommended on valves, or any other highly stressed components, as it will produce high stress points and may lead to early failure. Tie-on labels, suitably inscribed, are ideal for the purpose.
3 Before giving the valves and valve seats further attention, check the clearance between each valve stem and the guide in which it operates. Clearances are as follows:

	Standard	Service limit
Inlet valve/guide clearance	0.0008″ - 0.002″	0.004″
	(0.02 - 0.05 mm)	(0.1 mm)
Exhaust valve/guide clearance		
	0.0011″ - 0.0023″	0.004″
	(0.03 - 0.06 mm)	(0.1 mm)

Measure the valve stem at the point of greatest wear and then measure again at right-angles to the first measurement. If the valve stem is below the service limit it must be renewed.

	Standard	Service limit
Inlet valve stem	0.274″ - 0.2748″	0.270″
	(6.965 - 6.980 mm)	(6.86 mm)
Exhaust valve stem	0.2738″ - 0.2744″	0.269″
	(6.955 - 6.970 mm)	(6.85 mm)

The valve stem/guide clearance can be measured with the use of a dial guage and a new valve. Place the new valve into the guide and measure the amount of shake with the dial guage tip resting against the top of the stem. If the amount of wear is greater than the wear limit, the guide must be renewed.
4 To remove an old valve guide, place the cylinder head in an oven and heat it to about 150°C. The old guide can now be tapped out from the cylinder side. The correct drift should be

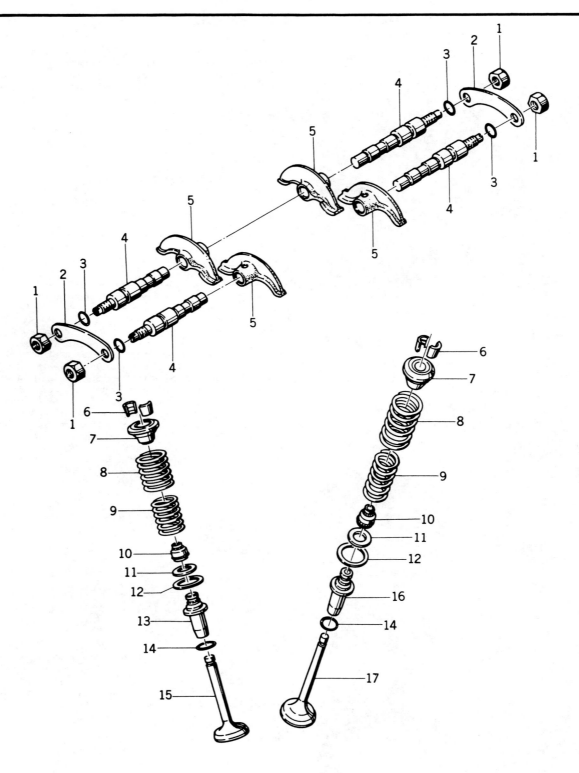

Fig. 1.9. Valves and valve gear

1 Locknut - 4 off
2 Lock washer plate - 2 off
3 'O' ring - 4 off
4 Rocker shaft - 4 off
5 Rocker arm - 4 off
6 Valve collet - 8 off

7 Valve spring collar - 4 off
8 Outer valve spring - 4 off
9 Inner valve spring - 4 off
10 Valve stem oil seal - 4 off

11 Inner valve spring seat - 4 off
12 Outer valve spring seat - 4 off
13 Exhaust valve guide - 2 off
14 Valve guide 'O' ring - 4 off

15 Exhaust valve - 2 off
16 Inlet valve guide - 2 off
17 Inlet valve guide - 2 off

shouldered with the smaller diameter the same size as the valve stem and the larger diameter slightly smaller than the O.D. of the valve guide. If a suitable drift is not available a plain brass drift may be utilised with great care. If an oven is not available for valve guide removal, local expansion may be effected by the use of a blow torch. Do not allow the flame to remain on one spot for too long, and ensure that the head is evenly heated. Each valve guide is fitted with an 'O' ring to ensure perfect sealing. The 'O' rings must be replaced with new components. New guides should be fitted with the head at the same heat as for removal.

5 Valve grinding is a simple task. Commence by smearing a trace of fine valve grinding compound (carborundum paste) on the valve seat and apply a suction tool to the head of the valve. Oil the valve stem and insert the valve in the guide so that the two surfaces to be ground in make contact with one another. With a semi-rotary motion, grind in the valve head to the seat, using a backward and forward action. Lift the valve occasionally so that the grinding compound is distributed evenly. Repeat the application until an unbroken ring of light grey matt finish is obtained on both valve and seat. This denotes the grinding operation is now complete. Before passing to the next valve, make sure that all traces of the valve grinding compound have been removed from both the valve and its seat and that none has entered the valve guide. If this precaution is not observed, rapid wear will take place due to the highly abrasive nature of the carborundum base.

6 When deep pits are encountered, it will be necessary to use a valve refacing machine and a valve seat cutter, set to an angle of 45°. Never resort to excessive grinding because this will only pocket the valves in the head and lead to reduced engine efficiency. If there is any doubt about the condition of a valve, fit a new one.

7 Examine the condition of the valve collets and the groove on the valve stem in which they seat. If there is any sign of damage, new parts should be fitted. Check that the valve spring collar is not cracked. If the collets work loose or the collar splits whilst the engine is running, a valve could drop into the cylinder and cause extensive damage.

8 Check the free length of each of the valve springs. The springs have reached their serviceable limit when they have compressed to the limit readings given in the Specifications Section of this Chapter.

9 Reassemble the valve and valve springs by reversing the dismantling procedure. Fit new oil seals to each valve guide and oil both the valve stem and the valve guide, prior to reassembly. Take special care to ensure the valve guide oil seal is not damaged when the valve is inserted. As a final check after assembly, give the end of each valve stem a light tap with a hammer, to make sure the split collets have located correctly.

10 Check the cylinder head for straightness, especially if it has shown a tendency to leak oil at the cylinder head joint. If there is any evidence of warpage, provided it is not too great, the cylinder head must be either machined flat or a new head fitted. Most cases of cylinder head warpage can be traced to unequal tensioning of the cylinder head nuts and bolts by tightening them in incorrect sequence.

29 Examination and renovation: rocker spindles and rocker arms

1 Undo the rocker spindle locking nuts and pull of the locking plate. Prise out each rocker spindle and lift out the rocker arms. Take care that each spindle remains with its original rocker arm.
2 Check the rocker arms for undue wear on their spindles and renew any that show excessive play. Examine each rocker arm where it bears on the cam and the opposite end which bears on the valve stem head. Arms that are badly hammered or worn should be renewed. Slight wear marks may be stoned out with an oil carborundum stone, but remember that if too much metal is removed it will not only weaken the component but may make correct adjustment of the tappet gap impossible.

28.2c Remove valve stem oil seal and . . .

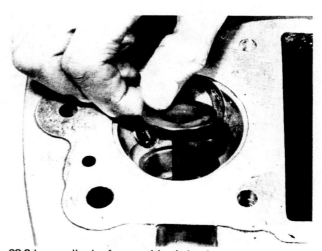
28.2d . . . pull valve from position in head

29.1a Loosen lock nuts and remove lock plate . . .

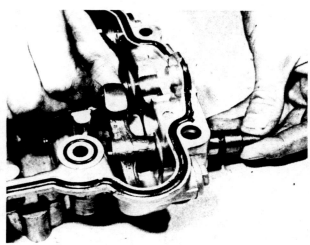

29.1b . . . to allow removal of rocker shafts and arms

30.2 Scuffing on camshaft bearing indicates poor lubrication

31.4 Ensure oil hole in gear housing aligns on replacement

3   Check the condition of the cam spindle 'O' rings and renew if necessary.

30 Examination and renovation: camshaft, camshaft bearings, drive chain and tensioner

1   The camshaft should be examined visually for wear, which will probably be most evident on the ramps of each cam and where the cam contour changes sharply. Also check the bearing surfaces for obvious wear and scoring. Cam lift can be checked by measuring the height of the cam from the bottom of the base circle to the top of the lobe. If the measurement is less than the service limit which is as follows the opening of that particular valve will be reduced resulting in poor performance.

	Standard	Service limit
Cam height	1.5114 in - 1.5145 in	1.508 in
	(38.39 - 38.47 mm)	(38.3 mm)

Measure the diameter of each bearing journal with a micrometer or vernier gauge. If the diameter is less than the service limit, renew the camshaft.
2   The camshaft bears directly on the cylinder head material and that of the cylinder head cover, there being no separate bearings. Check the bearing surfaces for wear and scoring. The clearance between the camshaft bearing journals and the aluminium bearing surfaces may be checked using plastigauge (press gauge) material in the same manner as described for crankshaft bearing clearance in Section 22.3 of this Chapter. If the clearance is greater than given for the service limit the recommended course is to replace the camshaft. If bad scuffing, is evident on the camshaft bearing surfaces of the cylinder head and cover, due to a lubrication failure, the only remedy is to renew the cylinder head and cylinder head cover, and the camshaft if it transpires that it has been damaged also.
3   Check the camshaft drive chain for wear and chipped or broken rollers and links. Check the wear by anchoring one end of the chain and pulling it taut. Measure a 20 link length from pin to pin. The correct measurements are as follows:

	Standard	Service limit
Camshaft chain	6.3 in	6.4 in
	(160 mm)	(162.4 mm)

If the chain is longer than the service limit or if any rollers are broken the chain must be renewed.
4   Check both chain guide tongues for wear on their rubber faces and measure the thickness of the rubber at about the centre of the tongues.

	Standard	Service limit
Front tongue thickness	0.12 in	0.060 in
	(3.3 mm)	(1.5 mm)
Rear tongue thickness	0.17 in	0.078 in
	(4.5 mm)	(2.0 mm)

31 Examination and renovation: camshaft drive chain sprockets and tachometer drive gears

1   The upper camshaft chain sprocket is bolted to the camshaft and in consequence is easily renewable if the teeth become hooked, worn, chipped or broken. The lower sprocket is integral with the crankshaft and if any of these defects are evident, the complete crankshaft assembly must be renewed. Fortunately, this drastic course of action is rarely necessary since the parts concerned are fully enclosed and well lubricated, working under ideal conditions.
2   If the sprockets are renewed, the chain should be renewed at the same time. It is bad practice to run old and new parts together since the rate of wear will be accelerated.

3 The worm drive to the tachometer is an integral part of the camshaft which meshes with a pinion attached to the cylinder head cover. If the worm is damaged or badly worn, it will be necessary to renew the camshaft complete.

4 The tachometer driven worm gear shaft is fitted in a housing which is a press fit in the cylinder head cover. If the worm gear is chipped or broken the gear and integral shaft should be removed. The shaft and housing can be eased from position in the cylinder head cover with the use of a screwdriver. Make certain when replacing these components that the oil hole drilled in the shaft housing is aligned with the oil hole in the cover, or lubrication failure will occur.

32 Examination and replacement: primary drive chain

1 The heavy duty primary drive chain should be examined carefully for signs of wear such as worn or bent side plates and worn link pins. The chain is of the endless type and under no circumstances should any form of quickly detachable link be fitted.

33 Examination and renovation: clutch assembly

1 After an extended period of service the clutch linings will wear and promote clutch slip. The limit of wear measured across each inserted plate and the standard measurement is as follows:

	Standard	Service limit
Clutch plate thickness	0.1141 in - 0.1220 in (2.9 - 3.1 mm)	0.0984 in (2.5 mm)

When the overall width reaches the limit, the inserted plates must be renewed, preferably as a complete set.

2 The plain plates should not show any excess heating (blueing). Check the warpage of each plate using plate glass or surface plate and a feeler gauge. The maximum allowable warpage is 0.011 in (0.30 mm).

3 Check the condition of the steel spring rings which lie between the clutch plates. Replace any that are bent or broken.

4 Check the free length of each clutch spring with a vernier gauge. After considerable use the springs will take a permanent set thereby reducing the pressure applied to the clutch plates. The correct measurements are as follows:

Standard	Service limit
Clutch springs 1.330 in (33.8 mm)	1.271 in (32.3 mm)

5 Examine the clutch assembly for burrs or indentation on the edges of the protruding tongues of the inserted plates and/or slots worn in the edges of the outer drum with which they engage. Similar wear can occur between the inner tongues of the plain clutch plates and the slots in the clutch inner drum. Wear of this nature will cause clutch drag and slow disengagement during gear changes, since the plates will become trapped and will not free fully when the clutch is withdrawn. A small amount of wear can be corrected by dressing with a fine file; more extensive wear will necessitate renewal of the worn parts.

6 The clutch release mechanism attached to the final drive sprocket cover does not normally require attention provided it is greased at regular intervals. It is held to the cover by two crosshead screws and operates on the worm and quick start thread principle.

34 Examination and renovation: gearbox components

1 Examine each of the gear pinions to ensure that there are no chipped or broken teeth and that the dogs on the end of the pinions are not rounded. Gear pinions with any of these defects must be renewed; there is no satisfactory method of reclaiming them.

2 The gearbox bearings must be free from play and show no signs of roughness when they are rotated. After thorough washing in petrol the bearings should be examined for roughness and play. Also check for pitting on the roller tracks.

3 It is advisable to renew the gearbox oil-seals irrespective of their condition. Should a re-used oil seal fail at a late date, a considerable amount of work is involved to gain access to renew it.

4 Check the gear selector rods for straightness by rolling them on a sheet of plate glass. A bent rod will cause difficulty in selecting gears and will make the gear change particularly heavy.

5 The selector forks should be examined closely, to ensure that they are not bent or badly worn. The case hardened pegs which engage with the cam channels are easily renewable if they are worn. Under normal conditions, the gear selector mechanism is unlikely to wear quickly, unless the gearbox oil level has been allowed to become low.

6 The tracks in the selector drum, with which the selector forks engage, should not show any undue signs of wear unless neglect has led to under lubrication of the gearbox. Check the tension of the gearchange pawl, gearchange arm and drum stopper arm springs. Weakness in the springs will lead to imprecise gear selection. Check the condition of the gear stopper arm roller and the pins in the change drum end with which it engages. It is unlikely that wear will take place here except after considerable mileage.

7 Check the condition of the kickstart components. If slipping has been encountered a worn ratchet and pawl will invariably be traced as the cause. Any other damage or wear to the components will be self-evident. If either the ratchet or pawl is found to be faulty, both components must be replaced as a pair. Examine the kickstart return spring, which should be renewed if there is any doubt about its condition.

35 Engine reassembly: general

1 Before reassembly of the engine/gear unit is commenced, the various component parts should be cleaned thoroughly and placed on a sheet of clean paper, close to the working area.

2 Make sure all traces of old gaskets have been removed and that the mating surfaces are clean and undamaged. One of the best ways to remove old gasket cement is to apply a rag soaked in methylated spirit. This acts as a solvent and will ensure that the cement is removed without resort to scraping and the consequent risk of damage.

3 Gather together all of the necessary tools and have available an oil can filled with clean engine oil. Make sure all new gaskets and oil seals are to hand, also all replacement parts required. Nothing is more frustrating than having to stop in the middle of a reassembly sequence because a vital gasket or replacement has been overlooked.

4 Make sure that the reassembly area is clean and that there is adequate working space. Refer to the torque and clearance settings wherever they are given. Many of the smaller bolts are easily sheared if over-tightened. Always use the correct size screwdriver bit for the crosshead screws and never an ordinary screwdriver or punch. If the existing screws show evidence of maltreatment in the past, it is advisable to renew them as a complete set.

36 Engine reassembly: replacing the crankshaft assembly and balance weights

1 Place the upper crankcase half so that it rests on the rear edge of the casing and the cylinder block studs.

2 Position the front camshaft chain tensioner tongue and replace the pivot shaft through the hole in the right-hand crankcase wall. The pivot pin should be replaced with its relieved end

36.2a Camshaft chain guide pivot shaft when replaced . . .

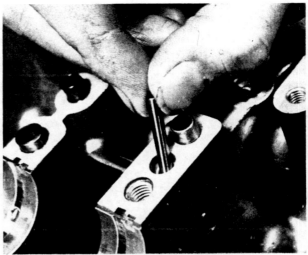

36.2b . . . must be locked by dowel pin

36.6a 'Bright' links on timing chain must align with 'dot'. . .

36.6b . . . with balance weights in position as shown

36.6c Tighten balance weight bearings to correct torque

36.8a Replace balance chain guide and . . .

36.8b . . . lubricate centre bearing cup before replacement

36.8c Tighten cap bolts to correct torque

37.2a Refit selector fork on change drum . . .

first so that the locking pin can be fitted and so render it secure.

3 Lubricate with engine oil the main bearing shells, after ensuring that they are correctly in place. Fit the camshaft drive chain onto the crankshaft sprocket. The correct sprocket is the smaller of the two. Place a new oil seal on the left-hand crankshaft end with the spring side facing inwards. The crankshaft can now be lowered into place, making certain that the chain falls into the tunnel between the two crankcase mouths, and that the oil seal sits in its groove in the crankcase.

4 Replace the five 'O' rings. Four equal sized small rings fit in recesses in the oil passages which feed the balance weight shafts. The fifth and larger ring lies to the rear of the outer crank web on the drive side.

5 The two balance weights, complete with bearing blocks must now be replaced and timed, together with the drive chain. Turn the crankshaft so that when viewed from the front of the engine the oil holes in the journals are half visible at the crankcase mating surface and the flywheels (webs) are facing upwards.

6 Lay the two balance weight assemblies on the bench so that the sprockets are facing upwards. Fit the drive chain on the sprockets with the two 'bright' links facing upwards, so that each 'bright' link engages with the punch marked tooth on each sprocket. The balance weights are now timed relative to each other. Keeping the two assemblies pulled apart so that drive chain is kept taut the complete assembly can be replaced in the crankcase. With the two balance weight assemblies positioned on their dowel pins in the crankcase and the drive chain meshed with the large crankshaft sprocket, recheck the timing relationship; refer to photographs. It must be correct.

7 Position the drive chain guide between the upper and lower chain runs. Fit the balance weight holder bolts, which should be tightened evenly and in a diagonal sequence. Complete the tightening with a torque wrench to 16.5 - 19.5 ft/lbs (2.3 - 2.7 kg/m).

8 Fit the main bearing centre cap so that the arrow faces the front. Apply non-permanent locking fluid to the balancer chain guide retaining screws and tighten the guide against the underside of the main bearing cap. The bosses through which the four main bearing cap retaining bolts are marked 1-2-3 and 4. This is the order in which the bolts should be tightened, at 18 - 22 ft/lbs (2.5 - 3.0 kg/m).

9 Check that the crankshaft is free to rotate. If this is not the case, the centre cap bolts should be removed and the two bearings in the cap checked.

37 Engine reassembly: replacing the gearbox components and kickstart shaft components

1 Insert the gearchange drum through the large hole in the drive side gearbox wall, until it is about half way through. Lightly lubricate the 3rd gear selector fork and slide it onto the change drum so that the locking pin hole faces the crankshaft.

2 Ensure that the change drum stopper plate drive pin is in place and position the stopper plate on the end of the change drum. The stopper plate must be fitted with the small projection (which operates the neutral warning switch) facing out, away from the change drum body. The stopper plate is retained by a circlip on the end of the change drum. The change drum can now be moved across and pushed into the needle bearing in the gearbox wall.

3 Fit the 3rd gear selector fork locking pin through the fork and into the middle channel in the change drum. Fit a new split pin through the selector fork and pin, and bend back the legs of the pin. Slide the selector fork rod part way into the gearbox and fit the two remaining selector forks. Viewed from the rear of the engine, fit the fork with the cutaway boss to the timing side, with the cutaway facing the timing side gearbox wall. Fit the second fork so that the drive pin is offset towards the drive side wall. Make certain that the fork pins engage correctly with the channels in the change drum.

4 Fit the clutch pushrod oil seal in the groove in the timing side

37.2b . . . which is located by a split pin

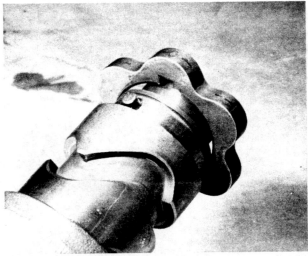

37.3a Cam stopper plate locates on drive pin . . ..

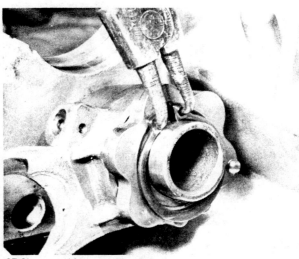

37.3b . . . and is secured by a circlip

37.3c Change drum located by a guide plate . . .

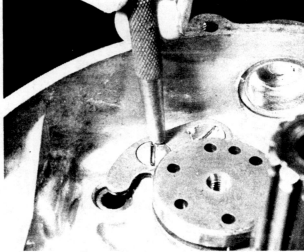

37.3d The screws must be punch locked

37.4a Refit the selector fork rod and forks ...

37.4b ...ensuring that the forks are correctly positioned

37.5a Replace the gearbox oil seal in the casing ...

37.5b ...and onto the shaft end .

37.5c Hole in needle roller bearing race locates ...

37.5d ...on peg in casing wall

37.5e Replace the two drive end bearing half clips and . . .

37.5f . . . refit the mainshaft assembly and . . .

37.5g . . . the layshaft assembly into the gearbox

37.5h Check that the selector forks engage correctly

37.6a Kickstart pawl cover held by circlip . . .

37.6b . . . as is the ratchet pawlwheel

37.6c Kickstart shaft and pawl wheel must be timed

wall next to the main shaft bearing recess. Replace the two gearbox bearing half clips in the grooves in the bearing recesses.

5 Replace the mainshaft, complete with gear clusters and bearings and then the layshaft, similarly complete. The selector forks must engage correctly with the sliding dogs on the gearshafts.

6 The kickstart shaft, complete with components, must now be replaced in the lower crankcase half. If the internal components such as the ratchet pawl and wheel have been removed for inspection, they must be replaced on the shaft before reassembly continues. See accompanying illustration. When replacing the kickstart pawl on the shaft bear in mind that the two components must be timed relative to each other, otherwise the kickstart shaft will not be suitably placed to fit the kickstart spring. A punch mark on the outer face of the pawl must align with a scribed line on the end of the kickstart shaft.

7 Place the kickshaft, complete with the internal components into the casing. Slide the kickstart shaft collar over the shaft and into the casing wall, so that the waisted portion of the collar faces outwards. Apply non-permanent locking fluid to the two countersunk screws which hold the shaft collar locking plate in place. Fit the plate and tighten the screws. Fit the shaft retaining circlip onto the shaft, ensuring that it engages the shaft groove and fits neatly up against the shaft collar. Fit the ratchet pawl stopper plate together with the double tab washer and tighten the bolts. Do not forget to bend up the tab washer ears against the two bolt heads.

37.7a Refit kickstarter shaft assembly into lower crankcase

38 Engine reassembly: joining the crankcase halves

1 Check that the oil return valve is replaced in the lower crankcase half. If the valve body has been removed, lightly coat the valve body threads with a non-permanent locking fluid before replacement. Check that the following items are correctly positioned in one or other of the crankcase halves: pushrod oil seal, timing side crankshaft seal, main oil passage 'O' ring, the two main bearing shells and the layshaft oil cup.

2 Make sure that the mating surfaces of the two crankcase halves are perfectly clean. Apply gasket compound to the face of the upper crankcase half. The lower casing can now be fitted over the upper crankcase and all the components. It is prudent to lubricate the various bearings with engine oil before fitting the lower casing. This will ensure that there is no oil starvation, however brief, when the engine is first run.

3 Insert the four (4) 8 mm screw and the ten (10) 6 mm bolts that secure the crankcase halves from the underside. First tighten the four 8 mm screws in an anticlockwise sequence, starting from the forward screw on the drive side. Tighten the screws to 18 - 22 ft/lbs (2.5 - 3.0 kg/m). Now tighten the ten 6 mm screws evenly and in as much a diagonal sequence as possible. Tighten the 6 mm screws to 69 - 87 in/lbs (0.8 - 1.0 kg/m).

4 Invert the engine so that it is the right way up and insert the six (6) upper crankcase screws. These again should be tightened evenly to a torque of 69 - 87 in/lbs (0.8 - 1.0 kg/m). Remember that the single screw on the rear most edge of the casing also holds the carburettor overflow tube retaining plate.

5 When inverting the engine for the first time, make certain that the camshaft drive chain does not fall back down into the crankcase. This can be avoided by tying the chain with string to one of the cylinder block studs.

37.7b Pawl guide bolts retained by tab washer

39 Engine reassembly: replacing the oil filter, the oil trap cover and drain plug

1 Place the engine so that the lower crankcase half faces upwards.

2 Ensure that the oil filter cover and bolt are perfectly clean and fit a new oil filter element. Check that the cover 'O' ring is in good condition and place the filter, together with the cover, in place. The cover bolt is adequately proportioned but is cross

38.1a Librally lubricate all bearings before joining crankcases

38.1b Ensure oil catch trough is in place

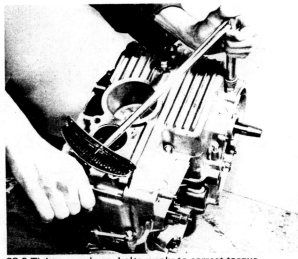

38.3 Tighten crankcase bolts evenly to correct torque

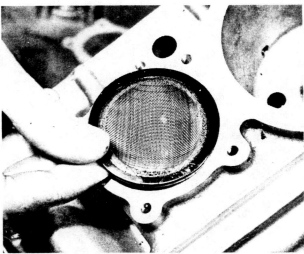

39.2a Oil filter gauze is retained by . . .

39.2b . . . aluminium cover and five screws

39.3 Fit new oil filter element

39.4 Ensure drain plug 'O' ring is in place

40.2 Replace the three 'O' rings before fitting oil pump

40.4a Ensure that change pawl engages with change pins

40.4b Gearchange shaft is retained by end plate

40.6a Tension kickstart spring and fit guide piece . . .

40.6b . . . which is retained by a circlip

41.2 Refit primary drive components as one unit

41.3a Replace thrust washer followed by . . .

41.3b . . . the clutch centre boss which . . .

41.3c . . . is retained by a circlip and shim(s)

41.4 Replace clutch plates one at a time

41.5a Insert the clutch push rod steel ball . . .

41.5b ...and lightly greased 'mushroom' headed thrust piece

drilled and axially drilled for oil feed purposes, it must therefore not be over tightened. The correct torque is 11 - 14.5 ft/lbs (1.5 - 2.0 kg/m).

3 Clean the mating surfaces of the oil trap cover. Place the oil trap gauze in position so that the dome faces inwards. Apply a little grease or gasket compound to a new gasket and replace the oil trap cover. Replace and tighten the screws evenly, to an equal torque.

4 Check that the drain plug 'O' ring is in place on the plug and replace the plug in the crankcase. Tighten to a torque of 14.5 - 18 ft/lbs (2.0 - 2.5 kg/m).

40 Engine reassembly: replacing the gearchange mechanism and the oil pump

1 Replace the gear change drum retaining plate, which is held by two countersunk screws. Punch lock the screws when they are in place, or better still apply a non-permanent locking fluid to the threads before assembly.

2 Fit the three (3) oil passage 'O' rings in the recesses in the crankcase wall where the oil pump sits. If there is any doubt about the condition of an 'O' ring it **MUST** be renewed otherwise expensive grating noises will occur eventually.

3 Place the five (5) change pins in the end of the gearchange drum. Note that there are six holes, but one hole is too small to accept a pin. Replace the pin cover and tighten the centre screw. Note that a lock washer is fitted under the screw head.

4 Lightly grease the gearchange splined shaft and introduce it through the hole in the gearbox wall. Gently push the shaft home through the oil seal in the timing side wall. This must be done with care or the seal lip will be damaged by the splines on the shaft. While pushing the shaft home, hold back the change pawl, which is spring loaded, on the end of the main arm, so that it clears the change pin assembly. The centralising spring on the main arm must be positioned correctly, with one spring leg either side of the stop screw. Replace the shaft locking plate and tighten the two retaining screws.

5 Replace the change drum stopper plunger, detent spring and bolt in the top of the gearbox casing, making certain that the 'O' ring is correctly positioned. Refit the oil pressure warning switch in the top of the casing. Note that the switch has a tapered thread, which aids oil tightness, and will therefore not screw in fully. Replace the neutral switch in the timing side of the gearbox.

6 Place the kickstart return spring over the kickstart shaft and engage the outer end of the spring with the anchor hole in the crankcase. Turn the kickstart shaft as far as it will go in a clockwise direction. Hold the inner end of the spring with a stout pair of pliers and tension the spring in an anticlockwise direction until the free end can be pushed into the radially drilled hole in the kickstart shaft. Replace the nylon spring guide and the retaining circlip.

41 Engine reassembly: replacing the clutch assembly and primary drive

1 If the oil pump drive gear was removed for inspection it should now be replaced on the boss at the rear of the clutch outer drum and the circlip refitted. The oil pump gear is not reversible and must be refitted with the recessed face away from the outer drum. **Ensure that the drive pin is replaced in the radial hole in the boss, otherwise no power will be transmitted to the gear.** The pin engages with a machined keyway in the inside of the gear.

2 Place the clutch outer drum on the bench together with the primary drive gear. Mesh the primary drive chain onto both sprockets then replace on their shafts at the same time. This method is much easier than replacing the two sprockets separately and then trying to fit the primary chain. Replace the primary drive gear circlip.

41.5c Align pressure plate 'dot' with mark on centre boss

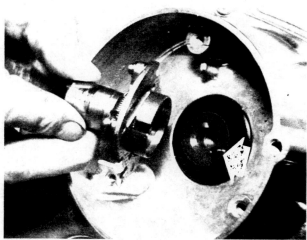

43.1 Automatic timing unit engages with roll pin on crankend

43.2 Fit contact breaker plate with condenser downwards

3 Fit the thrust washer onto the clutch shaft followed by the clutch centre boss. Replace the shim(s) followed by the circlip. These shims should take up all play between the centre boss and the circlip. If slop is still evident fit another shim.

4 The clutch plates and steel disengagement rings can now be replaced one at a time in the following order; friction plate, steel ring, steel plate, friction plate and so forth.

5 Insert the 3/8″ steel ball, followed by the 'mushroom head' pushrod piece into the hollow clutch shaft. Refit the clutch pressure plate, clutch springs, washers and bolts. The pressure plate should be replaced so that the small projections on the outer edge align with the punch marks on the outer face of the clutch centre boss. Tighten the four (4) spring bolts evenly, in a diagonal sequence, until they are tight.

42 Engine reassembly: replacing the primary drive cover

1 Before replacing the primary drive cover check that the oil seal for the timing side crankshaft is properly in position and that the spring band has not been misplaced. If a new seal is fitted it should be carefully knocked in, spring band innermost, so that the inner edge of the outer perimeter is flush with the edge of the casing.

2 Place a new gasket on the outer face of the crankcase; the dowels will hold it in position. Position the cover and knock it gently onto the dowels. Replace the twelve (12) crosshead screws and tighten them down evenly in a criss-cross sequence. Take care when fitting the outer cover that the kickstart shaft splines do not damage the oil seal lip. The forwardmost cover screw holds the contact breaker wire clip.

43 Engine reassembly: replacing the contact breaker assembly and the automatic timing unit

1 Fit the timing unit onto the end of the crankshaft. A short Mills pin projecting from the end of the shaft engages with a hole in the rear of the unit, to ensure its correct positioning with the crankshaft. Replace the crankshaft rotating hexagon (17 mm) on the end of the timing unit so that it is boss side inwards, and then replace the centre bolt. This should be tightened to a torque of 16.5 - 19.5 ft/lbs (2.3 - 2.7 kg/m). The rotation nut should, of course, be used to prevent the crankshaft turning while the bolt is being tightened.

2 Place the contact breaker plate, complete with contact breaker assembly in position in the casing. The correct position for the plate is when the condenser is at the lowest point possible. Replace the three (3) retaining screws through the sloppy holes in the plate but do not tighten fully. If the timing plate was punch marked as suggested during dismantling, it will only be necessary to rotate the contact breaker plate until the punch mark aligns with the punch mark on the top screw boss and the initial ignition timing should be correct. It is prudent to check the timing, however, as described in Chapter 3, Section 7. If the contact breaker plate wasn't marked for ease of retiming the ignition timing should be set as directed in Chapter 3, Section 7.

3 Make certain that the wiring grommet is in place in the edge of the casing and feed the wire through the clip that is held by the primary drive cover front screw. Replace the timing case cover and gasket.

44 Engine reassembly: replacing the alternator rotor, starter motor and casing

1 Place the starter motor driven sprocket onto the left-hand crankshaft with the centre boss side facing outwards. Fit the thrust washer, followed by the alternator rotor/starter clutch assembly. Replace the centre bolt and washer, tightening to a torque of 47 - 51 ft/lbs (6.5 - 7.0 kg/m). Remember that the

centre bolt has a left-hand thread and must be tightened in an anticlockwise direction.

2 Mesh the starter chain onto the driven sprocket, and with the chain placed in approximately the normal running position, mesh the starter motor sprocket with the free end of the chain. The sprocket lies with the centre boss face away from the engine.

3 Check that the large 'O' ring is in place on the drive end of the starter motor casing. Insert the starter motor into its casing at an angle, shaft first. Ease the motor over to the left so that it enters the hole in the casing wall and at the same time enter the splined shaft with the starter motor sprocket splines. Replace the two starter motor retaining bolts which pass through flanges on the motor end cover.

4 Replace the alternator cover and gasket which are held by eight (8) screws.

5 Some models do not have a starter motor as part of the machine specification.

45 Engine reassembly: replacing the pistons and cylinder block

1 Before replacing the pistons, place a clean rag in each crankcase mouth to prevent any displaced component from falling into the crankcase. It is only too easy to drop a circlip while it is being inserted into the piston boss, which would necessitate a further strip down for its retrieval.

2 Fit the pistons onto their original connecting rods, with the arrow embossed on each piston crown facing forwards. If the gudgeon pins are a tight fit in the piston bosses, warm each piston first to expand the metal. Do not forget to lubricate the gudgeon pin, small end eye and the piston bosses before reassembly.

3 Use new circlips. NEVER re-use old circlips. Check that each circlip has located correctly in its groove. A displaced circlip will cause severe engine damage.

4 Fit a new cylinder base gasket over the holding down studs. Gasket compound must not be used. Fit two new 'O' rings to the oil passage holes on the mating surface of the crankcase and, where fitted, fit new 'O' rings to each cylinder sleeve where they project from the cylinder barrel.

5 Position the piston rings so that their end gaps are out of line with each other and fit a piston ring clamp to each piston. It is highly recommended that ring clamps be used for cylinder block replacement. This operation can be done by hand but is a tedious task and it is all too easy to fracture a ring. Position the pistons at TDC.

6 Check that the camshaft rear chain guide is properly located and that the retaining pins are in place. Lubricate both cylinder bores thoroughly. Fit the cylinder block so that it rests at the top of the holding down studs and with a length of suitably bent wire hook the camshaft chain up through the chain tunnel between the cylinder bores. Run a screwdriver or rod through the chain across the top of the barrel to prevent the camshaft chain falling free.

7 Carefully slide the cylinder block down the holding down studs until the pistons enter the cylinder bores; Keeping the pistons square to the bores ease the block down until the piston clamps are displaced. Remove the two ring clamps and the rag padding from the crankcase mouths and push the cylinder block down onto the base gasket.

46 Engine reassembly: replacing the cylinder head, camshaft and timing the engine

1 Fit a new cylinder head gasket over the holding down studs, and replace the two 'square' 'O' rings. Using the hooked wire, pull the camshaft drive chain up through the chain tunnel in the cylinder head and fit the head onto the holding down studs. Place a screwdriver through the chain again, across the cylinder head.

2 Before refitting the camshaft, replace the two small cylinder

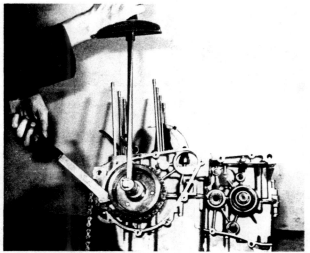
44.1 Tighten the left-hand thread bolt to correct torque

44.2 Refit starter motor and engage drive pinion

45.2a Always use new circlips when refitting piston

45.2b Arrow mark on piston crown must face forward

45.4a Replace 'O' rings on cylinder sleeves (where fitted) and . .

45.4b . . . place the 'O' rings and a new gasket on crankcase . . .

45.6 Use rod to hold cam chain in place

46.4a Place camshaft as shown when setting valve timings

46.4b 'T' mark on sprocket indicates correct position

46.5 Apply 'Locktite' to sprocket bolts before refitting

47.1a Check that the 'O' rings and sealing ring (where fitted) are correctly positioned...

47.1b ...and replace the cylinder head cover

head holding down bolts which fit adjacent to each spark plug hole. Tighten the bolts down very gently and evenly so that the cylinder head gasket is compressed and the cylinder head is pulled down into its correct position in relation to the cylinder barrel.

3 Position the camshaft sprocket onto the camshaft, with the arrow marks on the sprocket facing away from the sprocket flange Insert the camshaft through the chain from the right-hand side of the engine and fit the chain onto the sprocket. This is best accomplished by having the sprocket positioned, not up against the sprocket flange, but resting partway along the shaft on the inner bearing journal.

4 Rotate the crankshaft by means of the rotation hexagon on the automatic timing advancer until the scribed line next to the 'T' mark on the automatic timing unit aligns with the timing mark on the crankcase. Now turn the engine anticlockwise exactly 90° (¼ turn), slip the chain off the sprocket and turn the sprocket until the arrow on the sprocket, which has no letter adjacent to it, points to the front of the engine and is parallel to the cylinder head face. Turn the camshaft until the notch in the right-hand end faces directly up. Refit the chain onto the sprocket and refit the sprocket. Hold the camshaft steady and rotate the crankshaft forwards so that the sprocket bolt holes align with the bolt holes in the flange.

5 Apply a non-permanent locking fluid to the two camshaft bolts and tighten them to a torque of 10 - 11 ft/lbs (1.4 - 1.6 kg/m). Check that the valve timing is correct by turning the crankshaft until the 'T' mark line on the automatic timing unit aligns with the crankcase timing mark. The 'T' arrow on the camshaft sprocket should now face forwards and lie parallel to the cylinder head fitting face. If the marks do not align exactly, repeat the timing sequence and re-check. Absolute accuracy is essential.

47 Engine reassembly: replacing the chain tensioner unit and the cylinder head cover

1 Turn the crankshaft until the 'T' mark line on the automatic timing unit aligns with the timing mark in the crankcase. Loosen all four rocker spindle lock nuts and replace the large sealing ring and the four 'O' rings in the cylinder head cover. Use a gasket compound to hold the large sealing ring in place. Note that the large sealing ring located between the cylinder head and cover is only fitted on 1974 and 1975 models. Place the cylinder head cover on the holding down studs and then turn each rocker spindle until the punch mark next to the screwdriver slot is facing inwards (ie; towards the opposite spindle).

2 Replace and tighten the eight (8) cylinder head/cover sleeve nuts in an even and diagonal sequence. Finally tighten these nuts to a torque reading of 18 ft/lbs (2.5 kg/m). Retighten the two cylinder head flange bolts which lie next to the spark plug holes to a torque of 95 - 113 in/lbs (1.1 - 1.3 kg/m).

3 Using a new gasket replace the chain tensioner unit which is held by two crosshead screws. If the tensioner was dismantled, the sequence of assembly is as follows: pushrod, spring, tensioner body, pushrod guide and locknut. Turn the crankshaft anticlockwise and note when the pushrod is at its innermost position. Loosen the locknut and turn the pushrod guide until it is EXACTLY flush with the end of the pushrod. Retighten the locknut. This adjustment is critical, the crankshaft must be turned anticlockwise and the pushrod must be precisely flush with the guide when it is at its innermost position. Replace the 'O' ring and tensioner cap.

4 Remove the four valve clearance inspection caps and the two cylinder head side covers. With the right-hand crankcase inspection cover removed, observe the right-hand cylinder inlet valve and turn the crankshaft anticlockwise until the valve has just finished opening and closing, ie moving downwards and returning upwards. Continue turning the crankshaft anticlockwise for approximately ¼ turn until the 'T' mark on the ATU is in alignment with the timing mark pointer. The right-hand cylinder is now at the end of its compression stroke and

its inlet and exhaust valve clearances can be measured. Insert a feeler gauge of the correct thickness (see Specifications) between the valve stem and the rocker; the gauge should be a light sliding fit if the clearance is correct. If adjustment is necessary, slacken the adjuster locknut and turn the adjuster towards the + symbol to increase the clearance. Then insert the correct size feeler

47.3a Chain tension body held by two screws

47.3b Chain adjustment components

47.3c Replace the cap after adjustment

gauge between the valve stem and rocker, and turn the adjuster towards the — symbol until the feeler gauge is a light sliding fit. Retain this position whilst the locknut is tightened and recheck the setting. Repeat for the remaining valve of the right-hand cylinder. Note when making adjustment that the punch marks on the adjuster heads must face inwards, towards the

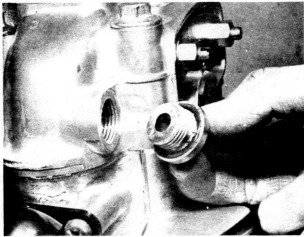

47.4a Remove the rocker caps to adjust rocker clearance

47.4b Marks on lockplate indicate direction for adjustment

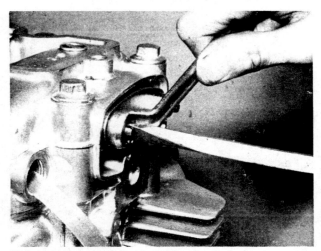

47.4c Hold rocker spindle when tightening the locknuts

+ and — symbols. When adjustment of the right-hand cylinder is complete turn the crankshaft over one full turn, realign the 'T' mark and repeat the procedure on the left-hand cylinder. Recheck all clearances after adjustment, tighten the adjuster locknuts and replace all inspection covers.

48 Engine reassembly: replacing the final drive sprocket

1 Push the 'O' ring onto the layshaft followed by the distance collar and then the sprocket. Place the lockwasher on the shaft, ensuring that the small tongue on the washer locates with the offset hole in the sprocket face. The sprocket will have to be prevented from rotating whilst the centre nut is tightened up; this may be accomplished by placing the engine in top gear and holding the crankshaft by the hexagon. Tighten the nut and bend up the tab washer against one of the nut flats. Check that the end of the gear selector rod is sealed off with a core plug.

49 Replacing the engine/gearbox unit in the frame

1 As is the case with removal, engine replacement requires considerable care and patience. Replacing the engine necessitates the use of two people and it is important that the machine is standing firmly on level ground. Lift the engine in from the right-hand side of the machine, with the front of the engine going in first. Tip the engine over to the left and then lift the rear of the engine up and into place.
2 Replace the two front engine mounting brackets. The top bolt is shared by both brackets. Lift the engine when necessary to stop the bolt threads fouling the brackets and insert the bottom rear engine bolt from the left. Note that both rear engine bolts pass through spacers which lie between the frame and the crankcase. The waisted spacer goes on the lower bolt. Replace the remaining rear bolt and front bolt. Before replacing the nuts on the engine mounting bolts, refit the head steady bracket which is held to the breather cover. Replace the breather cover on the head and insert and tighten the bolts. The head steady is held to the cover by a single through bolt and to the frame top tube by two bolts. The top rear mounting bolt also holds the stop lamp switch bracket and the earth lead terminal. Both components should be fitted before replacing the nuts.
3 Replace the starter motor lead and reconnect the oil pressure warning lead. Both leads connect within the starter motor case. Replace the chrome starter motor cover and also the gasket.
4 Track the two sets of wiring leads from the alternator up behind the final drive sprocket and secure them together with the starter motor lead, neutral indicator lead and oil pressure switch lead, with the wiring clip held by a screw just about the drive sprocket.
5 Lightly grease the clutch pushrod and insert it through the oil seal at the end of the mainshaft. Loop the final drive chain over the engine sprocket and mesh the two ends onto the rear wheel sprocket. Replace the master link making certain that the spring link is replaced the correct way round. That is with the closed end facing the direction of travel.
6 The final drive sprocket cover can now be replaced. Refit the clutch cable, making sure that the spring between the cable anchor and cable holder is not left out. The cover is held by four crosshead screws. The wiring leads, which are held by a clip above the final drive sprocket, must be positioned above the top chain guide, on the inside of the cover. If the leads are not correctly positioned they will be chafed by the drive chain, eventually leading to shorting out and total failure.
7 Replace both the gearchange lever and the kickstart lever on their respective shafts. Check the operating positions, before refitting and tightening the pinch bolts.
8 Refit the carburettors. It is easier to reconnect the throttle cables whilst the carburettors are off the machine. By turning the throttle twist grip ascertain which is the throttle accelera-tion cable. Fit the nipple into the rear nipple recess on the pulley and screw the adjuster screw as far in as possible. The deceleration cable can now be fitted in the same way. Centralise

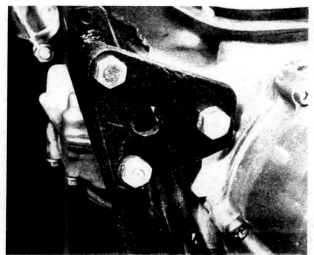

49.2a Replace the front engine bracket and bolt

49.2b The top rear mounting bolt is fitted with spacer as . . .

49.2c . . . is the lower rear mounting bolt

49.5 Connect drive chain while links are on sprocket

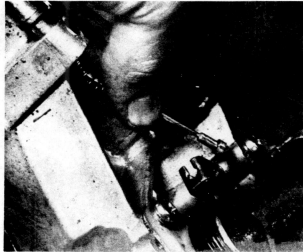

49.6a Replace the clutch cable assembly . . .

49.6b . . . ensuring the retaining split pin is not omitted

49.6c Replace the clutch pushrod before fitting cover

49.6d If necessary remove the cover and . . .

49.6e . . . adjust the clutch operating mechanism

49.13 Always use new exhaust gaskets

49.16a Replenish engine with correct grade of oil and . . .

49.16b . . . check the oil level in the sight glass

the two adjuster screws and tighten the locknuts. The carburettors can be refitted with ease if they are positioned just below the inlet rubber stubs. Insert the carburettor mouths into the stubs at an angle and then pull the carburettors up into the stubs. Refit the air cleaner box hoses and tighten up all four clamps.

9 Replace and tighten the two air filter box retaining bolts and insert the air filter element. Replace the lid. Track the four carburettor breather pipes so that they are secured by the retainer plate on the rear of the crankcase. Reconnect the breather tube that runs from the breather cover to the air filter box. The tube is held at both ends by screw clips.

10 Refit the ignition coil to the top frame tube, where it is held by two bolts. Connect the various wiring leads. If any difficulty is encountered in reconnecting, refer to the wiring diagram at the end of Chapter 6.

11 Track the wiring harness leads from the alternator across the machine and reconnect the plug ends with the sockets on the right-hand side of the machine. Replace the starter motor lead to the starter solenoid.

12 Replace the tachometer drive cable into the take-off point at the front of the cylinder head cover and tighten the knurled ring.

13 Refit each exhaust/silencer assembly. The rear of each silencer can be temporarily supported by a screwdriver passed through the bracket and into the footrest holder while the front pipe is fitted into the cylinder head and the split clamps and flanges bolted up. Always use new exhaust pipe gaskets. The pipe flanges are only finned on one side; this side must face out otherwise the fins will foul the frame downtubes. Replace the rear footrests through the silencer brackets, making sure that the projections on the footrest brackets locate with the holes on the inner end of the footrests. Replace the left-hand front footrest and the side stand extension spring.

14 Refit the petrol tank and connect the fuel lines. Do not omit the small spring clips.

15 Reconnect the spark plug caps to their respective spark plugs and reconnect the battery terminals. Give a final visual check to all electrical connections and replace the two side covers. Both are a push fit.

16 Pour 5.25 Imp. pint (3.0 litres) of SAE 20W/50 engine oil into the engine through the filler orifice to the rear of the cylinders. Kick the engine over smartly with the ignition off to help prime the oilways.

50 Starting and running the rebuilt engine

1 Open the petrol tap, close the carburettor chokes and start the engine, using either the kickstart or the electric starter. Raise the chokes as soon as the engine will run evenly and keep it running at a low speed for a few minutes to allow oil pressure to build up and the oil to circulate. If the red oil pressure indicator lamp is not extinguished, stop the engine immediately and investigate the lack of oil pressure.

2 The engine may tend to smoke through the exhausts initially, due to the amount of oil used when assembling the various components. The excess of oil should gradually burn away as the engine settles down.

3 Check the exterior of the machine for oil leaks or blowing gaskets. Make sure that each gear engages correctly and that all the controls function effectively, particularly the brakes. This is an essential last check before taking the machine on the road.

51 Taking the rebuilt machine on the road

1 Any rebuilt machine will need time to settle down, even if parts have been replaced in their original order. For this reason it is highly advisable to treat the machine gently for the first few miles to ensure oil has circulated throughout the lubrication system and that any new parts fitted have begun to bed down.

2 Even greater care is necessary if the engine has been rebored or if a new crankshaft has been fitted. In the case of a rebore, the engine will have to be run-in again, as if the machine were new. This means greater use of the gearbox and a restraining hand on the throttle until at least 500 miles have been covered. There is no point in keeping to any set speed limit; the main requirement is to keep a light loading on the engine and to gradually work up performance until the 500 mile mark is reached. These recommendations can be lessened to an extent when only a new crankshaft is fitted. Experience is the best guide since it is easy to tell when an engine is running freely.

3 If at any time a lubrication failure is suspected, stop the engine immediately, and investigate the cause. If an engine is run without oil, even for a short period, irreparable engine damage is inevitable.

4 When the engine has cooled down completely after the initial run, recheck the various settings, especially the valve clearances. During the run most of the engine components will have settled into their normal working locations.

52 Fault diagnosis

Symptom	Cause	Remedy
Engine will not start	Defective spark plugs	Remove the plugs and lay on cylinder heads. Check whether spark occurs when ignition is switched on and engine rotated.
	Dirty or closed contact breaker points	Check condition of points and whether gap is correct.
	Faulty or disconnected condenser	Check whether points arc when separated. Renew condenser if evidence of arcing.
Engine runs evenly	Ignition and/or fuel system fault	Check each system independently, as though engine will not start.
	Blowing cylinder head gasket	Leak should be evident from oil leakage where gas escapes.
	Incorrect ignition timing	Check accuracy and if necessary reset.
Lack of power	Fault in fuel system or incorrect ignition timing	See above.

Heavy oil consumption	Cylinder block in need of rebore	Check for bore wear, rebore and fit over-size pistons if required.
	Damaged oil seals	Check engine for oil leaks.
Excessive mechanical noise	Worn cylinder bores (piston slap)	Rebore and fit oversize pistons.
	Worn camshaft drive chain (rattle)	Adjust tensioner or replace chain.
	Worn big-end bearings (knock)	Fit replacement crankshaft assembly.
	Worn main bearings (rumble)	Fit new journal bearings and seals. Renew crankshaft assembly if centre bearings are worn.
Engine overheats and fades	Lubrication failure	Stop engine and check whether internal parts are receiving oil. Check oil level in crankcase.

53 Fault diagnosis - gearbox

Symptom	Cause	Remedy
Difficulty in engaging gears	Selector forks bent	Renew.
	Gear clusters not assembled correctly	Check gear cluster arrangement and position of thrust washers.
Machine jumps out of gear	Worn dogs on ends of gear pinions	Renew worn pinions.
	Stopper arms not seating correctly	Remove right-hand crankcase cover and check stopper arm action.
Gearchange lever does not return to original position	Broken return spring	Renew spring.
Kickstarter does not return when engine is turned over or started	Broken or poorly tensioned return spring	Renew spring or re-tension.
Kickstarter slips	Ratchet assembly worn	Part crankcase and renew all worn parts.

54 Fault diagnosis - clutch

Symptom	Cause	Remedy
Engine speed increases as shown by tachometer but machine does not respond	Clutch slip	Check clutch adjustment for free play at handlebar lever. Check thickness of inserted plates.
Difficulty in engaging gears. Gear changes jerky and machine creeps forward when clutch is withdrawn. Difficulty in selecting neutral	Clutch drag	Check clutch adjustment for too much free play. Check clutch drums for indentations in slots and clutch plates for burrs on tongues. Dress with file if damage not too great.
Clutch operation stiff	Damaged, trapped or frayed control cable	Check cable and renew if necessary. Make sure cable is lubricated and has no sharp bends.

Chapter 2 Fuel system and lubrication

Contents

Specifications

Fuel tank

Capacity	3.08 Imp galls. 3.7 US galls (14 litres)
Reserve	5.25 Imp pints. 3.2 US quarts (3 litres)

Carburettors

Make	Keihin
Type	CVB 36
Main jet	135
Main air jet	60
Slow air jet	110
Pilot jet	40
Air screw opening	7/8 $\pm$ ¼ turns out
Fuel level	2 - 4 mm (0.08 - 0.16 in)

Oil capacity ... ...   5.25 Imp pints. 3.2 US quarts (3 litres)

Oil pump

Clearance, outer rotor/pump body	0.0039 in - 0.0059 in (0.10 - 0.15 mm)
Clearance, between rotors	0.0009 in - 0.0045 in (0.025 - 0.115 mm)

1 General description

The fuel system comprises a petrol tank from which petrol is fed by gravity to the float chambers of the two Keihin carburettors. A single fuel tap with a detachable gauze filter is located beneath the tank, on the left-hand side. It contains provision for a reserve petrol supply when the main supply is exhausted.

For cold starting, a hand operated choke lever attached to the left-hand carburettor is linked to the right-hand instrument so that the mixture on both carburettors can be enriched temporarily. Throttle control is effected by the means of a push-pull cable arrangement which operate a 'butterfly' valve in each carburettor.

Lubrication is by the wet sump principle in which oil is delivered under pressure, from the sump, through a mechanical pump to the working parts of the engine. The pump is of the rotating vane type and is driven from the clutch by spur gears.

Oil is supplied under pressure via a release valve and a full flow oil filter fitted with a paper element. The engine oil supply is also shared by the primary drive and the gearbox.

2 Petrol tank: removal and replacement

1 The fuel tank is retained at the forward end by two rubber buffers fitted either side of the under side of the tank which fit into cups on the frame top tube. The rear of the tank sits on a small rubber saddle placed across the frame top tube and is retained by a rubber strap over a hook at the rear of the tank.
2 To remove the tank, pull off the fuel lines at the petrol tap unions where they are held by spring clips. Raise the seat, pull the rubber strap away from the hook at the rear of the tank, and lift the tank backwards and away from the machine.
3 When replacing the tank, reverse the above procedure. Make sure the tank seats correctly and does not trap any control cables or wires.

3.1a Petrol filter gauze is fitted in tap body

3.1b Petrol tap body retained on tank by two screws

3.2 Tap seal can be renewed with ease

4.1 Fuel feed and breather pipes held by small clip

5.1a Air hoses are handed and marked

5.1b Inlet stub must be positioned as directed

3 Petrol tap: removal and replacement

1 If only the petrol tap filter requires attention, there is no necessity to remove the tap or to drain the petrol tank. The filter bowl, which has a hexagon head to aid removal, is threaded into the base of the petrol tap and can be unscrewed after the tap has been turned to the 'off' position. The circular filter gauze will also be released and can be washed with petrol to remove any sediment. Before replacing, the filter bowl should be cleaned thoroughly.

2 It is seldom necessary to remove the lever which operates the petrol tap, although occasions may occur when a leakage develops at the joint. Although the tank must be drained before the lever assembly can be removed, there is no need to disturb the body of the tap.

3 To dismantle the lever assembly, remove the two crosshead screws passing through the plate on which the operating positions are inscribed. The plate can then be lifted away, followed by a spring, the lever itself and the seal behind the lever. The seal will have to be renewed if leakage has occurred. Reassemble the tap in the reverse order. Gasket cement or any other sealing medium is NOT necessary to secure a petrol tight seal.

4 If the tap body has to be removed, it is held to the underside of the petrol tank by two crosshead screws with washers. Note that there is an 'O' ring seal between the petrol tap body and the petrol tank, which must be renewed if it is damaged or if petrol leakage has occurred.

4 Petrol feed pipes: examination

1 Synthetic rubber feed pipes are used to convey the flow of petrol from the petrol tap to the float chamber of each of the four carburettors. Each pipe is retained by a wire clip, which must hold the pipe firmly in position. Check periodically to ensure the pipes have not begun to split or crack and that the wire clips have not worn through the surface.

2 Do NOT replace a broken pipe with one of natural rubber, even temporarily. Petrol causes natural rubber to swell very rapidly and disintegrate, with the result that minute particles of rubber would easily pass into the carburettors and cause blockages of the internal passageways. Plastic pipe of the correct bore size can be used as a temporary substitute but it should be replaced with the correct type of tubing as soon as possible since it will not have the same degree of flexibility.

5 Carburettors: removal

1 Slacken off the two screw clips which clamp the rubber inlet stubs around the carburettor mouths. Slacken off the two screw clips that hold the air box hoses and remove the air box retaining bolts.

2 Pull the air hoses off the carburettors and then pull the carburettors back and down, away from the inlet stubs. Disconnect the two cables from the throttle pulley, which is most easily accomplished as follows:

Loosen the locknuts on both cable adjusters and screw the rear most adjuster in as far as possible. Undo the forward adjuster until it can be pulled free from the holding bracket and slide the barrel nipple from position in the pulley. The rear adjuster may now be screwed right out and the cable disconnected from the pulley.

3 The carburettors are attached to a common mounting plate from which they should be removed before further dismantling. Starting with the left-hand carburettor, remove the two countersunk screws and pull the balance adjusting screw linkage and choke lever linkage out of their push fit connections. The right-hand carburettor can now be separated from the mounting plate, after removing the countersunk screws which hold it.

5.3 Countersunk screws hold carburettors to mounting plate

6.2 Pulley assembly retained by circlip and washer

6.4a Float chamber held by four screws

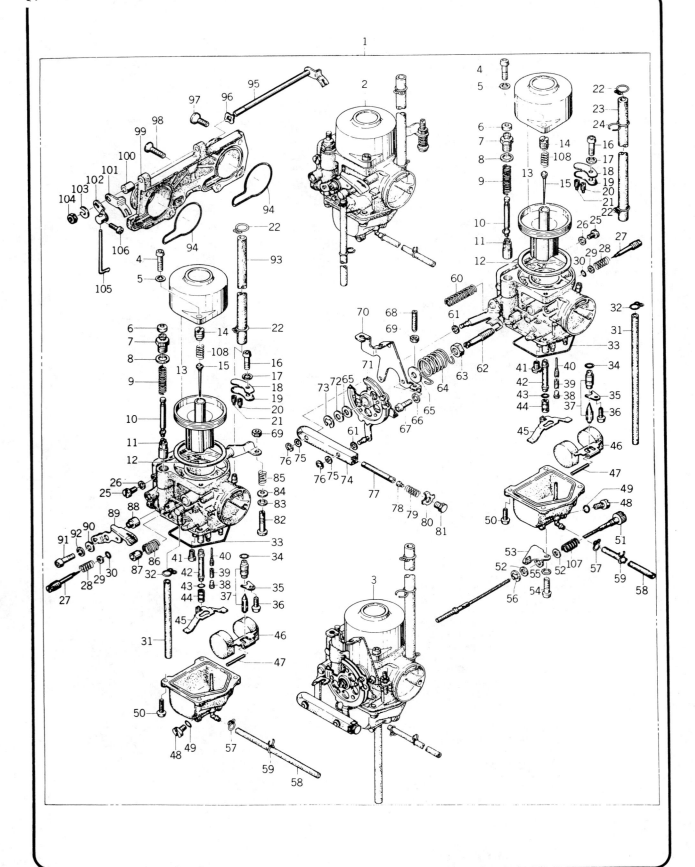

Fig. 2.1 Carburettor assemblies

  1 Carburettor assembly - complete
  2 Right-hand carburettor
  3 Left-hand carburettor
  4 Screw
  5 Spring washer - 4 off
  6 Dust cap rubber - 4 off
  7 Starter plunger nut - 2 off
  8 Plain washer - 2 off
  9 Spring - 2 off
 10 Starter plunger rod - 2 off
 11 Starter plunger
 12 Vacuum piston gasket - 2 off
 13 Vacuum piston and cover - 2 off
 14 Piston needle grub screw - 2 off
 15 Jet needle (piston needle) - 2 off
 16 Screw - 2 off
 17 Spring washer - 2 off
 18 Air jet cover plate - 2 off
 19 Cover plate gasket - 2 off
 20 Air jet   60 - 2 off
 21 Air jet   90 - 2 off
 22 Fuel pipe clip - 4 off
 23 Fuel pipe
 24 Fuel pipe clip
 25 Vacuum tester screw plug - 2 off
 26 Plain washer - 2 off
 27 Pilot adjuster screw - 2 off
 28 Pilot adjuster screw spring - 2 off
 29 Plain washer - 2 off
 30 Pilot screw 'O' ring - 2 off
 31 Breather pipe - 2 off
 32 Pipe clip - 2 off
 33 Float chamber sealing ring - 2 off
 34 Float valve sealing 'O' ring - 2 off
 35 Valve seat retaining plate - 2 off
 36 Screw - 2 off
 37 Float valve assembly - complete - 2 off
 38 Pilot jet cap - 2 off
 39 Pilot jet   35 - 2 off
 40 Slow jet   35 - 2 off
 41 Starter jet   72 - 2 off
 42 Needle jet - 2 off
 43 Main jet 'O' ring - 2 off
 44 Main jet   110 - 2 off
 45 Main jet holder plate - 2 off
 46 Float assembly - 2 off
 47 Float pivot pin - 2 off
 48 Drain plug - 2 off
 49 'O' ring - 2 off
 50 Screw - 7 off
 51 Throttle adjustment screw A
 52 Plain washer - 2 off
 53 Screw bracket
 54 Screw
 55 Spring washer
 56 Circlip
 57 Overflow pipe clip - 2 off
 58 Overflow pipe - 2 off
 59 Overflow pipe clip - 2 off
 60 Balance spring
 61 Wave washer - 2 off
 62 Balance adjusting screw
 63 Nut
 64 Throttle cable pulley swing
 65 Plain washer - 2 off
 66 Spring washer - 2 off
 67 Screw - 2 off
 68 Pulley adjustment screw
 69 Nut - 2 off
 70 Pulley bracket
 71 Throttle cable pulley
 72 Plain washer
 73 Circlip
 74 Throttle link
 75 Plain washer - 2 off
 76 Circlip - 2 off
 77 Throttle link adjusting rod
 78 Adjusting plug
 79 Spring
 80 Lock washer
 81 Bolt
 82 Throttle adjustment screw B
 83 Plain washer
 84 Plain washer
 85 Throttle stop screw spring
 86 Choke lever spring
 87 Choke lever contact
 88 Choke lever collar
 89 Choke lever collar
 90 Plain washer
 92 Spring washer
 93 Fuel pipe
 94 Mounting plate 'O' ring - 2 off
 95 Throttle valve shaft
 96 Wave washer - 2 off
 97 Screw - 2 off
 98 Screw - 2 off
 99 Mounting plate
100 Choke lever shaft collar
101 Starter plunger lever A
102 Starter plunger lever B
103 Lock washer
104 Nut
105 Choke link rod
106 Screw
107 Throttle screw spring
108 Piston spring - 2 off

6 Carburettors: dismantling, examination and reassembly

1 Before dismantling of the carburettors can be commenced, the linkage bar and pulley assembly should be removed. To dismantle the linkage mechanism bend up the bar washers from the bolt and unscrew the bolt, washer, spring and the plunger. Prise off the two 'C' rings that hold the bar in place and pull the bar from position.

2 The pulley assembly is retained on the pivot shaft by a circlip and two washers. Note the positions and pull each component off the shaft separately.

3 It is suggested that each carburettor is dismantled and reassembled separately, to avoid mixing up the components. The carburettors are handed and therefore components should not be interchanged.

4 Invert one carburettor and remove the four (4) float chamber screws. Lift the float chamber from position. Slide the jet keeper across in its sloppy hole and lift it out. The two floats, which are interconnected, can be lifted away, after the hinge pin has been pushed out, giving access to the float needle and needle seating. Place the float needle in a safe place until reassembly commences. The float needle seat is a push fit in the carburettor body and is retained by a claw and screw. With the claw removed, the seating will pull out. Note the 'O' ring on the inner end.

5 Pull out the push fit main jet and invert the carburettor which will let the needle jet fall free. The starter jet is the largest component in the carburettor base and should be unscrewed with a large screwdriver. Remove the small plug which was covered by the jet keeper plate and unscrew the pilot jet, followed by the slow running jet.

6 Remove the upper chamber screws and pull off the chamber cap and the helical spring. Pull the piston up and out of its slider and remove the piston gasket. The piston needle can be removed by unscrewing the plug in the top of the piston. The needle will drop out. The main air jet and slow running air jet are hidden below a plate and gasket, which is retained in the upper chamber by a single cross head screw. Remove the screw, plate and gasket and unscrew the two jets.

7 The starter plunger (choke) assembly is positioned in a tunnel to the side of the upper chamber. Unscrew the housing cap and pull the starter plunger assembly out. This consists of the plunger rod, spring and plunger piece.

8 It is not recommended that the 'butterfly' throttle valve assembly be removed as these components are not prone to wear. If wear occurs on the operating pivot a new carburettor will be required as air will find its way along the pivot bearings resulting in a weak mixture.

9 Check the condition of the floats. If they are damaged in any way, they should be renewed. The float needle and needle seating will wear after lengthy service and should be inspected carefully. Wear usually takes the form of a ridge or groove, which will cause the float needle to seat imperfectly. Always renew the seating and needle as a pair. An imperfection in one component will soon produce similar wear in the other.

10 After considerable service the piston needle and the needle jet in which it slides will wear, resulting in an increase in petrol consumption. Wear is caused by the passage of petrol and the two components rubbing together. It is advisable to renew the jet periodically in conjunction with the piston needle.

11 Before the carburettors are reassembled, using the reversed dismantling procedure, each should be cleaned out thoroughly using compressed air. Avoid using a piece of rag since there is always risk of particles of lint obstructing the internal passageways or the jet orifices.

12 Never use a piece of wire or any pointed metal object to clear a blocked jet. It is only too easy to enlarge the jet under these circumstances and increase the rate of petrol consumption. If compressed air is not available, a blast of air from a tyre pump will usually suffice.

13 Do not use excessive force when reassembling a carburettor because it is easy to shear a jet or some of the smaller screws.

6.4b Jet holder plate locates on offset hole

6.4c Note 'O' ring on push fit main jet

6.4d Remove pivot pin to free float assembly

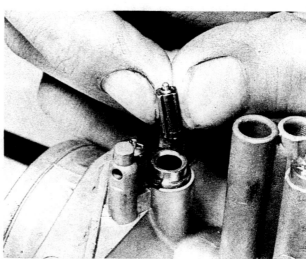

6.4e Do not mislay tiny float needle

6.4f Remove the retaining claw ...

6.4g ... to free the float needle seat

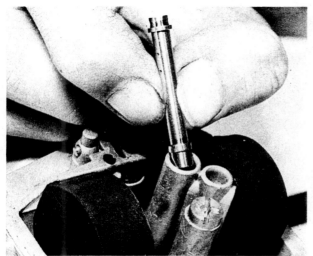

6.5a Needle jet is loose fit in bore

6.5b Starter jet is threaded

6.6a Remove upper chamber screws, lift off cover and ...

6.6b ... pull out the piston and needle

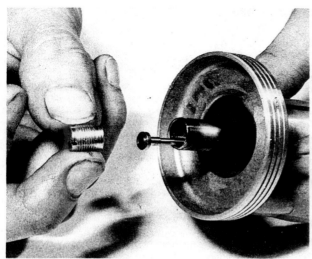

6.6c Needle retained by screw plug

6.6d Gasket held by single screw covers ...

6.6e ...the main and slow air jets

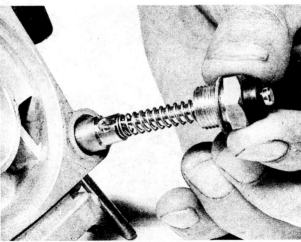

6.7 Starter (choke) plunger screws into carburettor body

6.10a Choke lever is connected by operating rods

6.10b Do not omit throttle cable pulley spring

7.3 Throttle stop screw is connected by flexi-link

Furthermore, the carburettors are cast in a zinc-based alloy which itself does not have a high tensile strength. Take particular care when replacing the throttle valves to ensure the needles align with the jet seats.

14 Avoid overtightening the screws which retain the carburettors to the mounting plate. Overtightening will cause the flanges to bow, giving rise to mysterious air leaks and a permanently weak mixture. If the flange is bowed, it can be rubbed down until it is flat once again using a rotary motion and a sheet of emery cloth wrapped around a sheet of glass. Make sure no particles of emery grit enter the carburettors and that the 'O' ring in the centre of each flange is replaced when the grinding operation is complete.

15 Do NOT remove either the throttle stop screw or the pilot jet screw without first making note of their exact positions. Failure to observe this precaution will make it necessary to re-synchronise both carburettors on reassembly.

7 Carburettors: adjustment for tickover

1 Before adjusting the carburettors, a check should be made to ensure that the following settings are correct: contact breaker

gap, ignition timing, valve clearance, spark plug gaps, crankcase oil level. It is also important that the engine is at normal running temperature. From cold the engine will take between 5 - 10 minutes to warm up satisfactorily.

2   Check that when the throttle is fully opened both 'butterfly' valves are in their fully open position (ie; parallel to the carburettor bore). This check can best be done when the carburettors are off the machine. A stop screw on the pulley bracket gives adjustment to the stop position.

3   Start the engine and bring it up to normal running temperature. Unscrew the throttle stop screw, which is syncronised to both carburettors and is mounted on a bracket on the right-hand carburettor, until the engine turns over at the slowest smooth speed obtainable. Turn each pilot screw on equal amount each until the engine reaches the highest rpm obtainable. Adjust the engine speed, using the throttle screw, until the engine is turning over at 1,100 - 1,300 as shown by the tachometer.

4   Alter the position of the pilot screws an equal amount to check whether the engine speed rises. If this is the case repeat the procedure in the previous paragraph.

5   With the idling speed (tickover) correct, screw each pilot screw in 1/16 turn.

8 Carburettors: synchronisation

1   For the best possible performance it is imperative that the carburettors are working in perfect harmony with each other. At any given throttle opening if the carburettors are not synchronised, not only will one cylinder be doing less work but it will also in effect have to be 'carried' by the other cylinder. This effect will reduce the performance considerably.

2   It is essential to use a vacuum gauge set consisting of two separate dial gauges, one of each being connected to each carburettor by means of a special adaptor tube. The adaptor pipe screws into the outside edge of each carburettor, the orifice of which is normally blocked by a crosshead screw. Most owners are unlikely to possess the necessary vacuum gauge set, which is somewhat expensive and is normally held by Kawasaki service agents who will carry out the synchronising operation for a nominal sum. In any event a special tool is required for adjusting the balancer mechanism.

3   If the vacuum gauge set is available together with the balancer screw adjustment tool (Kawasaki service tool No. 57001-167) the gauge reading at tick-over (1,100 - 1,300) should be 21 - 25 cm Hg with a variation of less than 3 cm Hg. If the variation is greater than 3 cm Hg the fuel tank must be removed and the balancer adjusting screw turned. Adjustment for the reading 21 - 25 cm Hg can be made on the pilot air screws.

9 Carburettor settings

1   Some of the carburettor settings, such as the sizes of the needle jets, main jets and needle positions, etc are predetermined by the manufacturer. Under normal circumstances it is unlikely that these settings will require modification, even though there is provision made. If a change appears necessary, it can often be attributed to a developing engine fault.

2   As an approximate guide the pilot jet setting controls engine speed up to 1/8 throttle. The throttle slide cutaway controls engine speed from 1/8 to 1/4 throttle and the position of the needle in the slide from 1/4 to 3/4 throttle. The size of the main jet is responsible for engine speed at the final 3/4 to full throttle. It should be added however that these are only guide lines. There is no clearly defined demarkation line due to a certain amount of overlap which occurs between the carburettor components involved.

3   Always err slightly on the side of a rich mixture, since a weak mixture will cause the engine to overheat. Reference to Chapter 3 will show how the condition of the spark plugs can be inter-

preted with some experience as a reliable guide to carburettor mixture strength. Flat spots in the carburation can usually be traced to a defective timing advancer. If the advancer action is suspect, it can be detected by checking the ignition timing with a stroboscope.

10 Exhaust system

1   Unlike a two-stroke, the exhaust system does not require such frequent attention because the exhaust gases are usually of a less oily nature.

2   Do not run the machine with the exhaust baffles removed, or with a quite different type of silencer fitted. The standard production silencers have been designed to give the best possible performance, whilst subduing the exhaust note to an acceptable level. Although a modified exhaust system or one without baffles, may give the illusion of greater speed as a result of the changed exhaust note, the chances are that performance will have suffered accordingly.

11 Air cleaner: dismantling and cleaning

1   On all models except the KZ400-D3 an air cleaner element of corrugated paper is fitted across the frame immediately beneath

11.2a Air filter box cover is held by single screw

11.2b Air filter element is push fit in box

12.1 Oil level can be checked by sight glass

12.2a Oil return valve is retained by circlip

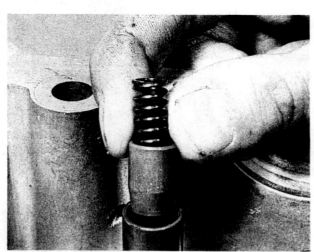

12.2b Plunger and spring can be lifted out

the nose of the dual seat. Air enters through a vent at the rear of the box containing the element and then passes through the element to ducts which lead to the carburettor mouths. A rubber pipe runs from the breather cover on the cylinder head to a union on the lower front edge of the filter box. This is fitted so that all carbon based vapours expelled from the engine are recirculated through the carburettors and then burnt in the cylinders.

2 To gain acces to the filter element, prise off the left-hand side cover and remove the box lid screw. The box lid hinges upwards allowing the element to be pulled from position.

3 On the KZ400-D3 models a cylindrical corrugated paper element is used. Access to the element is made by lifting the dual seat and unscrewing the air box cap. The filter will lift out.

4 To clean the element, tap it lightly to loosen the accumulation of dust and then use a soft brush to sweep the dust away. Alternatively, compressed air can be blown into the element from the inside. Remember the element is composed of corrugated paper and is easily damaged if handled roughly.

5 If the element is damp or oily it must be renewed. A damp or oily element will have a restrictive effect on the breathing of the carburettor and will almost certainly affect the engine performance.

6 On no account run without the air cleaners attached, or with the element missing. The jetting of the carburettors takes into account the presence of the air cleaner and engine performance will be seriously affected if this balance is upset.

7 To replace the element, reverse the dismantling procedure. Give a visual check to ensure that the inlet hoses are correctly located and not kinked, split or otherwise damaged. Check that the air cleaner cases are free from splits or cracks.

12 Engine lubrication

1 The engine oil, which is also shared with the gearbox and primary drive, is contained in the sump of the engine - not in a frame mounted oil tank as is usual on most other machines. The sump has a capacity of 5.25 Imp. pints (3.0 litres) including the oil filter, which holds approx. ¾ pint (0.4 litres).

2 A rotating vane type oil pump driven from a gear on the clutch, delivers oil from the sump to the rest of the engine. Oil is picked up in the sump through a wire gauze which protects the oil pump from any large particles of foreign matter. The delivery section of the pump feeds oil at a preset pressure via a pressure release valve, which by-passes oil to the sump if the pressure exceeds the preset limit. As a result, it is possible to maintain a constant pressure in the lubrication system. The standard pressure is 57 psi (4 kg/cm^2) when the engine running at 4,000 rpm and the oil is at a temperature of 80°C.

3 Since the oil flow will not, under normal circumstances, actuate the pressure release valve, it passes directly through the full flow filter which has a replaceable element, to filter out any impurities which may otherwise pass to the working parts of the engine. The oil filter unit has its own by-pass valve to prevent the cut-off of the oil supply if the filter element has become clogged.

4 Oil from the filter is fed direct to the crankshaft and big-end bearings with a separate pressure feed to the camshaft and valve assemblies. Oil is also fed directly to the balance weight assemblies. Surplus oil drains to the sump where it is picked up again and the cycle is repeated.

5 A fourth oil route is to the transmission through a passage at one end of the mainshaft bearings. After lubrication the oil is thrown down into the bottom of the crankcase.

6 An oil pressure warning light is included in the lubrication circuit to give visual warning by means of an indicator light, if the pressure should fall to a low level.

13 Oil pump: dismantling, examination and reassembly

1 The oil pump can be removed from the engine while the engine is still in the frame. However, it will be necessary to

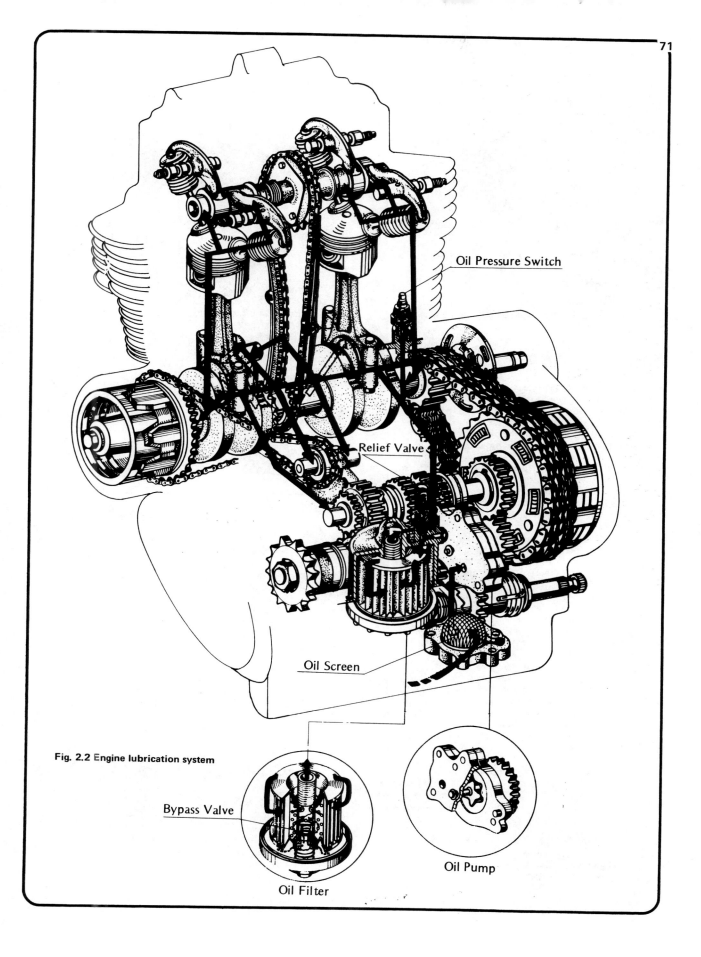

Oil Pressure Switch

Relief Valve

Oil Screen

Fig. 2.2 Engine lubrication system

Bypass Valve

Oil Filter

Oil Pump

13.3 Oil pump outer casing is retained by dowel pins

13.7 Punch marks on rotors must face out on reassembly

remove the automatic ignition timing unit, the primary drive cover, clutch assembly and primary drive pinion before access can be gained to the oil pump. Refer to Chapter 1, Sections 10 and 11. It is also necessary to drain the engine oil.

2 The oil pump is retained on the casing by four (4) crosshead screws which, when removed, will allow the pump assembly to be pulled off the two dowel pins.

3 Remove the 'C' clip and washer from the shaft projecting from the rear of the pump casing. The two halves of the pump body can now be gently prised apart. The casings are located on two dowel pins. Slide the inner rotor drive pin out of the centre shaft after lifting out the inner rotor and the outer rotor. The pump shaft and drive gear can be pulled out of the outer casing.

4 Wash all the pump components with petrol and allow them to dry before carrying out an examination. Before partially re-assembling the pump for various measurements to be carried out, check the casting for breakage or fracture, or scoring on the inside perimeter.

5 Reassemble the pump rotors and measure the clearance between the outer rotor and the pump body, using a feeler gauge. If the measurement exceeds the service limit of 0.010 in (0.25 mm) the rotor or the body must be renewed, whichever is worn. Measure the clearance between the outer rotor and the inner rotor, using a feeler gauge. If the clearance exceeds 0.008 in (0.21 mm) the rotors must be renewed as a set. It should be noted that one face of both the inner and outer rotor is punch marked. The punch marks should face away from the main pump casing during measurements and on reassembly. With the pump rotors installed in the pump body lay a straight edge across the mating surface of the pump body. Again with a feeler gauge measure the clearance between the rotor faces and the straight edge. If the clearance exceeds 0.006 in (0.15 mm) the rotors should be replaced as a set.

6 Examine the rotors and the pump body for signs of scoring, chipping or other surface damage which will occur if metallic particles find their way into the oil pump assembly. Renewal of the affected parts is the only remedy under these circumstances, bearing in mind that the rotors must always be replaced as a matched pair.

7 Reassemble the pump components by reversing the dis-mantling procedure. Remember that the punch marked faces of the rotors must face away from the main pump body. The component parts must be ABSOLUTELY clean or damage to the pump will result. Replace the rotors and lubricate them thoroughly before refitting the cover.

8 Check that the three (3) oil passage 'O' rings are in good condition and properly positioned in the crankcase and screw the oil pump up. Rotate the oil pump gear whilst tightening the screws to check that the rotors do not bind. A stiff pump is almost invariably due to dirty rotors.

9 Refit the clutch assembly, primary drive pinion and replace the cover and automatic timing unit as described in Chapter 1, Sections 37 and 39.

14 Oil filter: renewing the element

1 The oil filter is contained within a semi-isolated chamber within the crankcase. Access to the element is made by un-screwing the filter cover centre bolt which will bring with it the cover and also the element. Before removing the cover place a receptacle beneath the engine to catch the engine oil contained in the filter chamber.

2 When renewing the filter element it is wise to renew the filter cover 'O' ring at the same time. This will obviate the possibility of any oil leaks. Do not overtighten the centre bolt on replace-ment; the correct torque setting is 11 - 14.5 ft lbs (1.5 - 2.0 kg m).

3 The filter by-pass valve, comprising a plunger and spring, is situated in the bore of the filter cover centre bolt. It is recom-mended that the by-pass valve be checked for free movement during every filter change. The spring and plunger arc retained by a pin across the centre bolt. Knocking the pin out will allow the spring and plunger to be removed for cleaning.

4 Never run the engine without the filter element or increase the period between the recommended oil changes or oil filter changes.

Engine oil should be changed every 2,000 miles and the element changed every 4,000 miles. Use only the recommended viscosity.

15 Oil pressure warning lamp

1 An oil pressure warning lamp is incorporated in the lubrication system to give immediate warning of excessively low oil pressure.

2 The oil pressure switch is screwed into the crankcase, directly behind the right-hand cylinder. The switch is interconnected to a

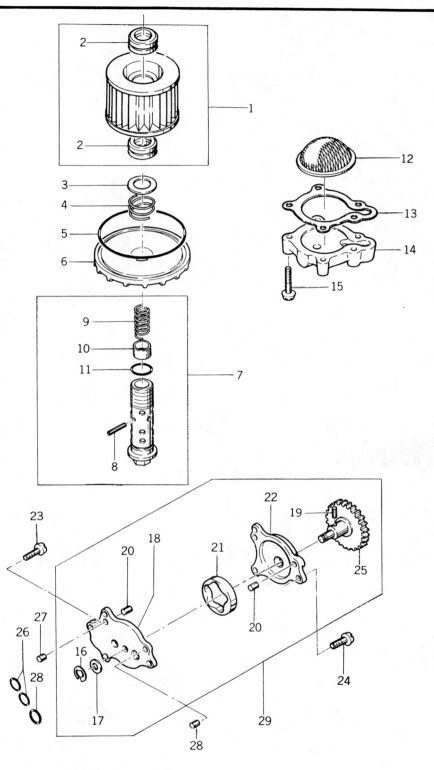

Fig. 2.3 Oil pump and oil filters

1 Oil filter - complete
2 Filter grommet - 2 off
3 Plain washer
4 Filter spring
5 'O' ring
6 Cover plate
7 Oil filter bolt
  assembly - complete

8 Spring anchor pin
9 Valve spring
10 Release valve
11 'O' ring
12 Oil strainer gauze
13 Gasket
14 Oil strainer cover
15 Screw - 5 off

16 Circlip
17 Thrust washer
18 Oil pump cover
19 Rotor drive pin
20 Dowel pin - 2 off
21 Outer rotor
22 Oil pump body
23 Screw

24 Screw - 3 off
25 Oil pump driven gear
26 'O' ring - 2 off
27 Dowel pin - 2 off
28 'O' ring
29 Oil pump
  assembly - complete

warning light on the lighting panel on the handlebars. The light should be on whenever the igntiion is on but will usually go out at about 1,500 rpm.

3 If the oil warning lamp comes on whilst the machine is being ridden the engine should be switched off immediately, otherwise there is a risk of severe engine damage due to lubrication failure.

The fault must be located and rectified before the engine is re-started and run, even for a brief moment. Machines fitted with plain shell bearings rely on high oil pressure to maintain a thin oil film between the bearing surfaces. Failure of the oil pressure will cause the working surfaces to come into direct contact, causing overheating and eventual seizure.

16 Fault diagnosis

Symptom	Cause	Remedy
Engine gradually fades and stops	Fuel starvation	Check vent hole in filler cap. Sediment in filter bowl or float chamber. Dismantle and clean.
Engine runs badly. Black smoke from exhausts	Carburettor flooding	Dismantle and clean carburettor. Check for punctured float or sticking float needle.
Engine lacks response and overheats	Weak mixture Air cleaner disconnected or hose split Modified silencer has upset carburation	Check for partial block in carburettors. Reconnect or renew hose. Replace with original design.
Oil pressure warning light comes on	Lubrication system failure	Stop engine immediately. Trace and rectify fault before re-starting.
Engine gets noisy	Failure to change engine oil when recommended	Drain off old oil and refill with new oil of correct grade. Renew oil filter element.

Chapter 3 Ignition system

Contents

Specifications

Alternator
Make	Nippon Denso
Model	021000 - 3560
Type	3-phase
Output	Nominal 12v.
Contact breaker gap	0.011 in - 0.015 in (0.3 - 0.4 mm)
Dwell angle	185° - 195° (51 - 54%)
Ignition timing	15° BTDC @ 1,500 rpm; 40° BTDC @ 2,670 rpm

Ignition coil
Make	Nippon Denso
Type	AJPG 30

Condensor
Capacity	0.22 ± 0.02 u fd

Spark plugs
Make	NGK or Nippon Denso
Type	B-8ES or W24ES
Reach	¾ in (19 mm)
Gap	0.027 in - 0.031 in (0.7 - 0.8 mm)

1 General description

1 The Kawasaki KZ400 series is fitted with a 12 volt electrical system powered by an alternator mounted on the left-hand crankshaft. Unlike most twin cylinder machines only one ignition coil and one control breaker set is fitted. Therefore a spark is provided at both sparking plugs at the same time inspite of the fact that only one cylinder is on the compression stroke.
2 Ignition source power is fed from the battery to the ignition coil primary windings. When the contact breaker opens, the low tension circuit is interrupted, and a high voltage is produced in the ignition coil secondary windings by magnetic induction.
3 The alternator current (AC) is passed through a rectifier where it is converted to DC (direct current) and used to charge the battery. Output of the alternator is controlled to 14-15v by a three-point electro-mechanical regulator which, together with the rectifier, is housed under the left-hand side cover directly below the dual seat.
4 A control-breaker assembly is fitted at the right-hand end of the crankshaft together with the automatic timing unit, which controls the precise point of firing relative to the engine speed.

2 Crankshaft alternator: checking the output

1 If the charging performance of the alternator is suspect, it can only satisfactorily be checked with the use of multi-meter test instrument that includes a voltmeter and ammeter. As most owner/riders are unlikely to possess equipment of this type it is advised that the machine be returned to a Kawasaki agent for testing.
2 If a multi-meter is available, an initial check on the alternator can be made as follows:

a) Remove the left-hand side cover and disconnect the 6 point plug connector. Disconnect the 9 point plug from the headlamp shell.

b) Ensure that the battery is fully charged and gives a reading of 12 volts or over.

c) Disconnect the white lead from the positive (+) battery terminal.

d) Set the multi-meter to the 30 volts DC range and connect the meter's positive lead to the rectifier white lead, and the meter's negative lead to the frame earth point.

e) Remove the right-hand side cover and disconnect the green and brown leads from the regulator (marked F and I respectively) Connect the green and brown leads together.

f) Start the engine and run it at 1,100 - 1,300 rpm (idling speed) and note the meter reading. The reading should be 14 volts or slightly more. If the reading is less, it indicates that the alternator is defective. The repair should then be entrusted to a Kawasaki agnet.

g) During this test the engine speed MUST NOT exceed 2,000 rpm or damage to the rectifier may result. As soon as the test is complete reconnect the green and brown leads to the regulator, which have been temporarily removed and interconnected.

3 Ignition coil: checking

1 The single ignition coil is a sealed unit, mounted on a bracket which is bolted to the frame top tube. If a weak spark and poor starting causes the performance of the coil to be suspected, it should be tested by a Kawasaki agent or an auto-electrical expert who will have the appropriate test equipment. A faulty coil must be renewed, it is not possible to effect a satisfactory repair.

2 A defective condenser in the contact breaker circuit can give the illusion of a defective coil and for this reason it is advisable to investigate the condition of the condenser before condemning the ignition coil. Refer to Section 7 of this Chapter.

4 Contact breaker: adjustment

1 To gain access to the contact breaker assembly, it is necessary to remove the cover plate which is held by two cross head screws to the primary drive cover. Note that the cover has a paper gasket to prevent the ingress of water.

2 Rotate the engine, by means of the rotation hexagon on the crankshaft end, until the points gap is in the fully open position. Examine the faces of the points. If they are blackened and burnt, or badly pitted, it will be necessary to remove them for further attention. See Section 5 of this Chapter.

3 Adjustment is effected by slackening the screw through the plate of the fixed contact breaker point and moving the point either closer to, or further away, from the moving contact until the gap is correct as measured by a feeler gauge. The correct gap with the points FULLY OPEN is 0.011 in - 0.015 in (0.3 - 0.4 mm). Two small projections on the contact breaker base plate

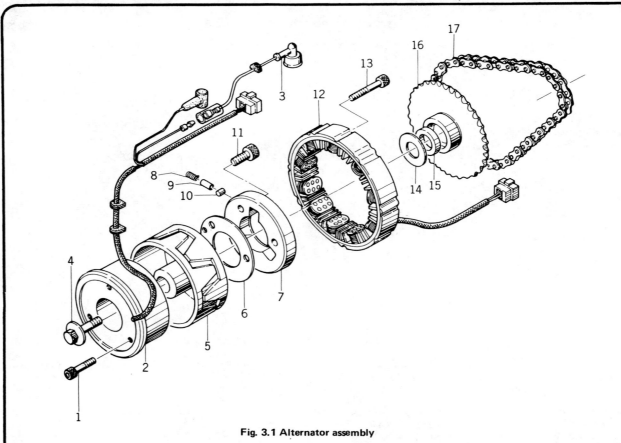

Fig. 3.1 Alternator assembly

1 Field coil bolt - 3 off	6 Starter clutch plate	10 Pin - 3 off	14 Thrust washer
2 Field coil	7 Starter clutch	11 Allen screw - 3 off	15 Oil seal
3 Oil pressure light wire	8 Spring - 3 off	12 Stator	16 Starter clutch sprocket
4 Rotor centre bolt	9 Plunger - 3 off	13 Allen bolt - 3 off	17 Starter motor chain
5 Rotor			

4.3 Check points when fully open

7.2 'F' mark on A.T.U. indicates firing point

permit the insertion of a screwdriver to lever the adjustable point into its correct location. Repeat this operation if there is any doubt about the accuracy of the measurement. Although this adjustment is relatively easy, it is of prime importance.

4   **Do not** slacken the three cross head screws which hold the contact breaker base plate in order to adjust the points gap. This will upset the ignition timing.

5   Before replacing the cover and gasket, place a few drops of thin oil on the cam lubrication wick. Do not over lubricate, as excess oil will eventually find its way onto the two contact points, causing the ignition circuit to malfunction.

5   Contact breaker points: removal, renovation and replacement

1   If the contact breaker points are burned, pitted or badly worn, they should be removed for dressing. If it is necessary to remove a substantial amount of material before the faces can be restored, the points should be renewed.

2   To remove the contact breaker points, detach the circlip which secures the moving contact to the pin on which it pivots. Remove the nut and bolt which holds the low tension lead to the contact point return spring and spring anchor. Carefully note the position of the insulating washers, which are fitted to the nut and bolt, so that they can be correctly replaced. Lift the moving contact off the pivot pin.

3   The fixed contact assembly is held to the base plate by a single cross head screw and washer.

4   The points should be dressed with an oil stone or fine emery cloth. Keep them absolutely square throughout the dressing operation, otherwise they will make angular contact on reassembly, and rapidly burn away. If emery cloth is used, it should be backed by a flat strip of steel. This will reduce the risk of rounding the edges of the points.

5   Replace the contacts by reversing the dismantling procedure, making quite certain that the insulating washers are fitted in the correct way. In order for the ignition system to function at all, the moving contact and the low-tension lead must be perfectly insulated from the base plate and fixed contact. It is advantageous to apply a very light smear of grease to the pivot pin, prior to replacement of the moving contact.

6   Check, and if necessary, re-adjust the contact breaker points when they are in the fully open position.

6   Condenser: removal and replacement

1   A condenser is included in the contact breaker circuit to prevent arcing across the contact breaker points as they separate. The condenser is connected in parallel with the points and if a fault develops, ignition failure is liable to occur.

2   If the engine proves difficult to start, or misfires when running, it is possible that the condenser is at fault. To check, view the contact points when the engine is running. If considerable sparking is apparent, and the points are badly blackened and burnt, the condenser can be regarded as unserviceable. In theory, no sparking at all should be evident between the points with the engine running. However, it is usually found in practice that a small amount of irregular sparking will occur. This should be disregarded.

3   The condenser is fitted in a recess on the contact breaker base plate where it is retained by a single screw through a bracket on the condenser body. Renewal is therefore straightforward.

7   Ignition timing: checking and resetting

1   In order to check the ignition timing, it is necessary to remove the contact breaker cover at the extreme right-hand end of the crankshaft, by detaching the two cross head screws. The cover will lift away complete with gasket. There is a circular aperture in the contact breaker base plate and the automatic timing unit, which lies behind the contact breaker base plate, is incribed with two sets of lines, marked 'T' and 'F'. There is also a fixed reference point in the form of a projection in the casing, with a timing mark formed in the centre. The timing unit has a dowelled fitting in the end of the crankshaft and can be replaced in one fixed position only. In consequence the timing marks cannot be varied in relationship to one another.

2   If the ignition timing is correct, the 'F' line will align exactly with the static timing mark when the contact breaker points are about to separate.

3   To adjust the position of the points in relation to the cam, slacken the three cross head screws which hold the base plate around the periphery. The base plate has 'sloppy' holes to permit a limited amount of movement; rotate the base plate in an anticlockwise direction to advance the ignition, and in a clockwise direction to retard the ignition.

4   The ignition timing can be checked or set with great accuracy if a bulb is used to indicate when the points separate. Disconnect the electrical leads to the moving contact and attach a lead from one terminal of the bulb in their place. Connect the other bulb terminal to the positive side of the battery and the negative lead of a battery to the crankcase. When the points separate the electrical circuit will be broken and the lamp will go out. A cycle lamp and battery are quite suitable for this operation.

5   It cannot be overstressed that optimum performance depends on the accuracy with which the ignition timing is set. Even a small error can cause a marked reduction in performance and in an extreme case, engine damage due to overheating. The contact breaker gap must be checked and if necessary re-adjusted BEFORE carrying out ignition timing checking or setting. When ignition timing evaluation is made it is essential that the automatic timing unit remains in the retarded (closed position).

8   Automatic timing unit: examination

1   The automatic timing mechanism rarely requires attention, although it is advisable to examine it periodically, when the contact breaker is receiving attention. It is retained by a small bolt and washer through the centre of the integral contact breaker cam and can be pulled off the end of the camshaft when the contact breaker plate is removed.

2   The unit comprises spring loaded balance weights, which move outward against the spring tension as centrifugal force increases. The balance weights must move freely on their pivots and be rust-free. The tension springs must also be in good condition. Keep the pivots lubricated and make sure the balance weights move easily, without binding. Most problems arise as a result of condensation, within the engine, which causes the unit to rust and balance weight movement to be restricted.

3   The automatic timing unit mechanism is fixed in relation to the crankshaft by means of a dowel. In consequence the mechanism cannot be replaced in anything other than the correct position. This ensures accuracy of ignition timing to within close limits, although a check should always be made when reassembly of the contact breakers is complete.

4   The correct functioning of the auto-advance unit can be checked when the engine is running by the use of a stroboscopic light. If a strobe light is available, connect it to the ignition circuit as directed by the manufacturer of the light. With the engine running, direct the beam of the light at the fixed timing

mark on the crankcase, through the aperture in the base plate. At tickover (1,100 - 1,300 rpm) the timing mark and the 'F' mark on the auto-advance unit should be precisely aligned. When the engine is running at 3,000 rpm or above, the timing mark should align with two parallel lines which are marked on the automatic timing unit slightly in advance of the 'F' mark. The above test relies, of course, on the static ignition timing being correct.

9   Spark plugs: checking and resetting the gaps

1   Two NGK B-8ES or ND WZ4ES spark plugs are fitted to the Kawasaki KZ400 series as standard. Certain operating conditions may indicate a change in spark plug grade, but generally the type recommended by the manufacturer gives the best all round serivce.

2   Check the gap of the plug points every three monthly or 2,000 mile serivce. To rest the gap, bend the outer electrode to bring it closer to, or further away from the central electrode until a 0.028 in (0.7 mm) feeler gauge can be inserted. Never bend the centre electrode or the insulator will crack, causing engine damage if the particles fall into the cylinder whilst the engine is running.

3   With some experience, the condition of the spark plug electrodes and insulator can be used as a reliable guide to engine operating conditions. See the accompanying diagram.

4   Always carry a spare pair of spark plugs of the recommended grade. In the rare event of plug failure, they will enable the engine to be restarted.

5   Beware of over-tightening the spark plugs, otherwise there is risk of stripping the threads from the aluminium alloy cylinder heads. The plugs should be sufficiently tight to seat firmly on their copper sealing washers, and no more. Use a spanner which is a good fit to prevent the spanner from slipping and breaking the insulator.

6   If the threads in the cylinder head strip as a result of over-tightening the spark plugs, it is possible to reclaim the head by the use of a Helicoil thread insert. This is a cheap and convenient method of replacing the threads; most motorcycle dealers operate a service of this nature at an economic price.

7   Make sure the plug insulating caps are a good fit and have their rubber seals. They should also be kept clean to prevent tracking. These caps contain the suppressors that eliminate both radio and TV interference.

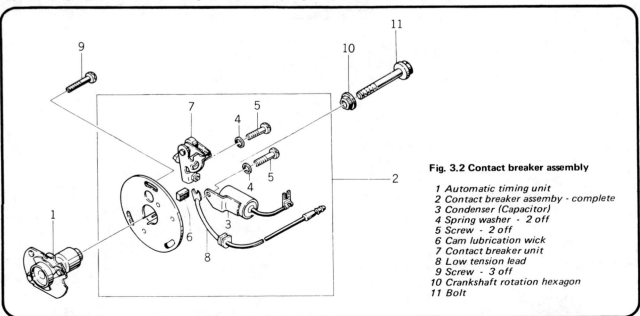

Fig. 3.2 Contact breaker assembly

1 *Automatic timing unit*
2 *Contact breaker assemby - complete*
3 *Condenser (Capacitor)*
4 *Spring washer - 2 off*
5 *Screw - 2 off*
6 *Cam lubrication wick*
7 *Contact breaker unit*
8 *Low tension lead*
9 *Screw   - 3 off*
10 *Crankshaft rotation hexagon*
11 *Bolt*

Electrode gap check - use a wire type gauge for best results

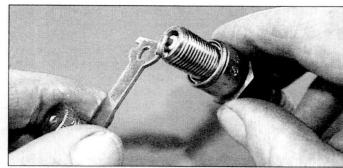

Electrode gap adjustment - bend the side electrode using the correct tool

Normal condition - A brown, tan or grey firing end indicates that the engine is in good condition and that the plug type is correct

Ash deposits - Light brown deposits encrusted on the electrodes and insulator, leading to misfire and hesitation. Caused by excessive amounts of oil in the combustion chamber or poor quality fuel/oil

Carbon fouling - Dry, black sooty deposits leading to misfire and weak spark. Caused by an over-rich fuel/air mixture, faulty choke operation or blocked air filter

Oil fouling - Wet oily deposits leading to misfire and weak spark. Caused by oil leakage past piston rings or valve guides (4-stroke engine), or excess lubricant (2-stroke engine)

Overheating - A blistered white insulator and glazed electrodes. Caused by ignition system fault, incorrect fuel, or cooling system fault

Worn plug - Worn electrodes will cause poor starting in damp or cold weather and will also waste fuel

10 Fault diagnosis

Symptom	Cause	Remedy
Engine will not start	Faulty ignition switch	Operate switch several times in case contacts are dirty. If lights and other electric function, switch may need renewal.
	Starter motor not working	Discharged battery. Use kickstart until battery is recharged.
	Short circuit in wiring	Check whether fuse is intact. Eliminate fault before switching on again.
	Completely discharged battery	If lights do not work, remove battery and recharge.
Engine misfires	Faulty condenser in ignition circuit	Renew condenser and re-test.
	Fouled spark plug	Renew plug and have original cleaned.
	Poor spark due to generator failure and discharged battery	Check output from generator. Remove and recharge battery
Engine lacks power and overheats	Retarded ignition timing	Check timing and also contact breaker gap. Check whether auto-timing unit has jammed.
Engine 'fades' when under load	Pre-ignition	Check grade of plugs fitted; use recommended grades only.

Chapter 4 Frame and forks

Contents

Specifications

Front forks
Spring free length	18.69 in (475 mm)
Spring free length service limit	18.30 in (465 mm)
Oil capacity (per leg):	
KZ400 and KZ400 D	155 – 165 cc
KZ400 S	161 – 166 cc
Oil level	13.4 – 14.2 in (340 – 360 mm)
Oil type	SAE 5W/20

Rear suspension
Pivot bush I.D.	0.8672 - 0.8684 in (22.03 - 22.063 mm)
Service limit	0.8747 in (22.26 mm)

1 General description

The Kawasaki KZ400 series have a duplex tube frame of the full cradle type; that is, with the engine not comprising any part of the frame. Rear suspension is of the swinging arm type, using oil filled suspension units to provide the necessary damping action. The units are adjustable so that the spring ratings can be effectively changed within certain limits to match the load carried.

The front forks are of the conventional telescopic type, having internal, oil-filled dampers. The fork springs are contained within the fork stanchions and each fork leg can be detached from the machine as a complete unit, without dismantling the steering head assembly.

2 Front forks: removal from the frame

1 It is unlikely that the front forks will have to be removed from the frame as a complete unit, unless the steering head

assembly requires attention or if the machine suffers frontal damage.

2 Commence front fork removal by disconnecting the main controls from the handlebars. In the case of machines fitted with a disc front brake the hydraulic master cylinder must be removed. The master cylinder and operating lever is clamped to the bars by two bolts and nuts. Disconnect the clutch cable and the front brake cable (where fitted).

3 Remove the combined starter/ignition switch from the right-hand end of the handlebars, and the indicator/lighting switch from the left-hand end of the bars.

4 Detach the headlamp glass and rim and disconnect the various snap connectors. The wires leading through to the handlebars can be pulled through the orifice in the rear of the headlamp, and the handlebar switches completely removed.

5 Slacken the four bolts that retain the handlebar clamps, and lift the handlebars away. Remove the tachometer and speedometer which are retained on a common bracket bolted to the top steering yoke. Disconnect the two drive cables by unscrewing the knurled ring on each cable end, and the indicator lamps.

6 Pull the two wires off the brake switch which is screwed into

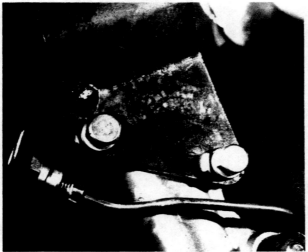
2.10a Mudguards are retained by two bolts inside fork legs ...

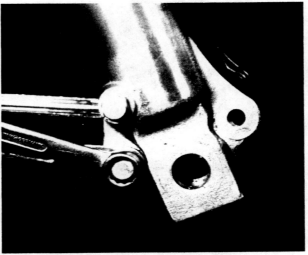
2.10b ... and by single bolts on rear stay

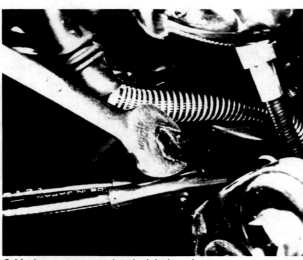
2.11a Loosen upper yoke pinch bolt and ...

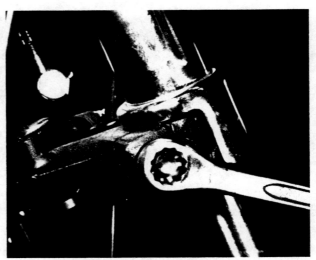
2.11b ... loosen lower yoke pinch bolt to ...

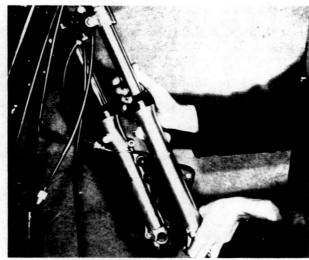
2.11c ... allow removal of complete fork leg

3.1 Drain plug next to wheel spindle hole

the hydraulic hose junction piece. The junction 'T' piece is retained on the steering lower yoke by two bolts (disc brake model).

7 Remove the headlamp shell which is retained by two bolts, one of which passes through each fork shroud bracket into the side of the headlamp shell.

8 Place a sturdy support below the crankcase so that the front wheel is raised well clear of the ground. Remove the speedometer cable from the gearbox on the right-hand side of the wheel, the cable is held by a screw ring. In the case of the drum brake machine the speedometer cable enters the brake plate on the left-hand side of the machine, where it is retained by a small bolt. The brake cable should also be disconnected by undoing the adjuster nut and pulling the cable through.

9 Remove the single bolt which holds the brake torque arm to the left-hand fork lower leg (drum brake only). Remove the split pin and undo the castellated nut on the wheel spindle. Loosen the bolts which hold the spindle clamp on the left-hand fork lower leg. Pull the wheel spindle from position and allow the front wheel to drop free.

10 On disc brake machines, remove the two bolts which retain the brake caliper assembly and remove the assembly together with the associate brake operating components. The brake hose is held by a clip and grommet and may be difficult to remove. It is better to bend the clip open to allow the brake hose and grommet to be freed than to try and force the hose out of the clip, which might cause damage.

11 When removing the various hydraulic brake parts it is important that care is taken not to bend or kink the brake hose or pipe. Under no circumstance should the front brake be operated at any time during removal or there is danger of the caliper piston being forced out of the cylinder with the resulting loss of fluid. Should this happen, the brake assembly must be bled after it has been replaced and the front wheel is in position. If any fluid is inadvertently spilled onto the paintwork it should be removed at once. Hydraulic fluids are most effective paint removers!

12 Remove the front mudguard, which is retained by one bolt on the lower end of each fork leg, and by two bolts through brackets on the inside of each fork lower leg. Remove the mudguard complete with centre bracket and stays.

13 Unscrew the upper and lower pinch bolts which clamp the fork legs to the two fork yokes. Each fork leg can now be removed as a complete unit. It may be necessary to spring the yoke clamps apart with a screwdriver to allow the fork legs to be pulled down, out of position.

14 Loosen the pinch bolt which clamps the steering head stem and undo the crown domed bolt. Remove the thick washer and wave washer. With the aid of a soft-nosed mallet the fork top yoke can be tapped upwards and off the steering stem.

15 To release the lower yoke and the steering head stem, unscrew the adjuster ring at the top with a suitable 'C' spanner. If such a spanner is not available a brass drift can be used to loosen the ring. As the steering head is lowered, the uncaged ball bearings from the lower race will be released, and care should be taken to catch them as they fall free. The bearings in the upper race will almost certainly stay in place.

16 It follows that much of this procedure can be avoided if it is necessary to remove the individual fork legs without disturbing the fork yokes and steering head bearings. Under these circumstances commence dismantling as described in paragraph 9 and work through to paragraph 11.

---

3 Front forks: dismantling

---

1 It is advisable to dismantle each fork leg separately using an identical procedure. There is less chance of unwittingly exchanging parts if this approach is adopted. Commence by draining the fork legs; there is a drain plug in each lower leg, located above the mudguard rear mounting stay.

2 Commence dismantling the fork leg by removing the Allen socket screw in the extreme lower end of the fork leg. Remove

3.2a Remove the Allen screw in lower leg then ...

3.2b ... undo the chrome top nut and ...

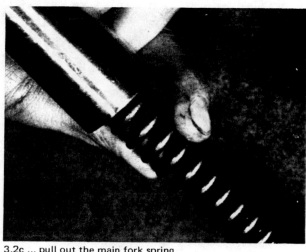
3.2c ... pull out the main fork spring

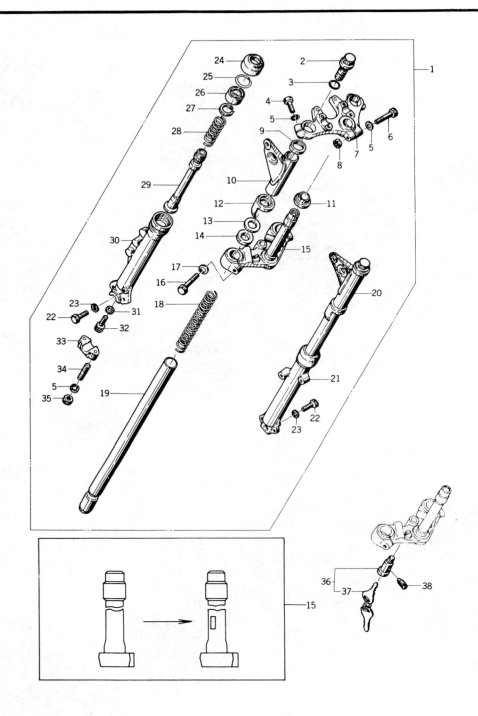

Fig. 4.1 Front forks

1 Front fork assembly complete
2 Fork tube cap bolt - 2 off
3 'O' ring - 2 off
4 Pinch bolt - 2 off
5 Spring washer - 5 off
6 Bolt
7 Top steering yoke
8 Lock nut
9 Upper shroud guide - 2 off

10 Left-hand fork shroud
11 Steering head bearing lower cone
12 Lower shroud guide - 2 off
13 Shroud washer - 2 off
14 Damper rubber - 2 off
15 Lower steering yoke
16 Pinch bolt - 2 off
17 Spring washer - 2 off
18 Upper fork spring - 2 off
19 Fork inner tube - 2 off

20 Right-hand fork shroud
21 Right-hand lower fork leg
22 Drain plug - 2 off
23 Drain plug washer - 2 off
24 Dust cover - 2 off
25 Oil seal circlip - 2 off
26 Oil seal - 2 off
27 Damper piston ring - 2 off
28 Lower fork spring - 2 off

29 Damper rod - 2 off
30 Left-hand lower fork leg
31 Fibre washer - 2 off
32 Damper rod holding screw - 2 off
33 Spindle clamp
34 Stud - 2 off
35 Nut - 2 off
36 Steering lock
37 Key set
38 Retainer screw

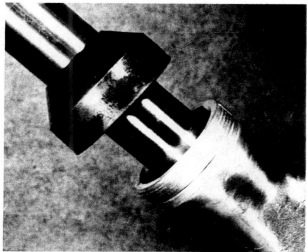

3.3a Prise the dust cap off and ...

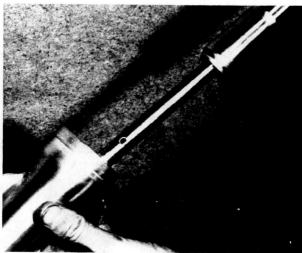

3.3b . . . pull out the fork tube and damper

3.3c Invert fork tube to free damper assembly

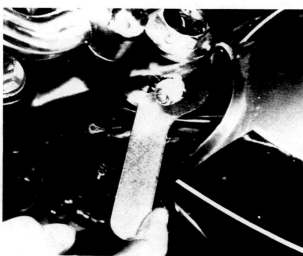

4.1 Use 'C' spanner to adjust head bearings

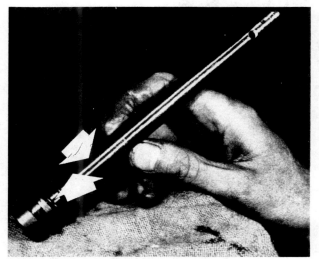

5.1a Oil orifices in damper rod must be clear as ...

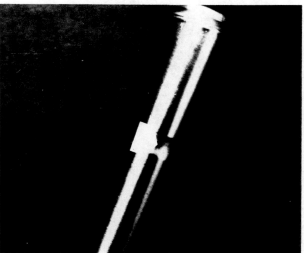

5.1b ... must be holes in fork tube

the chrome top bolt and pull out the spring. The fork leg may be held in the jaws of a vice in order to undo the chrome bolt, provided that the jaws are 'soft', or a length of inner tube is wrapped around the leg to protect it.

3   Prise the dust cover off the lower fork leg and pull the fork tube out of the lower leg. If the fork tube is now inverted the damper rod assembly will fall out. The various damper components can now be slipped off the damper rod for inspection.

4   Steering head bearings: examination and renovation

1   Before commencing reassembly of the forks, examine the steering head races. The ball bearing tracks of the respective cup and cone bearings should be polished and free from indentations, cracks or pitting. If signs of wear are evident, the cups and cones must be renewed. In order for the straight line steering on any motorcycle to be consistently good, the steering head bearings must be absolutely perfect. Even the smallest amount of wear on the cups and cones may cause steering wobble at high speeds and judder during heavy front wheel braking. The cups and cones are an interference fit on their respective seatings and can be tapped from position with a suitable dirft.

2   Ball bearings are relatively cheap. If the originals are marked or discoloured they must be renewed. To hold the steel balls in place during reassembly of the fork yokes, pack the bearings with grease. Both the upper race and the lower race contain nineteen (19) ¼ inch ball bearings. Although space will be left for one extra steel ball, making the number up to twenty, an extra steel ball must not be fitted. The gap allows the bearings to work correct, stopping them skidding and accelerating the rate of wear.

5   Front forks: examination and renovation

1   The parts most liable to wear over an extended period of service are the internal surfaces of the lower leg and the outer surfaces of the fork stanchion or tube. If there is excessive play between these two parts they must be replaced as a complete unit. Check the fork tube for scoring over the length which enters the oil seal. Bad scoring here will damage the oil seal and lead to fluid leakage.

2   It is advisable to renew the oil seals when the forks are dismantled even if they appear to be in good condition. This will save a strip-down of the forks at a later date if oil leakage occurs. The oil seal in the top of each lower fork leg is retained by an internal 'C' ring which can be prised out of position with a small

screwdriver. Check that the dust excluder rubbers are not split or worn where they bear on the fork tube. A worn excluder will allow the ingress of dust and water which will damage the oil seal and eventually cause wear of the fork tube.

3   It is not generally possible to straighten forks which have been badly damaged in an accident, particularly when the correct jigs are not available. It is always best to err on the side of safety and fit new ones, especially since there is no easy means to detect whether the forks have been over stressed or metal fatigued. Fork stanchions (tubes) can be checked, after removal from the lower legs by rolling them on a dead flat surface. Any misalignment will be immediately obvious.

4   The fork springs will take a permanent set after considerable usage and will need renewal if the fork action becomes spongy. The service limit for the total free length of each spring is 18.30 in (465 mm). Always renew them as a matched pair.

5   Fork damping is governed by the viscosity of the oil in the fork legs, normally SAE 5W20, and by the action of the damper assembly. Each fork leg holds 150 - 170 cc of damping fluid.

6   Front forks: replacement

1   Replace the front forks by following in reverse the dismantling procedures described in Section 2 and 3 of this Chapter. Before fully tightening the front wheel spindle clamps and the fork yoke pinch bolts, bounce the forks several times to ensure they work freely and are clamped in their original settings. Complete the final tightening from the wheel spindle clamps upward.

2   Check that the oil drain plugs are secure in the lower legs, then add the specified quantity and type of oil to each leg (see Specifications). With the forks fully extended (ie no weight on the front suspension) use a steel rule or length of welding rod passed down through the top of the stanchion to measure the oil level. If the oil level is not as specified, add or remove oil as necessary, noting that it is essential that the oil level is the same for each fork. Fit the top plugs to the forks.

3   If the fork stanchions prove difficult to re-locate through the fork yokes, make sure their outer surfaces are clean and polished so that they will slide more easily. It is often advantageous to use a screwdriver blade to open up the clamps as the stanchions are pushed upward into position.

4   Before the machine is used on the road, check the adjustment of the steering head bearings. If they are too slack, judder will occur. There should be no detectable play in the head races when the handlebars are pulled and pushed, with the front brake applied hard.

5.2 Fork oil seal held by spring clip

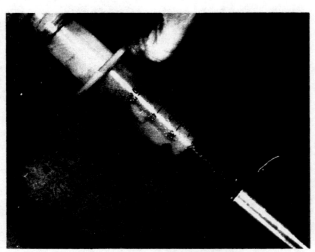

5.5 Refit each fork leg with 150-170 cc SAE 5W/20

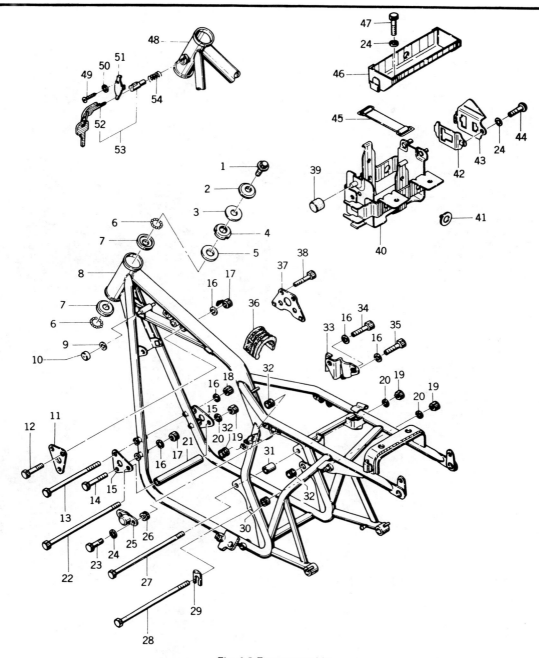

Fig. 4.2 Frame assembly

1 Steering head stem bolt	15 Front engine plate (lower) - 2 off	29 Shim
2 Steering head stem washer	16 Spring washer - 8 off	30 Spacer (rear lower)
3 Wave washer	17 Nut - 5 off	31 Spacer (rear upper)
4 Steering head stem nut	18 Locknut	32 Side cover grommet - 6 off
5 Steering head stem cap	19 Locknut - 3 off	33 Rear engine plate
6 Ball bearings - 38 off	20 Spring washer - 3 off	34 Bolt
7 Steering head cup - 2 off	21 Spacer (front)	35 Bolt
8 Frame assembly	22 Engine bolt (front)	36 Fuel tank mounting rubber (rear)
9 Plain washer - 2 off	23 Bolt - 2 off	37 Ignition coil bracket
10 Fuel tank mounting rubber (front) - 2 off	24 Spring washer - 5 off	38 Bolt - 2 off
11 Head steady plate	25 Battery carrier bracket	39 Damper rubber
12 Bolt - 3 off	26 Damper rubber - 2 off	40 Battery carrier
13 Bolt	27 Engine bolt (rear upper)	41 Battery case rubber - 6 off
14 Bolt - 2 off	28 Engine bolt (rear lower)	

42 Bracket
43 Bracket
44 Screw
45 Battery strap
46 Tool carrier
47 Bolt - 2 off
48 Head lug
49 Screw
50 Washer
51 Cover
52 Key set
53 Lock assembly
54 Spring

5 Overtight head races are equally undesirable. It is possible to unwittingly apply a loading of several tons on the head bearings by overtightening, even though the handlebars appear to turn quite freely. Overtight bearings will cause the machine to roll at low speeds and give generally imprecise handling with a tendency to weave. Adjustment is correct if there is no perceptible play in the bearings and the handlebars will swing to full lock in either direction, when the machine is on the centre stand with the front wheel clear of the ground. Only a slight tap should cause the handlebars to swing.

7 Steering head lock

1 The steering head lock is fitted in the underside of the lower yoke of the forks, where it is secured by a grub screw. When in the locked position, a bolt extends from the body of the lock when the forks are on full left-hand lock and abut against a portion of the steering head lug.
2 If the lock malfunctions it must be renewed. A repair is impracticable. When the lock is changed a new key must of course be used to match the new lock.

8 Frame: examination and renovation

1 The frame is unlikely to require attention unless accident damage has occurred. In some cases, replacement of the frame is the only satisfactory course of action if it is badly out of alignment. Only a few frame repair specialists have the jigs and mandrels necessary for resetting the frame to the required standard of accuracy and even then there is no easy means of assessing to what extent the frame may have been overstressed.
2 After the machine has covered a considerable mileage, it is advisable to examine the frame closely for signs of cracking or splitting at the welded joints. Rust can also cause weakness at these joints. Minor damage can be repaired by welding or brazing, depending on the extent and nature of the damage.
3 Remember that a frame which is out of alignment will cause handling problems and may even promote 'speed wobbles'. If misalignment is suspected, as the result of an accident, it will be necessary to strip the machine completely so that the frame can be checked and, if necessary, renewed.

9 Swinging arm rear fork: dismantling, examination and renovation

1 The rear fork assembly pivots on a detachable bush within each end of the fork crossmember and a pivot shaft which itself is surrounded by two bushes separated by a long distance piece. The pivot shaft passes through frame lugs on each side of the engine unit, and the two centre bushes and distance piece, so that the inner and outer bushes form the bearing surfaces. It is quite easy to renovate the swinging arm when wear necessitates attention.
2 To remove the rear swinging arm fork, first position the machine on the centre stand so that it rests firmly and securely. Remove the final drive chain by detaching the master link, and then unscrew the two cross head screws that hold the chain guard.
3 Detach the brake torque arm from the lug on the brake plate and from the lug on the frame. In both cases the torque arm bolt retaining nuts are secured by spring clips. Unscrew the adjuster ring on the brake operating arm and pull the rod through the trunnion on the brake arm. Replace the adjuster ring to avoid the loss of the brake rod spring.
4 Remove the split pin from the end of the wheel spindle and remove the castellated nut. The wheel spindle can now be pulled out to the left. Knock the wheel spacer out of position from between the brake plate and the fork end. The rear wheel can

9.3a Rear wheel spindle nut secured by split pin

9.3b Brake torque arm nuts secured by spring pins

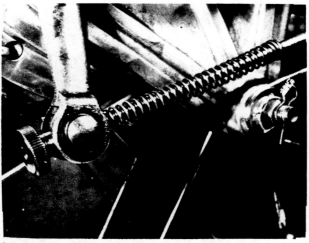

9.3c Loosen adjuster screw to free brake rod

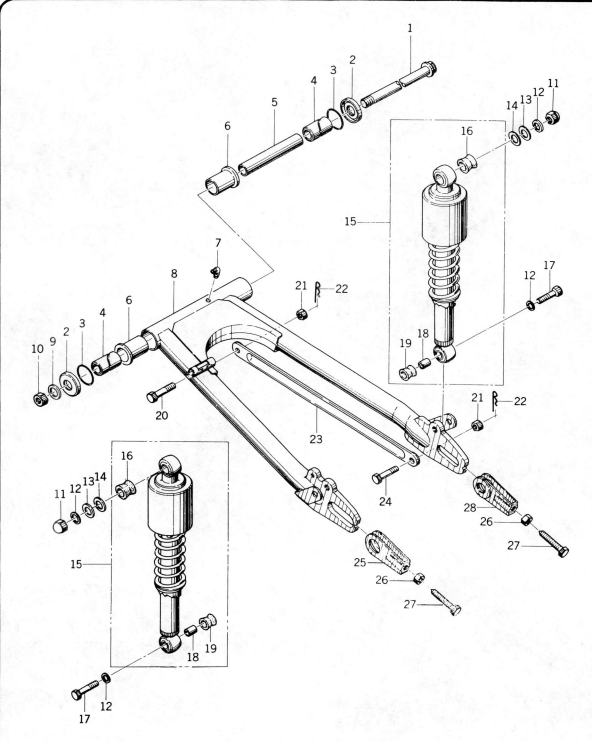

Fig. 4.3 Rear swinging arm assembly

1 Swinging arm
  pivot shaft
2 Dust cap - 2 off
3 'O' ring - 2 off
4 Inner bush - 2 off
5 Distance piece
6 Outer bush - 2 off
7 Grease nipple
8 Swinging arm fork

9 Washer
10 Nut
11 Domed nut - 2 off
12 Spring washer - 4 off
13 Plain washer - 2 off
14 Plain washer - 2 off
15 Suspension unit
  complete

16 Rubber bush - 2 off
17 Pivot bolt - 2 off
18 Bush - 2 off
19 Rubber bush - 2 off
20 Bolt
21 Nut
22 Spring pin
23 Brake torque arm

24 Bolt
25 Left-hand chain
  adjuster
26 Lock nut - 2 off
27 Adjuster bolt - 2 off
28 Right-hand
  adjuster

9.4a Pull wheel spindle out and ...

9.4b ... pull wheel away from cush drive hub

9.6 Remove suspension unit lower bolts

9.7a Remove swinging arm pivot nut and knock shaft out

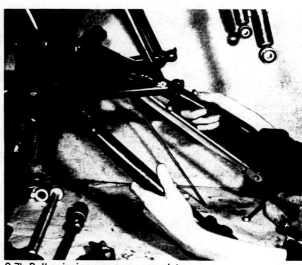
9.7b Pull swinging arm away complete

9.8a Remove dust excluder caps ...

9.8b ... noting the grease retaining 'O' ring

9.9 Outer bushes can be driven from position

9.8c Remove the inner bushes and ...

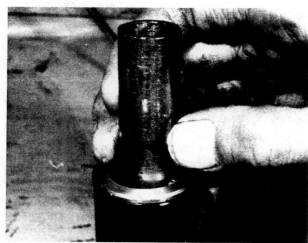

9.8d ... the long distance piece

now be pulled over to the right, off the cush drive assembly, and can be removed from the frame. The cush drive hub complete with the rear wheel sprocket will be left in position attached to the left-hand rear fork member.

5   Undo the large nut which holds the cush drive hub and sprocket ,in position. This assembly and the wheel position adjuster can now be pulled free.

6   Detach both rear suspension units at their lugs on the swinging arm fork. Each unit is held by a single bolt screwed into a threaded hole in the swinging arm.

7   Remove the locknut from the end of the pivot shaft, which can then be tapped out from the left-hand side. Working the swinging arm fork up and down will aid removal of the shaft. The swinging arm fork is now free to be pulled from position between the two frame lugs.

8   Remove the dust excluder caps from each end of the fork crossmember. Note the presence of the two 'O' rings in the caps. Push out the two inner bushes together with the distance piece.

9   Wash the inner and outer bushes carefully in petrol or an other solvent. Do not remove the outer bushes from positon in the fork crossmember unless they need renewal as they are made of a brittle material that will probably fracture while being drifted out. With a micrometer or vernier gauge, measure the internal diameter of the outer bushes and the outside diameter of the inner bushes. If any component is outside the service limit as follows, the bearings should be renewed as a complete set.

Check the pivot shaft for straightness by rolling it on the edge of a dead flat surface. If the shaft is bent it must be renewed or straightened.

10 Reassemble the swinging arm fork by reversing the dismantling procedure. Grease the pivot shaft and bearings liberally before reassembly and check that the 'O' rings in the dust caps are in good condition.

11 Worn swinging arm pivot bearings will give imprecise handling with a tendency for the rear end of the machine to twitch or hop. The play can be detected by placing the machine on its centre stand and with the rear wheel clear of the ground, pulling and pushing on the fork ends in a horizontal direction. Any play will be magnified by the leverage effect. In the UK, excess play will cause the machine to fail an MoT test.

10 Rear suspension units: examination

1   The rear suspension units fitted to the Kawasaki KZ400 machine are of the normal hydraulically damped type, adjustable to give five different spring settings. A 'C' spanner included in the tool kit should be used to turn the lower spring seat and so

alter its position on the adjustment projection. When the spring seat is turned so that the effective length of the spring is shortened the suspension will become heavier.

2   If a suspension unit leaks, or if the damping efficiency is reduced in any other way the two units must be replaced as a pair. For precise roadholding it is imperative that both units react to movement in the same way. It follows that the units must always be set at the same spring loading.

11 Centre stand: examination

1   The centre stand pivots on a shaft running across the bottom frame tubes, which is retained by a split pin and washer. The pivot assemblies on centre stands are often neglected with regard to lubrication and this will eventually lead to wear. It is prudent to remove the pivot shaft from time to time and grease it thoroughly. This will prolong the effective life of the stand.

2   Check that the return spring is in good condition. A broken or weak spring may cause the stand to fall whilst the machine is being ridden, and catch in some obstacle, unseating the rider.

12 Prop stand: examination

1   The prop stand is attached to a lug welded to the left-hand lower frame tube. An extension spring anchored to the left-hand footrest ensures that the stand is retracted when the weight of the machine is taken off the stand.

2   Check that the pivot bolt is secured and that the extension spring is in good condition and not overstretched. An accident is almost certain if the stand extends whilst the machine is on the move.

13 Footrests: examination and renovation

1   The front footrests are bolted to lugs welded to the frame lower engine tubes. The left-hand footrest sharing a lug with the side stand assembly. The footrests pivot upwards on their mounting brackets and are spring loaded to keep them in their horizontal position. If an obstacle is struck they will fold upwards, reducing the risk of damage to the rider's foot or to the main frame.

2   If the footrests are damaged in an accident, it is possible to dismantle the assembly into its component parts. Detach each footrest from the frame lugs and separate the folding foot piece from the bracket on which it pivots by withdrawing out the split pin and pulling out the pivot shaft. It is preferable to renew the damaged parts, but if necessary, they can be bent straight by clamping them in a vice and heating to a dull red with a blow lamp whilst the appropriate pressure is applied. Do not attempt to straighten the footrests while they are attached to the frame.

3   If heat is applied to the main footrest piece during any straighting operation it follows that the footrest rubber must be removed temporarily.

14 Rear brake pedal: examination and renovation

1   The rear brake pedal pivots on a shaft which passes through a welded lug on the forward end of the silencer/rear footrest mounting tube. The pivot shaft is itself welded to the lug, the pedal assembly being held in place by a nut and two washers.

2   If the brake pedal is bent or twisted it can be removed from the shaft after unscrewing the retaining nut and straightened by adopting the same method as recommended for bent footrests. It should be borne in mind that heating the pedal will almost certainly destroy the chrome plate with which the component is finished, therefore if the cosmetic appearance of the machine is important the part should be renewed.

3   The rear brake pedal is returned to its normal position by an extension spring. This should be checked to ensure that it is not stretched, and pulls the brake off cleanly.

15 Dual seat: removal

1   The dualseat is attached to two small lugs welded to the right-hand side of the subframe, and pivots on two clevis pins which pass through these lugs. The seat opens from the right where it is kept locked by a safety catch that also acts as a helmet security hook. The catch can only be released by the matching key.

2   Although it is seldom necessary to remove the dual seat, it can be lifted away after the clevis pins are pushed out. The clevis pins are retained by spring pins.

16 Speedometer heads and tachometer heads: removal and replacement

1   The speedometer and tachometer heads are freed quite easily by removing their four mounting nuts, washers, collars and rubber mountings. They can then be lifted upwards off their mounting plate. Detach the drive cables at the screwed couplings and withdraw the bulb holders from the base of each instrument.

2   Apart from defects in either the drive or drive cables, a speedometer or tachometer which malfunctions is difficult to repair. Fit a replacement or alternatively entrust the repair to a competent instrument repair specialist.

3   Remember that a speedometer in correct working order is a statutory requirement in the UK. Apart from this legal necessity, reference to the odometer readings is the most satisfactory means of keeping pace with the maintenance schedules.

17 Speedometer and tachometer drive cables: examination and maintenance

1   It is advisable to detach the drive cable(s) from time to time in order to check whether they are lubricated adequately, and whether the outer coverings are damaged or compressed at any point along their run. Jerky or sluggish movements can often be traced to a damaged drive cable.

2   For greasing, withdraw the inner cable. After removing all the old grease, clean with a petrol-soaked rag and examine the cable for broken strands or other damage.

3   Regrease the cable with high melting point grease, taking care not to grease the last six inches at the point where the cable enters the instrument head. If this precaution is not observed, grease will work into the head and immobilise the instrument movement.

4   If any instrument head stops working suspect a broken drive cable unless the odometer readings continue. Inspection will show whether the inner cable has broken; if so, the inner cable alone can be replaced and re-inserted in the outer casing, after greasing. Never fit a new inner cable alone if the covering is damaged or compressed at any point along its run.

18 Speedometer and tachometer drives: location and examination

1   In the case of the disc front brake machines, the speedometer drive gearbox is fitted on the right-hand side of the front wheel hub. On drum front brake machines the gearbox is an integral part of the brake plate and is driven internally from the front hub. In both cases the drive rarely gives trouble provided it is kept properly lubricated. Lubrication should take place whenever the front wheel is removed for wheel bearing inspection or replacement.

2   The tachometer drive is taken from the cylinder head cover, between the two cylinders. The drive is taken from the overhead

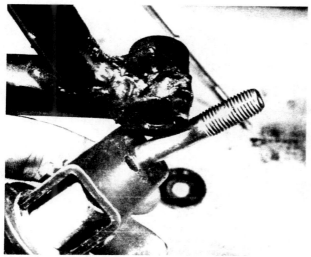
13.1 Rear footrests locate on peg on mounting

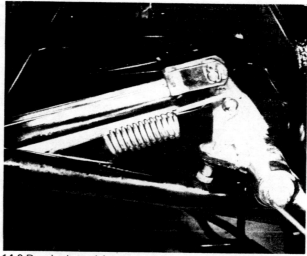
14.3 Rear brake pedal return spring

18.1a Speedometer cable is driven by gearbox on front wheel

18.1b The speedometer gearbox drive gear which ...

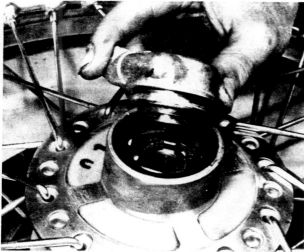
18.1c ... is a sliding fit in the gearbox ...

18.1d ... engages with dogged ring on wheel hub

camshaft by means of skew-cut pinions and then by a flexible cable to the tachometer head. It is unlikely that the internal drive will give trouble during the normal service life of the machine, particularly since it is fully enclosed and effectively lubricated.

19 Cleaning the machine

1 After removing all surface dirt with a rag or sponge which is washed frequently in clean water, the machine should be allowed to dry thoroughly. Application of car polish or wax to the cycle parts will give a good finish, particularly if the machine receives this attention at regular intervals.

2 The plated parts should require only a wipe with a damp rag, but if they are badly corroded, as may occur during the winter when the roads are salted, it is permissible to use one of the proprietary chrome cleaners. These often have an oily base which will help to prevent corrosion from recurring.

3 If the engine parts are particularly oily, use a cleaning compound such as Gunk or Jizer. Apply the compound whilst the parts are dry and work it in with a brush so that it has an opportunity to penetrate and soak into the film of oil and grease. Finish off by washing down liberally, taking care that water does not enter the carburettors, air cleaners or the electrics. If desired, the now clean aluminium alloy parts can be enhanced still further when they are dry by using a special polish such as Solvol Autosol. This will restore the full lustre.

4 If possible, the machine should be wiped down immediately after it has been used in the wet, so that it is not garaged under damp conditions which will promote rusting. Make sure that the the chain is wiped and re-oiled, to prevent water from entering the rollers and causing harshness with an accompanying rapid rate of wear. Remember there is less chance of water entering the control cables and causing stiffness if they are lubricated regularly as described in the Routine Maintenance Section.

20 Fault diagnosis - frame and forks

Symptom	Cause	Remedy
Machine veers either to the left or the right with hands off handlebars	Bent frame Twisted forks Wheels out of alignment	Check and renew. Check and replace. Check and re-align.
Machine rolls at low speed	Overtight steering head bearings	Slacken until adjustment is correct.
Machine judders when front brake is applied	Slack steering head bearings Worn fork bushes	Tighten until adjustment is correct. Dismantle forks and renew bushes.
Machine pitches on uneven surfaces	Ineffective fork dampers Ineffective rear suspension units Suspension too soft	Check oil content. Check whether units still have damping action. Raise suspension unit adjustment one notch.
Fork action stiff	Fork legs out of alignment (twisted in yokes)	Slacken yoke clamps, and fork top bolts. Pump fork several times then retighten from bottom upwards.
Machine wanders. Steering imprecise. Rear wheel tends to hop	Worn swinging arm pivot	Dismantle and renew bushes and pivot shaft.

Chapter 5 Wheels, brakes and tyres

Contents

Specifications

Tyres
Front ... ... 3.25 - 18 in
Rear ... ... 3.50 - 18 in

Tyre pressures
Front ... ... 27 p.s.i. (31 p.s.i.*)
Rear ... ... 28 p.s.i. (33 p.s.i.*)

Higher pressures for sustained high speeds.

Brakes
Front ... ... Hydraulic 11 in (277 mm) disc brake*
Rear ... ... 7 in (180 mm) single leading shoe drum brake

* Some European models are fitted with twin leading shoe drum front brakes.

1 General description

1 The Kawasaki KZ400 series are fitted with 18 in steel rim wheel on the front and rear. The front tyre section is 3.25 in and the rear 3.50 in. The original fitted tyres are manufactured by Yokohama. Depending on the model, the front brake is a hydraulically operated 11 in disc brake, with the master cylinder mounted on the right-hand handlebar, or a twin leading shoe internally expanding drum brake operated by cable. The rear wheel on all models is fitted with a single leading shoe drum brake.

2 Front wheel: examination and renovation

1 Place the machine on the centre stand so that the front wheel is raised clear of the ground. Spin the wheel and check the rim alignment. Small irregularities can be corrected by tightening the spokes in the affected area although a certain amount of experience is necessary to prevent over-correction. Any flats in the wheel rim will be evident at the same time. These are more difficult to remove and in most cases it will be necessary to have the wheel rebuilt on a new rim. Apart from the effect on stability, a flat will expose the tyre bead and walls to greater risk of damage if the machine is run with a deformed wheel.

2 Check for loose and broken spokes. Tapping the spokes is the best guide to tension. A loose spoke will produce a quite different sound and should be tightened by turning the nipple in an anticlockwise direction. Always check for run out by spinning the wheel again. If the spokes have to be tightened by an excessive amount, it is advisable to remove the tyre and tube as detailed in Section 16 of this Chapter. This will enable the protruding ends of the spokes to be ground off, thus preventing them from chafing the inner tube and causing punctures.

3 Front wheel disc brake: examination and renovation

1 Check the front brake master cylinder, hose and caliper unit for signs of fluid leakage. Pay particular attention to the

3.4a Removal of screw and plate will allow ...

3.4b ... removal of inner disc pad

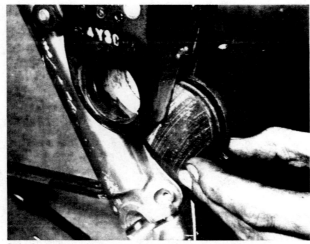

3.4c Squeeze brake lever gently to eject piston disc pad

condition of the synthetic rubber hose, which should be renewed without question if there are signs of cracking, splitting or other exterior damage.

2   Check the level of hydraulic fluid by removing the cap on the brake fluid reservoir and lifting out the diaphragm and diaphragm plate. This is one of the maintenance tasks, which should never be neglected. Make certain that the handlebars are in the central position when removing the reservoir cap, because if the fluid level is high, the fluid will spill over the reservoir brim. If the level is particularly low, the fluid delivery passage will be allowed direct contact with the air and may necessitate the bleeding of the system at a later date. A level mark is given on the inside of the reservoir cylinder; if the level is below the mark, brake fluid of the correct grade must be added. **NEVER USE ENGINE OIL** or anything other than the recommended fluid. Other fluids have unsatisfactory characteristics and will quickly destroy the seals.

3   The brake pads should be inspected for wear. Each brake pad is stepped ie; it has more than one diameter. If either brake pad is worn down by the amount of the first stepped portion, both brake pads must be renewed as a set. The brake pads can be checked while they are still in position in the caliper and the front wheel is still in situ. If the front brake is operated the extent of wear can be easily seen.

4   The brake pads can be removed from the caliper after the front wheel has been taken out. Commence by removing the retaining screw and backplate on the inside pad. The pad will push out of position. **Very gently** apply the front brake lever, which will operate the caliper piston and so push the outer pad from position. Do not pump the brake when carrying out this operation or there is a danger of the piston being pushed out of the cylinder. It will be noted that the outer pad (piston pad) has a steel shim on the rear face. The shim is fitted to prevent the disc brake assembly squeaking during operation, and is located by a small projection on the brake pad.

When fitting new pads, it will probably be found that the increased size of the pads will prevent the brake disc from fitting between the pads when the front wheel is being replaced. To overcome this, press hard on the outer (piston) pad and at the same time slightly loosen the brake bleed valve. The pad will move inwards slowly and then stop at which point the bleed valve must be tightened immediately. It will be found that a small amount of fluid will have been ejected from the bleed valve. Wipe up the fluid immediately and then check the level in the master cylinder.

5   If brake action becomes spongy, or if any part of the hydraulic system is dismantled (such as when the hose is replaced) it is necessary to bleed the system in order to remove all traces of air. The following procedure should be followed:

6   Attach a tube to the bleed valve at the top of the caliper unit, after removing the dust cap. It is preferable to use a transparent plastic tube, so that the presence of air bubbles is seen more readily.

7   The far end of the tube should rest in a small bottle so that it is submerged in hydraulic fluid. This is essential, to prevent air from passing back into the system. In consequence, the end of the tube must remain submerged at all times.

8   Check that the reservoir on the handlebars is full of fluid and replace the cap to keep the fluid clean.

9   If spongy brake action necessitates the bleeding operation, squeeze and release the brake lever several times in rapid succession, to allow the pressure in the system to build up. Then open the bleed valve by unscrewing it one complete turn whilst maintaining pressure on the lever. This is a two-person operation. Squeeze the lever fully until it meets the handlebar, then close the bleed valve. If parts of the system have been replaced, the bleed valve can be opened from the beginning and the brake lever worked until fluid issues from the bleed tube. Note that it may be necessary to top up the reservoir during this operation; if it empties, air will enter the system and the whole operation will have to be repeated.

10 Repeat operation 9 until bubbles disappear from the bleed

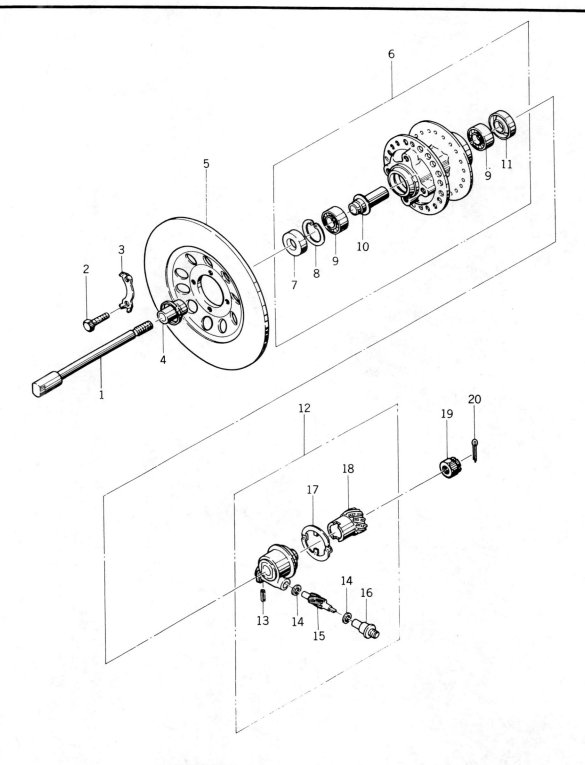

Fig. 5.1 Front hub assembly (Disc brake model)

1 Front wheel spindle
2 Bolt - 4 off
3 Tab washer - 2 off
4 Dust collar
5 Brake disc
6 Front hub
  assembly - complete

7 Oil seal
8 Bearing circlip
9 Wheel bearing - 2 off
10 Distance piece
11 Oil seal

12 Speedometer gearbox -
  complete
13 Mills pin
14 Thrust washer
15 Gear shaft

16 Shaft housing
17 Speedometer drive ring
18 Speedometer drive gear
19 Castellated nut
20 Split pin

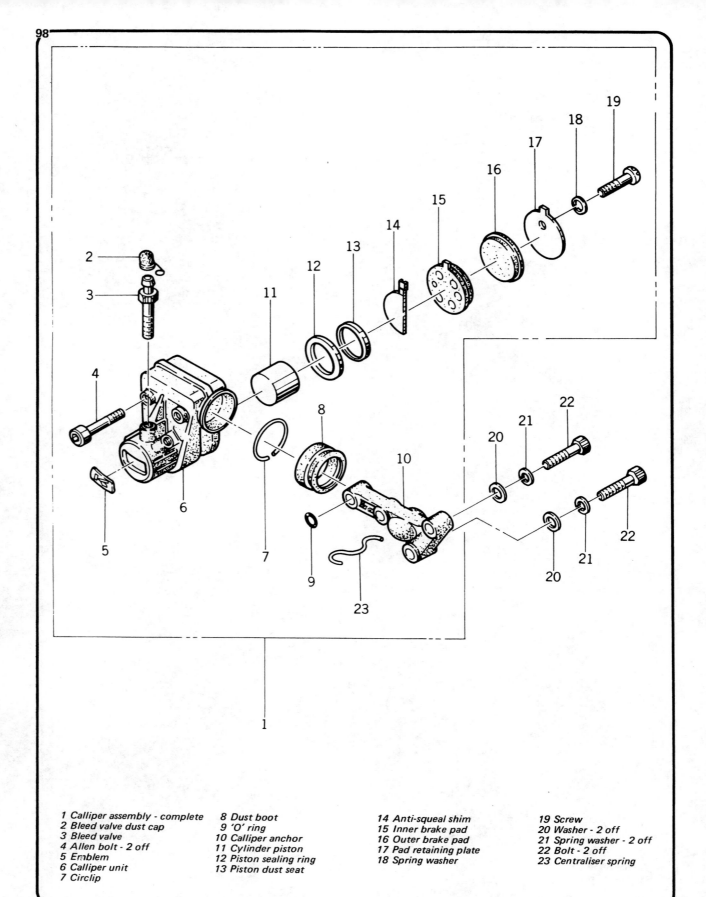

1 Calliper assembly - complete
2 Bleed valve dust cap
3 Bleed valve
4 Allen bolt - 2 off
5 Emblem
6 Calliper unit
7 Circlip

8 Dust boot
9 'O' ring
10 Calliper anchor
11 Cylinder piston
12 Piston sealing ring
13 Piston dust seat

14 Anti-squeal shim
15 Inner brake pad
16 Outer brake pad
17 Pad retaining plate
18 Spring washer

19 Screw
20 Washer - 2 off
21 Spring washer - 2 off
22 Bolt - 2 off
23 Centraliser spring

3.4d Half plate on rear ot pad is anti-squeal device

3.9 Attach a bleed tube to bleed valve

3.10 Always replace bleed valve cap after bleeding

tube. Close the bleed valve fully, remove the bleed tube and replace the dust cap.

11 Check the lever in the reservoir and top up if necessary. Never use the fluid which has drained into the bottles at the end of the bleed tube because this contains air bubbles which will re-introduce air into the system. It must stand for 24 hours before it can be re-used.

12 Refit the diamphragm and diaphragm plate and tighten the reservoir cap securely.

13 Do not spill fluid on the cycle parts. It is a very effective paint stripper! Also, the plastic glasses in the speedometer and tachometer heads will be badly obscured if fluid is spilt on them.

4   Removing and replacing the brake disc

1   It is unlikely that the disc will require attention until a considerable mileage has been covered, unless premature scoring of the disc has taken place thereby reducing braking efficiency. To remove the disc, first detach the front wheel as described in Chapter 4, Section 2.8 and 9. The disc is bolted to the front wheel on the left-hand side by four bolts, which are secured in pairs by a common tab washer. Bend back the tab washers and remove the bolts, to free the disc.

2   The brake disc can be checked for wear and for warpage whilst the front wheel is still in the machine. Using a micrometer measure the thickness of the disc at the point of greatest wear. If the measurement is much less than the recommended service limit of 0.21 in (5.5 mm) the disc should be renewed. Check the warpage of the disc by setting up a suitable pointer close to the outer periphery of the disc and spinning the front wheel slowly. If the total warpage is more than 0.011 in (0.3 mm) the disc should be renewed. A warped disc, apart from reducing the braking efficiency, is likely to cause juddering during braking and will also cause the brake to bind when it is not in use.

5   Master cylinder: examination and renovation

1   The master cylinder is unlikely to give trouble unless the machine has been stored for a lengthy period or until a considerable mileage has been covered. The usual signs of trouble are leakage of hydraulic fluid and a gradual fall in the fluid reservoir content.

2   To gain full access to the master cylinder, commence the dismantling operation by attaching a bleed tube to the caliper unit bleed nipple. Open the bleed nipple one complete turn, then operate the front brake lever until all fluid is pumped out of the reservoir. Close the bleed nipple, detach the tube and store the fluid in a closed container for subsequent re-use.

3   Detach the hose and also the stop lamp switch. Remove the handlebar lever pivot bolt and the lever itself.

4   Access is now available to the piston and the cylinder and it is possible to remove the piston assembly, together with all the relevant seals. Take note of the way in which the seals are arranged because they must be replaced in the same order. Failure to observe this necessity will result in brake failure.

5   Clean the master cylinder and piston with either hydraulic fluid or alcohol. On no account use either abrasives or other solvents such as petrol. If any signs of wear or damage are evident, renewal is necessary. It is not practicable to reclaim either the piston or the cylinder bore.

6   Soak the new seals in hydraulic fluid for about 15 minutes prior to fitting, then reassemble the parts IN EXACTLY THE SAME ORDER, using the reversal of the dismantling procedure. Lubricate with hydraulic fluid and make sure the feather edges of the various seals are not damaged.

7   Refit the assembled master cylinder unit to the handlebar, and reconnect the handlebar lever, hose, stop lamp etc. Refill the reservoir with hydraulic fluid and bleed the entire system by following the procedure detailed in Section 3.5 of this Chapter.

8   Check that the brake is working correctly before taking the machine on the road, to restore pressure and align the pads

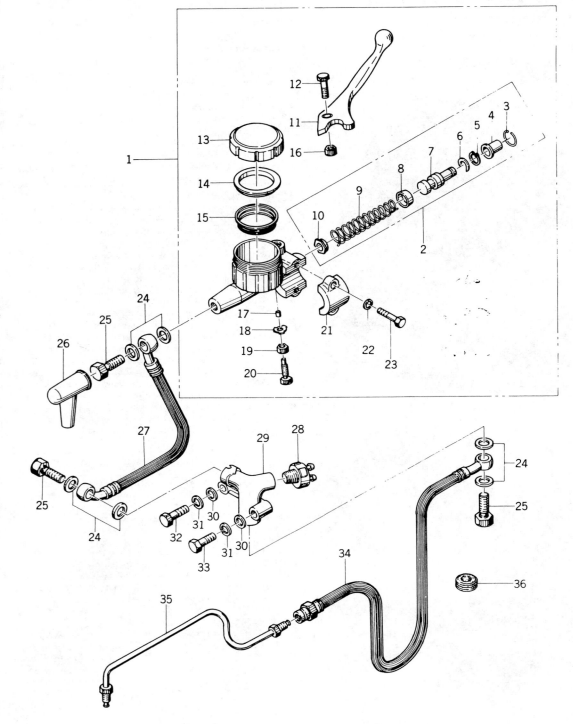

Fig. 5.3 Master cylinder (Disc brake model)

1 Master cylinder - complete	10 Valve assembly	19 Lock nut	28 Stop lamp switch
2 Piston assembly - complete	11 Brake lever	20 Lever adjustment screw	29 'T' union
3 Circlip	12 Pivot bolt	21 Cylinder clamp	30 Plain washer - 2 off
4 Dust cover	13 Reservoir cap	22 Washer - 2 off	31 Spring washer - 2 off
5 Circlip	14 Diaphragm plate	23 Bolt - 2 off	32 Bolt
6 Stopper clip	15 Diaphragm	24 Fibre washer - 6 off	33 Bolt
7 Piston	16 Nut	25 Union bolt - 3 off	34 Calliper brake hose
8 Piston seal	17 Tube	26 Dust cover	35 Bridge pipe
9 Return spring	18 Lock washer	27 Cylinder brake hose	36 Brake hose grommet

7.1a Remove the end cap from the hub and ...

7.1b ... prise out the oil seal

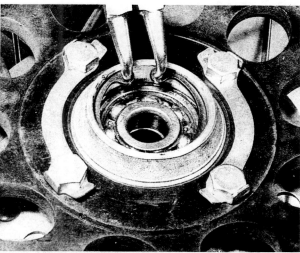

7.1c The bearing is held by a circlip

7.1d Oil seal retains speedometer dog ring

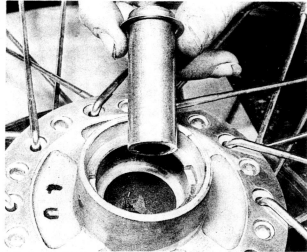

7.2a Spacer lies between front wheel bearings

7.2b Pack bearings with grease before reassembly

correctly. Use the brake gently for the first 50 miles or so to enable all the new parts to bed down correctly.

9 It should be emphasised that repairs to the master cylinder are best entrusted to a Kawasaki agent, or alternatively, that the defective part should be replaced by a new unit. Dismantling and reassembly requires a certain amount of skill and it is imperative that the entire operation is carried out under cleaner than average conditions.

6 Front wheel drum brake: examination and renovation

After removal of the front wheel the brake plate complete with brake shoes and speedometer gear can be removed from the wheel hub.

2 Examine the brake linings for oil, dirt or grease. Surface dirt can be removed with a stiff brush but oil soaked linings should be replaced. High spots can be carefully eased down with emery cloth.

3 Examine the condition of the brake linings and if they have worn thin they should be renewed. The brake linings are bonded to the brake shoes and thus separate linings are not available.

4 To remove the shoes, pull them away from the two cams and then pull them away from the plate in a 'V' formation so that they can be removed together complete with the return springs. When they are well clear of the brake plate the springs can be removed. Check the springs for any signs of wear or stretching and renew if necessary. Check the surface of the brake drum for wear or scoring.

5 Whilst the brake plate is off, the brake cam spindle should be lubricated sparingly with grease. Before removing the linkage between the cams, check that both the cams and the levers are marked (usually centre punched) so that they can be replaced in the same positions. Mark them clearly, if not. Slacken both pinch bolts noting the washer under both the bolt head and nut. Pull off the linkage assembly complete. It will probably be tight and will have to be levered off gently with a screwdriver, being careful not to damage the alloy brake plate. Do not undo the connecting brake rod lock nut otherwise realignment will be required on reassembly.

6 Brush all the dust from the brake plate and reassemble in the reverse order to the above. Do not forget the felt dust seals on the cam spindles and to lightly grease the cams, spindles and the fixed spindle at the other end of the brake shoe.

9.1a Brake plate will pull out of drum

9.1b Inspect linings for wear

10.1a Hollow spindle runs on bearing in cush drive hub

10.1b Spacer collar fits in oil seal on cush drive hub

7 The speedometer drive located in the brake plate should not require attention except for cleaning and new grease. Examine the oil seal and obtain a replacement, if required.

8 Dust out the brake drum and examine it for score marks and damage. It should have a shiny, smooth surface. Clean the drum with a petrol soaked rag to remove all traces of grease.

9 When reassembling the wheel and brake do not forget to replace the spacing shims and do not get any grease or oil on the brake shoes or drum.

10 When replacing the front wheel in the forks make sure the torque arm is reconnected and the bolt tightened fully. Failure to heed this warning may result in a serious accident if the bolt drops out and the brake is applied hard.

7 Front wheel bearings: examination and replacement

All models

1 Place the machine on the centre stand and remove the front wheel as described in Chapter 4, Section 2.8 and 2.9. On disc brake machines remove the speedometer gearbox, drive gear and oil seal on the right-hand side of the hub and remove the spacer, oil seal and bearing retainer circlip from the left-hand side. To give access to the bearings on drum brake machines, first remove the brake plate on the left-hand side of the hub and the dust excluder and oil seal from the right-hand side of the hub.

2 The wheel bearings can now be tapped out from each side with the use of a suitable long drift. Careful and even tapping will prevent the bearing 'tying' and damage to the races.

3 Remove all the old grease from the hub and bearings, giving the latter a final wash in petrol. When the bearings are dirty, lubricate them sparingly with a very light oil. Check the bearings for play and roughness when they are spun by hand. All used bearings will emit a small amount of noise when spun but they should not chatter or sound rough. If there is any doubt about the conditions of the bearings they should be renewed.

4 Before replacing the bearings pack them with high melting point grease. Do not overfill the hub centre with grease as it will expand when hot and may find its way past the oil seals. The hub space should be about 2/3 full of grease. Drift the bearings in, using a soft drift on the outside ring of the bearing. Do not drift the centre ring of the bearing or damage will be incurred. Replace the oil seals carefully, drifting them into place with a thick walled tube of approximately the same dimension as the oil seal. A large socket spanner is ideal.

8 Rear wheel: examination, removal and renovation

1 Place the machine on the centre stand so that the rear wheel is raised clear of the ground. Check for rim alignment, damage to the rim and loose or broken spokes by following the procedure relating to the front wheel, as described in Section 2 of this Chapter.

2 To remove the rear wheel, use the procedure described in Chapter 4, Section 9.3 and 9.4. The rear brake plate can be lifted off the right-hand end of the wheel hub as a complete unit.

3 When replacing the rear wheel, check to ensure both torque arm bolts are tightened fully. If they work loose, a serious accident may well result from the ensuing skid.

9 Rear brake: examination and renovation

1 Examine the conditions of the brake linings as described in Section 6.2-4 of this Chapter. Measure the thickness of the brake linings at their thinnest points. If they are below 0.098 in (2.5 mm) they must be renewed. As with the front brake lining they must be renewed together with the brake shoes to which they are bonded. A pointer on the outside of the brake back plate, attached to the operating cam, indicates the wear limit approximately.

10 Rear wheel bearings: removal and replacement

1 The rear wheel assembly has three journal ball bearings. One bearing lies each side of the wheel hub and the third bearing is fitted in the cush drive assembly to which is attached the sprocket. The cush drive/sprocket assembly can be removed after separating the final drive chain at the master link and removing the large nut which holds the hollow bearing spindle.

2 Drift the wheel bearings from position using the same method as described for the front wheel. Before the cush drive bearing is tapped out the hollow spindle and oil seal should be removed. It is not necessary to remove the sprocket.

11 Adjusting the front brake (twin leading shoe drum brake only)

1 In order for the twin leading shoe front brake to operate at full efficiency the leading edges of the brake linings must come into contact with the brake drum at exactly the same time when the brake is applied. It is also important that an equal amount of leverage is applied to the two brake operating cams. This is affected by ensuring that the two brake arms are set parallel to each other. If the arms are not parallel to each other, the effective length of the rear most operating lever is reduced, thereby lowering the leverage ratio on the operating cam.

2 If, during front brake maintenance the relative positions of the two operating levers were not punch marked to ensure easy and accurate reassembly the brake can be reset with the wheel in place in the forks as follows:

Place the main (long) brake operating arm on the splines of the front operating cam so that when the operating cable is attached to the arm and the arm is pulled into the 'ON' position, the angle between the arm and the cable is slightly less than 90°. If the angle is found to be more than 90° pull the arm off the splines and refit it in the next position in a clockwise direction.

3 Fit the brake operating cable, and whilst spinning the front wheel, adjust the nut on the cable end until the brake just begins to bite. Slacken off the nut ½ a turn. Loosen the locknut on the cam arm connecting rod and fit the rear brake arm onto the camshaft splines so that the two arms are parallel. Spin the wheel again and turn the adjusting rod until the rear arm moves sufficiently to make the brake just bite. Slacken the adjuster rod half a turn. The two operating arms should now to all intents and purposes be parallel. Tighten the locknut on the connecting rod and tighten the two brake arm pinch bolts.

4 Adjust the operating cable at the handlebar lever so that there is approximately 1 in (25 mm) movement at the lever end before braking action is commenced.

12 Adjusting the rear brake

All models

1 Adjustment of the rear brake is correct when there is ¾ - 1¼ in (20 - 30 mm) up and down movement measured at the rear brake pedal foot piece, between the fully 'off' and 'on' position.

2 If, when the brake is fully applied, the angle between the brake arm and the operating rod is more than 90° the brake arm should be pulled off the camshaft, after loosening the pinch bolt. Reset the brake arm so that the right angle is produced.

3 Note that it may be necessary to adjust the height-setting of the stop lamp switch after adjustment of the brake pedal position.

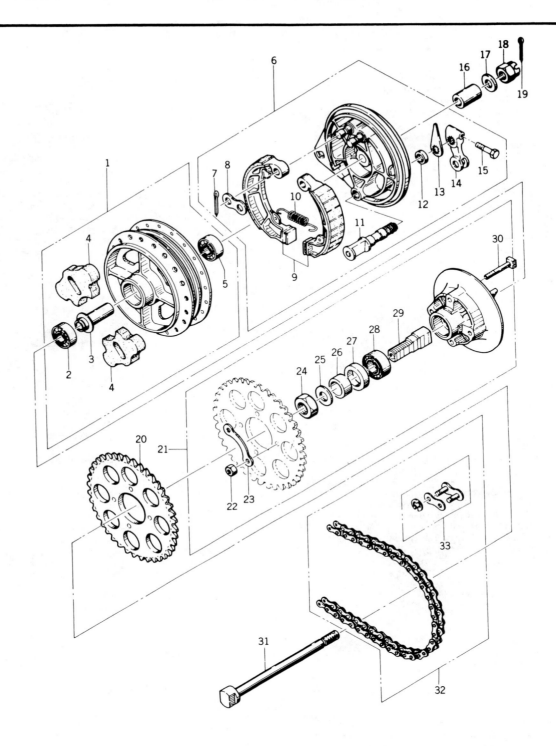

Fig. 5.4 Rear wheel hub assembly

1 Rear hub - complete
2 Wheel bearing
3 Distance piece
4 Cush drive rubber - 4 off
5 Wheel bearing
6 Rear brake assembly - complete
9 Brake shoe lining - 2 off
10 Brake shoe return spring - 2 off
11 Operating camshaft
12 Collar
13 Wear indicator
14 Brake arm
15 Pinch bolt
16 Distance piece
17 Washer
18 Castellated nut
19 Split pin
20 Rear wheel sprocket
21 Cush drive sprocket hub - complete
22 Nut - 4 off
23 Tab washer - 2 off
24 Nut
25 Washer
26 Collar
27 Oil seal
28 Hub bearing
29 Hollow spindle
30 Sprocket bolt
31 Rear wheel spindle
32 Rear chain - complete
33 Master link

13.1 Rear wheel sprocket is retained by four nuts

14.1 Cush drive rubbers are easily removed

14.2 Note 'O' ring on rear wheel hub

13 Rear wheel sprocket: removal and examination

1   The rear wheel sprocket is retained on the cush drive assembly flange by four bolts and nuts. The nuts are secured in pairs by common tab washers.
2   Examine the sprocket for chipped, hooked or worn teeth. If renewal is necessary unbend the tab washers and remove the four retaining nuts. It is a good policy to renew the tab washers when fitting the new sprocket.
3   If a new rear sprocket is required it is almost certain that the engine drive sprocket will also require replacement. In any case, it is generally considered good practice to renew the two sprockets and the rear chain at the same time.

14 Rear wheel cush drive: examination and renovation

1   The cush drive assembly consists of four rubber buffers which are housed between the rear hub and the cush drive flange casting. Four blocks cast on the inside of the drive flange transmit power from the sprocket to the rubber blocks which are held against webs cast in the wheel hub. In this way a limited amount of controlled movement is allowed between the sprocket and the rear hub, which cushions out any roughness or surging transmitted by the engine.
2   When the rear wheel is removed, it is advisable to examine the rubber buffers for signs of damage or deterioration which might render them ineffective. After extended service the rubber buffers will become permanently compacted, giving rise to excess sprocket/hub movement.

15 Chain: examination, lubrication and adjustment

1   The final drive chain is fully exposed apart from the protection given by a short chainguard along the upper run, and if not properly maintained will have a short life. A worn chain will cause rapid wear of the sprockets and they too will need replacement.
2   The chain tension will need adjustment at regular intervals, to compensate for wear. This is accomplished by loosening the rear wheel nut, which is secured by a split pin, and loosening the large nut holding the cush drive/sprocket hub hollow spindle, with the machine on the centre stand. The brake torque arm nuts should be loosened, but it is not necessary to remove the spring security pins.
3   Slacken the locknuts on the chain adjusters on the fork ends. Screw the adjusters inwards an equal amount to tighten the chain. The tension is correct if there is ¾ in - 1 in (15 - 20 mm) up and down movement in the centre of the lower chain run. Always check the chain when it is at its tightest point; a chain rarely wears evenly. This may be accomplished by turning the wheel whilst applying a finger to the lower chain run. The tightest point is easily found.
4   Always adjust the draw bolts an even amount so that correct wheel alignment is preserved. The fork ends are marked with a series of vertical lines to provide a visual check. If desired, wheel alignment can be checked by running a plank of wood parallel to the machine so that it touches both walls of the rear tyre. If wheel alignment is correct, it should be equidistant from either side of the front wheel tyre when tested on both sides of the rear wheel; it will not touch the front tyre because this tyre has a smaller cross section. See the accompanying diagram.
5   Do not run the chain overtight to compensate for uneven wear. A tight chain will place excessive stresses on the gearbox and rear wheel bearings leading to their early failure. It will also absorb a surprising amount of power.
6   After a period of running, the chain will require lubrication. Lack of oil will accelerate the rate of wear of both chain and sprockets and will lead to harsh transmission. The application of engine oil will act as a temporary expedient, but it is preferable

15.1 Chain spring link must be replaced correctly

15.2 Marks on fork end facilitate wheel alignment

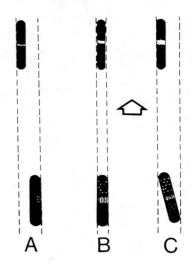

Fig. 5.5 Checking wheel alignment

A & C Incorrect   *B Correct*

to remove the chain and immerse it in a molten lubricant such as Linklyfe or Chainguard after it has been cleaned in a paraffin bath. These latter lubricants achieve better penetration of the chain links and rollers and are less likely to be thrown off when the chain is in motion.

7 To check whether the chain is due for replacement, lay it lengthwise in a straight line and compress it endwise until all play is taken up. Anchor one end, then pull in the opposite direction to take up the play which develops. If the chain extends by more than ¼ inch per foot, it should be renewed in conjunction with the sprockets. Note that this check should ALWAYS be made after the chain has been washed out, but before any lubricant is applied, otherwise the lubricant may take up some of the play.

8 When fitting the chain on the machine, make sure the spring link is positioned correctly with the closed end facing the direction of travel.

16 Tyres - removal and replacement

1 At some time or other the need will arise to remove and replace the tyres, either as the result of a puncture or because a renewal is required to offset wear. To the inexperienced tyre changing represents a formidable task yet if a few simple rules are observed and the technique learned, the whole operation is surprisingly simple.

2 To remove the tyre from either wheel, first detach the wheel from the machine by following the procedure in Chapters 4.2, paragraph 7 or 4.9, paragraphs 2 to 4, depending on whether the front or the rear wheel is involved. Deflate the tyre by removing the valve insert and when it is fully deflated, push the bead of the tyre away from the wheel rim on both sides so that the bead enters the centre well of the rim. Remove the locking cap and push the tyre valve into the tyre itself.

3 Insert a tyre lever close to the valve and lever the edge of the tyre over the outside of the wheel rim. Very little force should be necessary; if resistance is encountered it is probably due to the fact that the tyre beads have not entered the well of the wheel rim all the way round the tyre.

4 Once the tyre has been edged over the wheel rim, it is easy to work around the wheel rim so that the tyre is completely free on one side. At this stage, the inner tube can be removed.

5 Working from the other side of the wheel, ease the other edge of the tyre over the outside of the wheel rim which is furthest away. Continue to work around the rim until the tyre is free completely from the rim.

6 If a puncture has necessitated the removal of the tyre, re-inflate the inner tube and immerse it in a bowl of water to trace the source of the leak. Mark its position and deflate the tube. Dry the tube and clean the area around the puncture with a petrol soaked rag. When the surface has dried, apply the rubber solution and allow this to dry before removing the backing from the patch and applying the patch to the surface.

7 It is best to use a patch of the self-vulcanising type which will form a very permanent repair. Note that it may be necessary to remove a protective covering from the top surface of the patch, after it has sealed in position. Inner tubes made from synthetic rubber may require a special type of patch and adhesive if a satisfactory bond is to be achieved.

8 Before refitting the tyre, check the inside to make sure that the agent which caused the   puncture is not trapped. Check the outside of the tyre, particularly the tread area, to make sure nothing is trapped that may cause a further puncture.

9 If the inner tube has been patched on a number of past occasions, or if there is a tear or large hole. it is preferable to discard it and fit a new one. Sudden deflation may cause an accident, particularly if it occurs with the front wheel.

10 To replace the tyre, inflate the inner tube sufficiently for it to assume a circular shape but only just. Then push it into the tyre so that it is enclosed completely. Lay the tyre on the wheel at an angle and insert the valve through the rim tape and the hole in the wheel rim. Attach the locking cap on the first few threads,

Tyre changing sequence - tubed tyres

 A

Deflate tyre. After pushing tyre beads away from rim flanges push tyre bead into well of rim at point opposite valve. Insert tyre lever adjacent to valve and work bead over edge of rim.

Use two levers to work bead over edge of rim. Note use of rim protectors

 B

 C

Remove inner tube from tyre

When first bead is clear, remove tyre as shown

 D

 E

When fitting, partially inflate inner tube and insert in tyre

Work first bead over rim and feed valve through hole in rim. Partially screw on retaining nut to hold valve in place.

 F

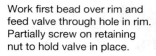

 G

Check that inner tube is positioned correctly and work second bead over rim using tyre levers. Start at a point opposite valve.

Work final area of bead over rim whilst pushing valve inwards to ensure that inner tube is not trapped

 H

sufficient to hold the valve captive in its correct location.

11 Starting at the point furthest from the valve, push the tyre bead over the edge of the wheel rim until it is located in the central well. Continue to work around the tyre in this fashion until the whole of one side of the tyre is on the rim. It may be necessary to use a tyre lever during the final stages.

12 Make sure that there is no pull on the tyre valve and again commencing with the area furthest from the valve, ease the other bead of the tyre over the edge of the rim. Finish with the area close to the valve, pushing the valve up into the tyre until the locking cap touches the rim. This will ensure the inner tube is not trapped when the last section of the bead is edged over the rim with a tyre lever.

13 Check that the inner tube is not trapped at any point. Re-inflate the inner tube and check that the tyre is seating correctly around the wheel rim. There should be a thin rib moulded around the wall of the tyre on both sides which should be equidistant from the wheel rim at all points. If the tyre is unevenly located on the rim, try bouncing the wheel when the tyre is at the recommended pressure. It is probable that one of the beads has not pulled clear of the centre well.

14 Always run the tyres at the recommended pressures and never under or over-inflate. The correct pressures for solo use are given in the Specifications Section of this Chapter. If a pillion passenger is carried, increase the rear tyre pressure only by approximately 4 psi.

15 Tyre replacement is aided by dusting the side walls, particularly in the vicinity of the beads, with a liberal coating of French chalk. Washing up liquid can also be used to good effect, but this has the disadvantage of causing the inner surfaces of the wheel rim to rust.

16 Never replace the inner tube and tyre without the rim tape in position. If this precaution is overlooked there is good chance of the ends of the spoke nipples chafing the inner tube and causing a crop of punctures.

17 Never fit a tyre which has a damaged tread or side walls. Apart from the legal aspects, there is a very great risk of a blow-out, which can have serious consequences.

17 Fault diagnosis

Symptom	Cause	Remedy
Handlebars oscillate at low speeds	Buckle or flat in wheel rim, most probably front wheel	Check rim alignment by spinning wheel. Correct by retensioning spokes or rebuilding on new rim.
	Tyre not straight on rim	Check tyre alignment.
Machine lacks power and accelerates poorly	Rear brake binding	Warm brake drum provides best evidence. Re-adjust brake.
Rear brake grabs when applied gently	Ends of brake shoes not chamfered	Chamfer with file.
	Elliptical brake drum	Lightly skim in lathe (specialist attention required).
Front brake feels spongy	Air in hydraulic system	Bleed brake.
Brake pull-off sluggish	Brake cam binding in housing	Free and grease.
	Weak brake shoe springs	Renew if springs have not become displaced.
	Sticking pistons in brake caliper	Overhaul caliper unit.
Harsh transmission	Worn or badly adjusted final drive chain	Adjust or renew as necessary.
	Hooked or badly worn sprockets	Renew as a pair.
	Worn or deteriorating cush drive rubbers	Renew rubbers.

Chapter 6 Electrical system

Contents

Specifications

Battery
Make	Yuasa
Type	12N12A - 4A - 1
Voltage	12v.
Capacity	12 A.H.
Earth	Negative

Alternator
Make	Nippon Denso
Model	021000 - 3560
Type	3-phase
Output	Nominal 12v.

Starter motor ... ...
	Mitsuba SM242	
Brush length	0.43 - 0.49 in	(11.0 - 12.5 mm)
Service length	0.24 in	(6 mm)

Bulbs
Headlight	50/35w
Tail/brake	8/27w
Speedometer	3.4w x 2
Tachometer	3.4w x 2
Neutral indicator	3.4w
High beam indicator	1.7w
Flashing indicators	23w x 4
Flasher indicator bulb	3.4w
Oil pressure indicator	3.4w
Brake light failure indicator	3.4w

All bulbs rated 12 volt

1 General description

The Kawasaki KZ400 series are fitted with a 12 volt electrical system. The system comprises a crankshaft driven AC (alternating current) generator of the 3-phase type, the output of which is controlled by an electro-mechanical three point regulator to match the electrical demand. A silicon rectifier is incorporated in the circuit to convert the current to DC (direct current) so it can be used to charge the battery.

2 Crankshaft alternator: checking the output

1 As explained in Chapter 3, Section 2, the output from the alternator can be checked by connecting an ammeter into the battery circuit. Refer to that Chapter for details.

2 Note that the test described gives only an approximate indication of whether the generator is functioning correctly. The assistance of a Kawasaki agent or auto-electrician should be sought to determine whether the generator is working at peak efficiency and when under load. Bear in mind that a faulty regulator unit can give the impression that the generator is malfunctioning.

3 Battery: examination and maintenance

1 A Yuasa 12N12A - 4A, 12 volt, 12 amp hour battery is fitted to the Kawasaki KZ400 models.

2 The transparent plastic case of the battery permits the upper and lower levels of the electrolyte to be observed without disturbing the battery by removing the left-hand side cover. Maintenance is normally limited to keeping the electrolyte level between the prescribed upper and lower limits and making sure that the vent tube is not blocked. The lead plates and their separators are also visible through the transparent case, a further guide to the general condition of the battery.

3 Unless acid is spilt, as may occur if the machine falls over, the electrolyte should always be topped up with distilled water to restore the correct level. If acid is spilt onto any part of the machine, it should be neutralised with an alkali such as washing soda or baking powder and washed away with plenty of water, otherwise serious corrosion will occur. Top up with sulphuric acid of the correct specific gravity (1.260 to 1.280) only when spillage has occured. Check that the vent pipe is well clear of the frame or any of the other cycle parts.

4 It is seldom practicable to repair a cracked battery case because the acid present in the joint will prevent the formation of an effective seal. It is always best to renew a cracked battery, especially in view of the corrosion which will be casued if the acid continues to leak.

5 If the machine is not used for a period, it is advisable to remove the battery and give it a 'refresher' charge every six weeks or so from a battery charger. If the battery is permitted to discharge completely, the plates will sulphate and render the battery useless.

6 Occasionally, check the condition of the battery terminals to ensure that corrosion is not taking place and that the electrical connections are tight. If corrosion has occurred, it should be cleaned away by scraping with a knife and then using emery cloth to remove the final traces. Remake the electrical connections whilst the joint is still clean, then smear the assembly with petroleum jelly (NOT grease) to prevent recurrence of the corrosion. Badly corroded connections can have a high electrical resistance and may give the impression of a complete battery failure.

4 Battery: charging procedure

1 Since the ignition system is dependent on the battery for its operation, if the battery discharges completely it must be removed and recharged before the machine can be used. A battery charger is necessary for this purpose.

2 The normal charge rate is 3 amps for about 4 hours for a 12 amp hour battery. A more rapid charge at a higher rate can be given in an emergency, but this should be avoided if at all possible because it will shorten the useful working life of the battery. Always ensure the battery is topped up before charging.

3 When the battery is replaced on the machine, make sure that it is protected by the rubber pads in the battery compartment, which help damp out the undersirable effects of vibration. Do not reverse connect the battery, or the silicon rectifier may be damaged by the reverse flow of current.

5 Silicon rectifier: general description

1 The function of the silicon rectifier is to convert the AC current produced by the alternator into DC so that it can be used to charge the battery.

2 The rectifier is located to the rear of the battery, beneath the dual seat, a location where it is afforded reasonable protection. The question of access is of relatively little importance because the rectifier is unlikely to give trouble during normal service. Should it malfunction, a repair is not practicable. It must be renewed.

3 Damage to the rectifier will occur if the machine is run without a battery for any period of time, or with one that no longer holds its charge. A high voltage will develop in the absence of any load across the coils of the alternator which will cause a reverse flow of current and subsequent damage to the rectifier

3.1 Battery is positioned below dual seat

5.1 Silicon rectifier and flasher relay

cells. Reverse connection of the battery will have a similar undersirable effect.

4 There is no simple means of checking whether the rectifier is functioning correctly without the appropriate test equipment. A Kawasaki agent or an auto-electrician are best qualified to advise, particularly if the battery is in a low state of charge.

5 Do not disturb the rectifier retaining nut or in any way damage the surfaces of the assembly. Any such action may cause the coating over the electrodes to peel or flake and destroy the working action.

6 Voltage regulator: examination

1 The voltage regulator unit is fitted behind the right-hand side cover, directly in front of the starter motor solenoid. If the battery is continually overcharged or discharged, the regulator may be defective. Symptoms of overcharging include a battery that requires continual topping up of the electrolyte and lamp bulbs which burn out at high engine speeds.

2 If the regulator unit is suspect, a preliminary check may be made as follows:

Ensure that the battery has a charge of not less than 12 volts. If the battery is undercharged or defective it is likely that the regulator unit will not function correctly. Remove the left-hand side cover and disconnect the six (6) point electrical connector. Remove the headlamp rim and reflector and disconnect the nine (9) point connector. This will remove the load from the alternator. Set a multimeter to the 30 volts DC range and connect the positive (+) meter lead to the positive (+) terminal of the battery. Connect the negative (−) meter lead to the negative (−) terminal of the battery.

3 Start the engine and hold the speed to 1600 rpm. The meter reading should be 14-15v. Gradually increase the engine speed to 4000 rpm and the reading should again be 14-15 volts. During this test the engine speed must NOT be reduced at all. If the speed is inadvertently dropped, increase the speed to 1600 rpm again and start the test again. Engine speed should not be reduced due to an electrical phenomena known as hysteresis (residual current) which produces a difference in voltage depending on whether the engine speed is rising or falling.

4 If the multimeter readings are incorrect the regulator unit will require adjustment and more specific testing. It is recommended that this work be carried out by a Kawasaki dealer or an auto-electrician.

7 Fuses: location and replacement

1 The fuse holder is located behind the left-hand side cover.

2 If a fuse blows, it should not be renewed until a check has shown whether a short circuit has occurred. This will involve checking the electrical circuit to identify and correct the fault. If this precaution is not observed, the replacement fuse, which may be the only spare, may blow immediately on connection.

3 When a fuse blows whilst the machine is running and no spare is available a 'get you home' remedy is to remove the blown fuse and wrap it in silver paper before replacing it in the fuse holder. The silver paper will restore electrical continuity by bridging the broken wire within the fuse. This expedient should never be used if there is evidence of a short circuit or other major electrical fault, otherwise more serious damage will be caused. Renew the 'doctored' fuse at the earliest possible opportunity to restore full circuit protection.

8 Starter motor: removal, examination and replacement

1 An electric starter motor, operated from a small push-button on the right-hand side of the handlebars, provides an alternative and more convenient method of starting the engine, without

having to use the kickstart. The starter motor is mounted within a compartment at the rear of the cylinder block, closed by an oblong, chromium plated cover. Current is supplied from the battery via a heavy duty solenoid switch and a cable capable of carrying the very high current demanded by the starter motor on the initial start-up.

2 The starter motor drives a free running clutch immediately behind the generator rotor. The clutch ensures the starter motor drive is disconnected from the primary transmission immediately the engine starts. It operates on the centrifugal principle; spring loaded rollers take up the drive until the centrifugal force of the rotating engine overcomes their resistance and the drive is automatically disconnected.

3 To remove the starter motor from the engine unit, first disconnect the positive lead from the battery, then the starter motor cable from the solenoid switch. Remove the starter lead from the starter motor, where it is retained by a nut and spring washer, two bolts in the chromium plated cover over the starter motor housing and lift the cover away, complete with gasket. The starter motor is secured to the crankcase by two bolts which pass through the left-hand end of the motor casing. When these bolts are withdrawn, the motor can be prised out of position and lifted out of its compartment, with the heavy duty cable still attached. If necessary, temporarily detach the lead and grommet from the oil pressure switch, which pass through the starter motor compartment.

4 The parts of the starter motor most likely to require attention are the brushes. The end cover is retained by the two long screws which pass through the lugs cast on both pieces. If the screws are withdrawn, the end cover is retained by the two long screws which pass through the lugs cast on both end pieces. If the screws are withdrawn, the end cover can be lifted away and the brush gear exposed.

5 Lift up the spring clips which bear on the end of each brush and remove the brushes from their holders. Each brush should have a length of 0.43 - 0.49 in (11.0 - 12.5 mm). The minimum allowable brush length is ¼ in (6 mm). If the brush is shorter it must be renewed.

6 Before the brushes are replaced, make sure that the commutator is clean. The commutator is the copper segments on which the brushes bear. Clean the commutator with a strip of glass paper. Never use emery cloth or 'wet-and-dry' as the small

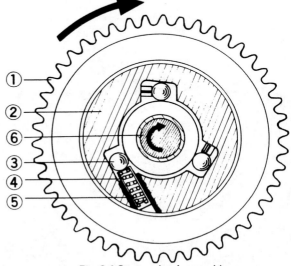

Fig. 6.1 Starter clutch assembly

1 *Driven sprocket*
2 *Clutch block*
3 *Roller - 3 off*
4 *Spring cap - 3 off*
5 *Spring - 3 off*
6 *Crankshaft*

6.1 Voltage regulator is fitted behind right-hand side cover

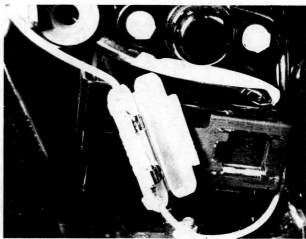

7.1 Fuse holder retained in rubber block

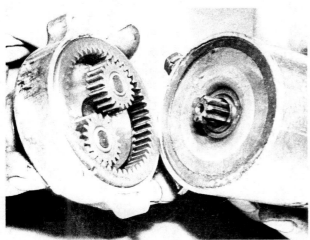

8.1 Starter motor drives through planetary gears

8.4a Armature commutator must be clean and polished

abrasive fragments may embed themselves in the soft brass of the commutator and cause excessive wear of the brushes. Finish off the commutator with metal polish to give a smooth surface and finally wipe the segments over with a methylated spirits soaked rag to ensure a grease free surface. Check that the mica insulators, which lie between the segments of the commutator, are undercut. The standard groove depth is 0.02 - 0.03 in (0.5 - 0.8 mm), but if the average groove depth is less than 0.008 in (0.2 mm) the armature should be renewed or returned to a Kawasaki dealer for re-cutting.

7   Replace the brushes in their holders and check that they slide quite freely. Make sure the brushes are replaced in their original positions because they will have worn to the profile of the commutator. Replace and tighten the end cover, then replace the starter motor and cable in the housing, tighten down and re-make the electrical connection to the solenoid switch. Check that the starter motor functions correctly before replacing the compartment cover and sealing gasket.

9   Starter solenoid switch: function and location

1   The starter motor switch is designed to work on the electro-magnetic principle. When the starter motor button is depressed, current from the battery passes through windings in the switch

8.4b Renew badly worn brushes

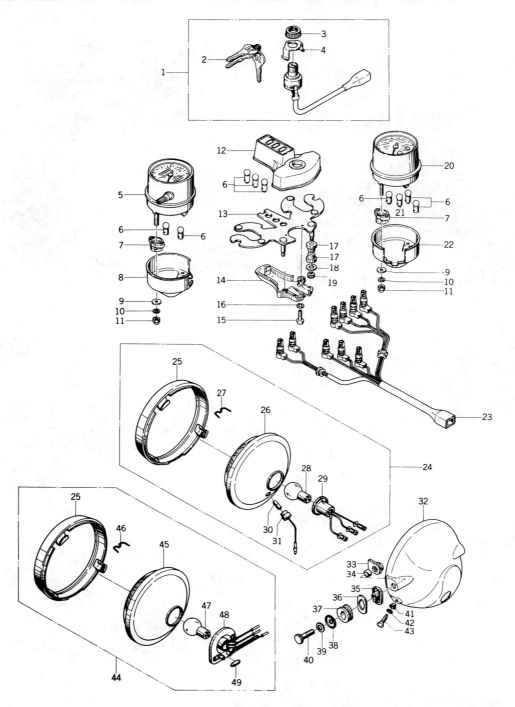

Fig. 6.2 Headlamp assembly and instruments

1 Ignition switch - complete
2 Key set
3 Switch retaining ring
4 Switch bracket
5 Speedometer head
6 Bulb 12 3.4w - 8 off
7 Damper rubber - 4 off
8 Speedometer cowl
9 Plain washer - 4 off
10 Spring washer - 4 off
11 Nut - 4 off
12 Warning light cover
13 Instrument mounting bracket

14 Lower cover
15 Screw - 2 off
16 Spring washer - 2 off
17 Damper rubber - 4 off
18 Washer - 2 off
19 Nut - 2 off
20 Tachometer head
21 Bulb 12v 1.7w
22 Tachometer cowl
23 Bulb holder assembly
24 Headlamp unit - complete
25 Rim

26 Lens unit
27 Retainer clip - 4 off
28 Bulb 12v 35/35w
29 Bulb holder
30 Pilot bulb 12v 4w
31 Pilot bulb holder
32 Headlamp shell
33 Nut - 2 off
34 Collar - 2 off
35 Collar - 2 off
36 Plate - 2 off
37 Damper rubber - 2 off

38 Plain washer - 2 off
39 Plain washer - 2 off
40 Mounting bolt - 2 off
41 Insert - 2 off
42 Spring washer - 2 off
43 Screw - 2 off
44 Headlamp unit - complete
45 Lens assembly
46 Retainer clip
47 Bulb 12v 36/36w
48 Bulb holder
49 Bulb 12v 4w

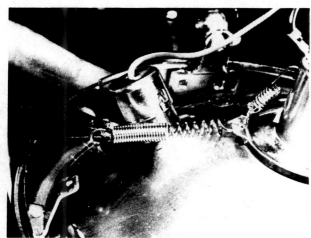

10.2a Main bulb holder is retained by spring

10.2b Bulb is held in holder by off-set pins

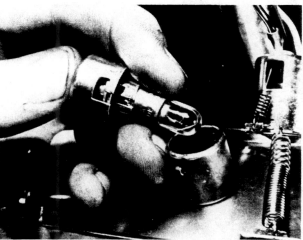

10.2c Pilot bulb and bulb holder have bayonet fixing

solenoid and generate an electro-magnetic force which causes a set of contact points to close. Immediately the points close, the starter motor is energised and a very heavy current is drawn from the battery.

2   This arrangement is used for at least two reasons. Firstly, the starter motor current is drawn only when the button is depressed and is cut off again when pressure on the button is released. This ensures minimum drainage on the battery. Secondly, if the battery is in a low state of charge, there will not be sufficient current to cause the solenoid contacts to close. In consequence, it is not possible to place an excessive drain on the battery which, in some circumstances, can cause the plates to overheat and shed their coatings. If the starter will not operate, first suspect a discharged battery. This can be checked by trying the horn or switching on the lights. If this check shows the battery to be in good shape, suspect the starter switch which should come into action with a pronounced click. It is located behind the left-hand side panel and can be identified by the heavy duty starter cable connected to it. It is not possible to effect a satisfactory repair if the switch malfunctions; it must be renewed.

10 Headlamp: replacing the bulbs and adjusting beam height

1   In order to gain access to the headlamp bulbs it is necessary to first remove the rim, complete with the reflector and headlamp glass. The rim is retained by two screws which pass through the headlamp shell just below the two headlamp mounting bolts.
2   The headlamp unit fitted to the KZ400-D3 model is of the sealed beam type and therefore if either of the headlamp filaments blow the complete unit should be replaced. On other models the headlamp bulb has a bayonet fixing in the bulb holder which is a push fit in the rear of the reflector. A reflector that accepts a pilot bulb is fitted to all models delivered to countries or states where parking lights are a statutory requirement. The pilot bulb is held in the bulb holder by a bayonet fixing.
3   Beam height on all models is effected by tilting the headlamp shell after the mounting bolts have been loosened slightly. On sealed beam units the horizontal alignment of the beam can be adjusted by altering the position of the screw which passes through the headlamp rim. The screw is fitted at the 9 o'clock position when viewed from the front of the machine. Turning the screw in a clockwise direction will move the beam direction over to the left-hand side.
4   In the UK, regulations stipulate that the headlamp must be arranged so that the light will not dazzle a person standing at a distance greater than 25 yards from the lamp, whose eye level is not less than 3 feet 6 inches above that plane. It is easy to approximate this setting by placing the machine 25 yards away from a wall, on a level road, and setting the beam height so that it is concentrated at the same height as the distance of the centre of the headlamp from the ground. The rider must be seated normally during this operation and also the pillion passenger, if one is carried regularly.

11 Stop and tail lamp: replacement of bulbs

1   The combined stop and tail lamp bulb contains two filaments, one for the stop lamp and one for the tail lamp.
2   The offset pin bayonet fixing bulb can be renewed after the plastic lens cover and screws has been removed.

12 Flashing indicator lamps: replacing bulbs

1   Flashing indicator lamps are fitted to the front and rear of the machine. They are mounted on short stalks through which the wires pass. Access to each bulb is gained by removing the two screws holding the plastic lens cover. The bulbs are of 23W rating and are retained by a bayonet fixing.

11.2a Tail/stop lamp lens cover is held by two screws ...

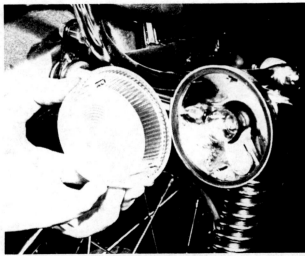

11.2b ... as are all the indicator lens covers

15.1 Warning light console is between instruments

18.1 Stop lamp switch is adjustable for height

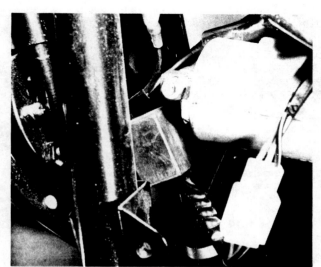

18.2a Brake light failure switch is forward of coil

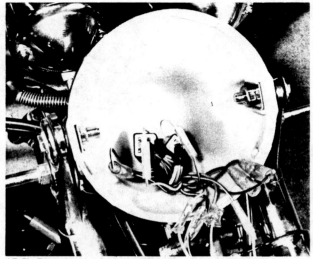

18.2b Electrical leads are colour coded; have snap connectors

13 Flashing indicator relay: location and replacement

1 The flashing indicator relay fitted in conjunction with the flashing indicator lamps is located behind the rectifier, behind the left-hand side cover. It is mounted in a rubber 'box' which isolates it from the harmful effects of vibration.

2 When the relay malfunctions, it must be renewed; a repair is impracticable. When the unit is in working order audible clicks will be heard which coincide with the flash of the indicator lamps. If the lamps malfunction, check firstly that a bulb has not blown, or the handlebar switch is not faulty. The usual symptom of a fault is one initial flash before the unit goes dead.

3 Take great care when handling a flasher unit. It is easily damaged, if dropped.

14 Speedometer and tachometer heads: replacement of bulbs

1 Bulbs fitted to each instrument illuminate the dials during the hours of darkness when the headlamp is switched on. All bulbs fitted to either instrument head have the same type of bulb holder which is a push fit in the instrument base.

2 Access to the bulbs and holders is gained by removing the nuts and washers which secure the rubber mounted instruments to their common mounting plate. Lift the instruments clear of the mounting plate and pull out the bulb holders.

15 Indicator panel lamps

1 An indicator lamp panel which holds three warning bulbs is fitted between the speedometer and tachometer heads. The panel is held to the instrument mounting bracket by a single screw from underneath. The bulbs are fitted in a holder which is a push fit in the panel base.

16 Horn: adjustment

1 The horn is mounted on a spring plate between the two frame down tubes. After considerable use the contacts inside the horn will wear. To compensate for wear an adjusting screw is fitted at the rear of the horn. If the horn tone becomes inaudible or poor, turn the screw in slowly until the tone is correct again. Do not turn the screw in too far or the current increase may burn out the horn coil.

17 Ignition switch: removal and replacement

1 The combined ignition and lighting master switch is mounted in the warning light panel mounting plate.

2 If the switch proves defective it can be removed only after the headlamp has been detached from its mounting brackets. Remove the ignition switch nut and take off the upper switch cover. Disconnect the switch wiring socket. The switch and lower cover can be removed after unscrewing the two mounting bolts.

3 Reassembly of the switch can be made in the reverse procedure as described for dismantling. Repair is rarely practicable. It is preferable to purchase a new switch unit, which will probably necessitate the use of a different key.

18 Stop lamp switch: adjustment

1 All models have a stop lamp switch fitted to operate in conjunction with the rear brake pedal. The switch is located immediately to the rear of the crankcase, on the right-hand side of the machine. It has a threaded body giving a range of adjustment.

2 If the stop lamp is late in operating, slacken the locknuts and turn the body of the lamp in an anticlockwise direction so that the switch rises from the bracket to which it is attached. When the adjustment seems near correct, tighten the locknuts and test.

3 If the lamp operates too early, the locknuts should be slackened and the switch body turned clockwise so that it is lowered in relation to the mounting bracket.

4 As a guide, the light should operate after the brake pedal has been depressed by about 2 cm (¾ inch).

5 A stop lamp switch is also incorporated in the front brake cable, to give warning when the front brake is applied. This is not yet a statutory requirement in the UK, although it applies in many other countries and states.

6 The front brake stop lamp switch is built into the hydraulic system and contains no provision for adjustment. If the switch malfunctions, it must be renewed.

19 Handlebar switches: general

1 Generally speaking, the switches give little trouble, but if necessary they can be dismantled by separating the halves which form a split clamp around the handlebars. Note that the machine cannot be started until the ignition cut-out on the right-hand end of the handlebars is turned to the central 'ON' position.

2 Always disconnect the battery before removing any of the switches, to prevent the possibility of a short circuit. Most troubles are caused by dirty contacts, but in the event of the breakage of some internal part, it will be necessary to renew the complete switch.

Fault diagnosis overleaf

20 Fault diagnosis

Fault	Cause	Remedy
Complete electrical failure	Blown fuse	Check wiring and electrical components for short circuit before fitting new 15 amp fuse.
	Isolated battery	Check battery connections, also whether connections show signs of corrosion.
Dim lights, horn and starter inoperative	Discharged battery	Remove battery and charge with battery charger. Check generator output and voltage regulator settings.
Constantly blowing bulbs	Vibration or poor earth connection	Check security of bulb holders. Check earth return connections.
Starter motor sluggish	Worn brushes	Remove starter motor and renew brushes.
Parking lights dim rapidly	Battery will not hold charge	Renew battery at earliest opportunity.
Flashing indicators do not operate	Blown bulb	Renew bulb.
	Damaged flasher unit	Renew flasher unit.

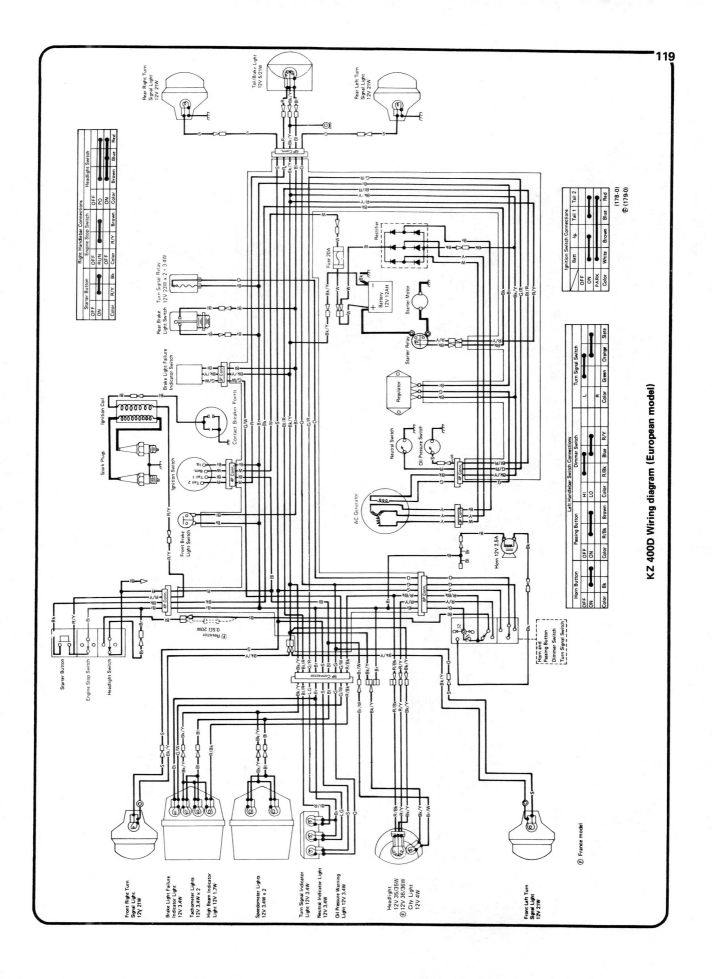

KZ 400D Wiring diagram (European model)

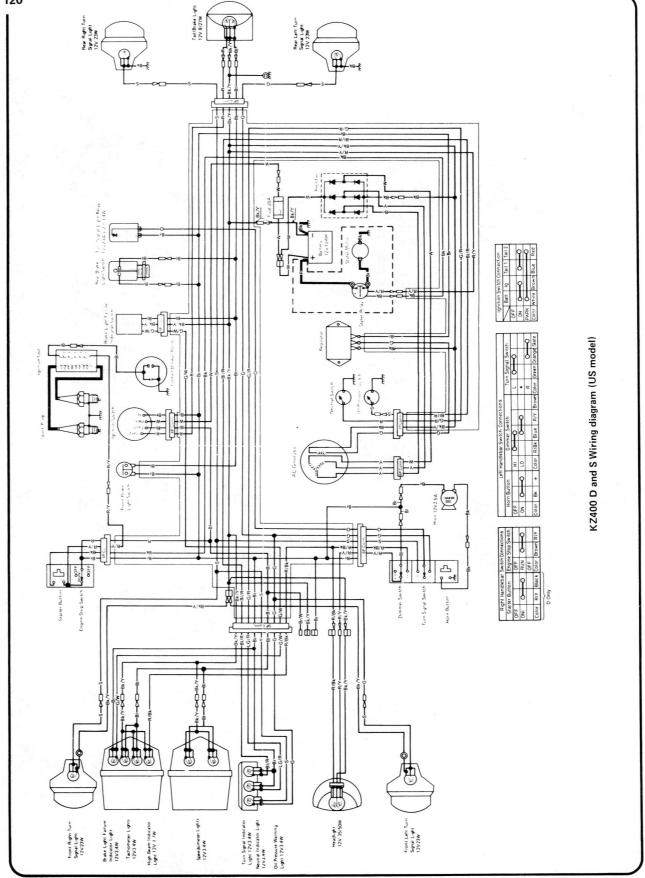

KZ400 D and S Wiring diagram (US model)

Left-hand view of the Z400 B

Left-hand view of the Z400 G

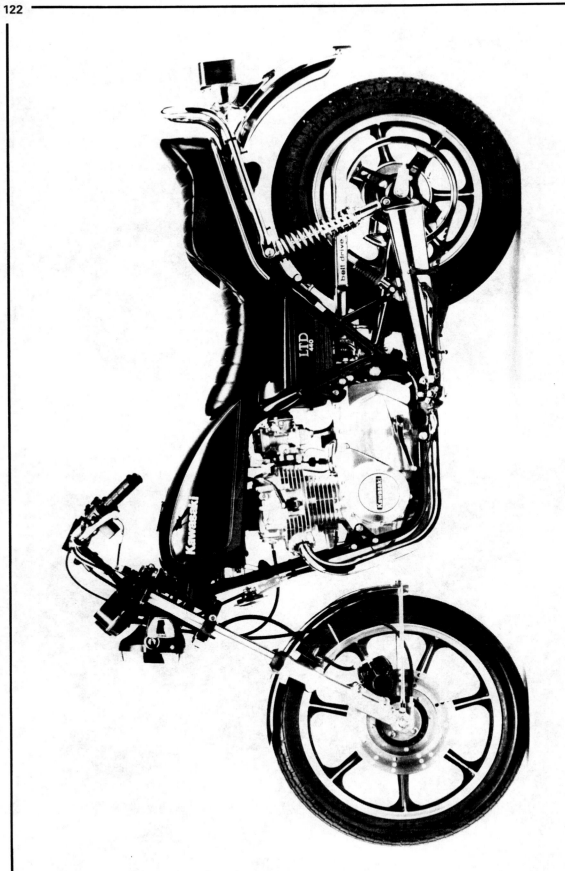

Left-hand view of the Z440 D

Chapter 7
KZ 400 and KZ 440 models from 1977 to 1981

Contents

Specifications

The following specifications relate to the 400 cc models bearing the suffixes B1, B2, B3, B4, C1, C2, G1, G2, G3, H3. At the time of publication comprehensive specifications for the H1 model were not available. The H1, however, is similar in many respects to the H3, the main difference being in the type of ignition system fitted. For specifications relating to the 440 cc models see the following section of specifications.

Specifications relating to Chapter 1
Engine

Type	Vertical parallel twin cylinder, SOHC, four-stroke
Bore	64 mm (2.60 in)
Stroke...	62 mm (2.44 in)
Displacement...	398 cc (24.3 cu in)
Compression ratio	9.5 : 1
Max. bhp:	
C1 and C2 models	34.5 @ 8500 rpm
All others	36.0 @ 8500 rpm

Pistons

	B1/B2/C1/C2	B3/B4/G1/G2/G3/H1/H3
Oversizes	+0.5 mm and +1.0 mm (+0.020 in and +0.040 in)	
Ring end gap (installed)	0.2 — 0.4 mm (0.0079 — 0.0157 in)	
Service limit	0.7 mm (0.0276 in)	
Ring to groove clearance:		
Top ring	0.040 — 0.080 mm (0.0016 — 0.0031 in)	0.05 — 0.09 mm (0.0020 — 0.0035 in)
Service limit ...	0.18 mm (0.0071 in)	0.19 mm (0.0075 in)
2nd ring	0.010 — 0.045 mm (0.0004 — 0.0018 in)	0.01 — 0.05 mm (0.0004 — 0.0020 in)
Service limit ...	0.145 mm (0.0057 in)	0.15 mm (0.0059 in)
Oil ring	0.020 — 0.055 mm (0.0008 — 0.0022 in)	Not applicable
Service limit ...	0.15 mm (0.006 in)	Not applicable
Piston to bore clearance	0.037 — 0.064 mm (0.0015 — 0.0025 in)	0.037 — 0.064 mm (0.0015 — 0.0025 in)

Valves

	All models
Valve seat angle	45°
Valve stem diameter:	
Inlet	6.965 — 6.980 mm (0.2742 — 0.2748 in)
Service limit	6.90 mm (0.271 in)
Exhaust	6.950 — 6.970 mm (0.2736 — 0.2744 in)
Service limit	6.90 mm (0.2717 in)
Valve guide bore diameter	7.000 — 7.018 mm (0.2756 — 0.2763 in)
Service limit	7.08 mm (0.2787 in)
Valve stem to guide clearance:	
Inlet	0.053 — 0.139 mm (0.0021 — 0.0055 in)
Service limit	0.26 mm (0.0102 in)
Exhaust	0.075 — 0.169 mm (0.0030 — 0.0067 in)
Service limit	0.25 mm (0.0098 in)
Valve seat width	0.5 — 1.0 mm (0.197 — 0.039 in)
Valve spring pressure at prescribed length:	
Inner at 22.2 mm (0.874 in)	28.5 — 31.5 kg (62.83 — 69.45 lb)
Service limit	27.3 kg (60.19 lb)
Outer at 25.7 mm (1.0118 in)	53.2 — 58.8 kg (117.29 — 129.63 lb)
Service limit	51.4 kg (113.32 lb)
Valve spring warpage	0 — 1.0 mm (0 — 0.04 in)
Service limit	1.5 mm (0.06 in)

Valve clearances and timing

Valve clearance (engine cold):	
Inlet	0.17 — 0.22 mm (0.0067 — 0.0087 in)
Exhaust	0.17 — 0.22 mm (0.0067 — 0.0087 in)
Valve timing:	
Inlet opens	27° BTDC
Inlet closes	73° ABDC
Duration	280°
Exhaust opens	70° BBDC
Exhaust closes	30° ATDC
Duration	280°

Camshaft and drive

	B1/B2/C1/C2/G1/H1	B3/B4/G2/G3/H3
Lobe height	38.339 — 38.479 mm (1.5094 — 1.5149 in)	
Service limit	38.25 mm (1.506 in)	
Camshaft journal diameter	24.950 — 24.970 mm (0.9823 — 0.9831 in)	
Service limit	24.93 mm (0.9815 in)	
Camshaft journal to head clearance	0.130 — 0.240 mm (0.0051 — 0.0094 in)	
Service limit	0.29 mm (0.0114 in)	
Camshaft radial run-out	0 — 0.01 mm (0 — 0.0004 in)	
Service limit	0.1 mm (0.0039 in)	
Camshaft chain length (20 pin length under 5 kg/ll lb tension)	160.0 — 160.3 mm (6.299 — 6.311 in)	Not available
Service limit	162.4 mm (6.3937 in)	128.8 mm (5.0709 in)
Chain guide max. wear depth:		
Front	1.5 mm (0.0591 in)	3.6 mm (0.1417 in)
Rear	2.5 mm (0.0984 in)	4.5 mm (0.1772 in)
Chain tensioner spring free length	About 44.2 mm (1.74 in)	Not available
Service limit	42.0 mm (1.65 in)	40.0 mm (1.5748 in)

Crankshaft assembly

All models

Big-end bearing radial play	0.040 − 0.069 mm (0.0016 − 0.0027 in)
Service limit	0.1 mm (0.0039 in)
Big-end bearing axial play (end float)	0.15 − 0.25 mm (0.0059 − 0.0098 in)
Service limit	0.45 mm (0.0177 in)
Big-end eye internal diameter:	
Unmarked	38.000 − 38.008 mm (1.4961 − 1.4964 in)
'O' marked	38.009 − 38.016 mm (1.4964 − 1.4967 in)
Crankshaft big-end journal diameter:	
Unmarked	34.984 − 34.994 mm (1.3773 − 1.3777 in)
'O' marked	34.995 − 35.000 mm (1.3778 − 1.3780 in)
Service limit	34.97 mm (1.3768 in)
Big-end bearing shell thickness:	
Green	1.485 − 1.490 mm (0.0585 − 0.0587 in)
Black	1.480 − 1.485 mm (0.0583 − 0.0585 in)
Brown	1.475 − 1.480 mm (0.0581 − 0.0583 in)
Big-end bearing clearance:	
B1/B2/C1/C2/G1 models	0.040 − 0.069 mm (0.0016 − 0.0027 in)
Service limit	0.1 mm (0.0039 in)
All others	Not available
Service limit	0.08 mm (0.0031 in)
Connecting rod straightness:	
Bend	Less than 0.10 mm (0.0039 in)
Service limit	0.2 mm (0.0079 in)
Twist	Less than 0.15 mm (0.0059 in)
Service limit	0.2 mm (0.0079 in)
Crankshaft centre journal runout	0 − 0.02 mm (0 − 0.0008 in)
Service limit	0.05 mm (0.0020 in)
Main bearing clearance:	
B1/B2/C1/C2/G1 models	0.034 − 0.076 mm (0.0013 − 0.0030 in)
Service limit	0.11 mm (0.0043 in)
All others	Not available
Service limit	0.08 mm (0.0031 in)
Crankshaft journal diameter:	
1978−79 models	35.984 − 36.000 mm (1.4167 − 1.4173 in)
Service limit	35.96 mm (1.4157 in)
Crankshaft journal diameter:	
1980−81 models	
Marked '1'	35.992 − 36.000 mm (1.4170 − 1.4173 in)
Unmarked	35.984 − 35.992 mm (1.4467 − 1.4170 in)
Service limit	35.96 mm (1.4157 in)
Crankshaft main bearing bore diameter:	
Marked 'O'	39.000 − 39.008 mm (1.5354 − 1.5357 in)
Unmarked	39.009 − 39.016 mm (1.5358 − 1.5361 in)
Crankshaft end float	0.20 − 0.30 mm (0.0079 − 0.0118 in)
Service limit	9.45 mm (0.0177 in)
Small-end bearing diameter...	15.003 − 15.014 mm (0.5907 − 0.5911 in)
Service limit	15.05 mm (0.5925 in)
Gudgeon (piston) pin diameter	14.994 − 14.998 mm (0.5903 − 0.5905 in)
Service limit	14.96 mm (0.5890 in)
Piston bore diameter	15.004 − 15.009 mm (0.5907 − 0.5909 in)
Service limit	15.08 mm (0.5937 in)

Balancer mechanism

Balancer shaft diameter	19.967 − 19.980 mm (0.7861 − 0.7866 in)
Service limit	19.93 mm (0.7846 in)
Balancer shaft bore diameter	20.000 − 20.030 mm (0.7874 − 0.7886 in)
Service limit	20.08 mm (0.7905 in)
Balancer spring free length	9.8 − 10.4 mm (0.3858 − 0.4094 in)
Service limit	9.3 mm (0.3661 in)
Balancer chain length (20 pin length under 5 kg/11 lb tension)	160.0 − 160.3 mm (6.299 − 6.311 in)
Service limit	162.4 mm (6.394 in)
Balancer chain guide wear limit:	
Upper	1.0 mm (0.04 in)
Lower	1.5 mm (0.06 in)

Clutch

Number of plain plates	5
Number of friction plates	6
Number of springs	4
Friction plate thickness	2.9 − 3.1 mm (0.114 − 0.122 in)

Service limit	2.7 mm (0.106 in)
Plain plate warpage	0 — 0.2 mm (0 — 0.008 in)
Service limit	0.4 mm (0.016 in)
Friction plate tang/housing clearance	0.15 — 0.45 mm (0.006 — 0.018 in)
Service limit	0.7 mm (0.28 in)
Housing bore internal diameter	25.000 — 25.021 mm (0.9843 — 0.9851 in)
Service limit	25.03 mm (0.9854 in)
Mainshaft outside diameter	24.959 — 24.980 mm (1.0220 — 0.9835 in)
Service limit	24.94 mm (0.982 in)

Primary drive

Type	Hy-Vo chain
Make	Tsubakimoto
Size	3/8 P — 5/8 W
No. of links	74
Maximum free play	30 mm (1.18 in)
Primary chain guide thickness:	
Upper	4.5 mm (0.18 in)
Lower	6.0 mm (0.24 in)
Service limit (both)	2.0 mm (0.08 in)

Gearbox

	Six-speed models	Five-speed models
Type ...	Six-speed constant mesh	Five-speed constant mesh
Ratios:		
Bottom	2.54 : 1 (33/13 T)	2.57 : 1 (36/14 T)
2nd	1.75 : 1 (28/16 T)	1.68 : 1 (32/19 T)
3rd	1.32 : 1 (25/19 T)	1.27 : 1 (28/22 T)
4th	1.10 : 1 (23/21 T)	1.04 : 1 (26/25 T)
5th	0.96 : 1 (22/23 T)	0.89 : 1 (24/27 T)
6th	0.88 : 1 (21/24 T)	Not applicable
Primary drive ratio	2.43 : 1 (56/23 T)	2.43 : 1 (56/23 T)
Final drive ratio	3.00 : 1 (45/15 T)	3.00 : 1 (45/15 T)
Overall drive ratio (top gear)	6.39 : 1	6.49 : 1

Specifications relating to Chapter 2

Fuel tank

	B4/G3/H3	All other models
Overall capacity	12 lit (2.64/3.1 US/Imp gal)	14 lit (3.08/3.7 Imp/US gal)
Reserve	Not available	3 lit (5.25/6.4 Imp/US pint)

Carburettors

	D4/S3	B1/B3/C1/G1/G2	B2/C2	B4/G3	H1/H3
Make	Keihin	Keihin	Keihin	Keihin	Keihin
Type	VB32	VB32	CV32	CV32	CV32
Primary main jet	70	70	70	70	70
Secondary main jet	95	90	90R	88	80
Pilot air jet	—	115	130	130	130
Primary air jet	—	150	120	150	150
Secondary air jet	—	60	50	60	50
Pilot (slow) jet	35	35	35	35	35
Jet needle	—	003303	003001	003303	003002
Pilot screw (turns out)	1½ ± 3/8	1¼ ± ½	1¼ ± ½	2¼	2¼
Fuel level:					
D4/S3	2.0 — 4.0 mm (0.08 — 0.16 in)				
All others	1.5 — 3.5 mm (0.06 — 0.14 in)				

Engine lubrication system

	D4/S3	All other models
Type	Pressure fed, wet sump	
Overall capacity	3.0 lit (5.3/6.3 Imp/US pint)	2.9 lit (5.1/6.0 Imp/US pint)
Capacity less filter	2.6 lit (4.6/5.5 Imp/US pint)	Not available

Oil pump

	D4/S3	All other models
Type	Trochoid	Trochoid
Inner/outer rotor clearance	0.025 — 0.115 mm (0.0010 — 0.0045 in)	Less than 0.15 mm (0.006 in)
Service limit	0.21 mm (0.0083 in)	0.21 mm (0.0083 in)
Rotor end float	0.03 — 0.09 mm (0.0012 — 0.0035 in)	0.04 — 0.10 mm (0.0016 — 0.0039 in)
Service limit	0.15 mm (0.006 in)	0.15 mm (0.006 in)
Outer rotor/body clearance	0.10 — 0.15 mm (0.004 — 0.006 in)	0.10 — 0.18 mm (0.004 — 0.0071 in)

Service limit	0.25 mm (0.0098 in)	0.25 mm (0.0098 in)

Pressure:

At 4000 rpm/80°C	More than 1.5 kg cm^2 (21 psi)	—
At 4000 rpm/90°C	—	More than 2.0 kg cm^2 (28 psi)

Specifications relating to Chapter 3

Ignition system

	D4/S3	H3/G3	All other models
Type	Contact breaker	Electronic	Contact breaker

Ignition timing:

	D4/S3	H3/G3	All other models
Retarded	10° BTDC @ 1100 rpm	10° BTDC @ 1100 rpm	10° BTDC @ 1100 rpm
Full advance	40° BTDC @ 2800 rpm	40° BTDC @ 3200 rpm	35° BTDC @ 3200 rpm
Advance begins at	Not available	1400 − 1600 rpm	Not available
Full advance at	Not available	3000 − 3400 rpm	Not available
Contact breaker gap	0.3 − 0.4 mm (0.012 − 0.016 in)	Not applicable	0.3 − 0.4 mm (0.012 − 0.016 in)
Dwell angle	185 − 195° (51 − 54%)	Not applicable	185 − 200° (51.5 − 55.5%)

Ignition coil resistance

Primary windings	3.2 − 4.8 ohm	1.8 − 2.8 ohm	3.2 − 4.8 ohm
Secondary windings	10.4 − 15.6 K ohm	10.4 − 15.6 K ohm	10.4 − 15.6 K ohm

Pick-up coil resistance ... ...

	Not applicable	360 − 540 ohm	Not applicable

Spark plugs

Make	NGK or ND	NGK or ND	NGK or ND
Type	B8ES or W24ES	B7ES or W22ES-U	B7ES or W22ES-U
Reach	19 mm (¾ in)	19 mm (¾ in)	19 mm (¾ in)
Gap		0.7 − 0.8 mm (0.028 − 0.031 in)	

Specifications relating to Chapter 4

Front forks

	H1/H3	All other models
Type	Oil damped telescopic	

Damping oil capacity (per leg):

	H1/H3	All other models
Dry	145 − 155 cc	145 − 155 cc
At oil change	About 125 cc	About 125 cc
Oil level	417 mm (16.4 in) from top of stanchion with fork spring installed	
Oil grade	SAE 5W/20 or fork oil	
Spring free length	519.5 mm (20.45 in)	484.5 mm (19.07 in)
Service limit	510.0 mm (20.08 in)	475.0 mm (18.70 in)

Rear suspension

	All models
Type	Pivoted rear fork supported by oil-damped units
Pivot bearings	Caged needle roller
Pivot sleeve diameter	21.987 − 22.000 mm (0.8656 − 0.8661 in)
Service limit	21.96 mm (0.8646 in)
Pivot shaft runout	Less than 0.10 mm (0.004 in)
Service limit	0.14 mm (0.0055 in)
Repair limit	0.7 mm (0.0276 in)

Suspension travel

Front	150 mm (5.9055 in)

Rear:

H1/H3	115 mm (4.5276 in)
All others	95 mm (3.7402 in)

Specifications relating to Chapter 5

Wheels

	B1/B2/B3/B4/C1/C2	G1/G2/G3	H1/H3
Type	Steel rim, wire spoked	Cast alloy	Cast alloy

Rim sizes:

	B1/B2/B3/B4/C1/C2	G1/G2/G3	H1/H3
Front	1.60 x 18	1.60 x 18	1.85 x 19
Rear	1.85 x 18	1.85 x 18	2.50 x 16

Maximum rim runout:

	B1/B2/B3/B4/C1/C2	G1/G2/G3	H1/H3
Axial	0 − 0.8 mm (0 − 0.0315 in)	Not available	Not available
Service limit	2.0 mm (0.08 in)	0.5 mm (0.020 in)	0.5 mm (0.020 in)
Radial	0 − 1.0 mm (0 − 0.04 in)	Not available	Not available
Service limit	2.0 mm (0.08 in)	0.8 mm (0.031 in)	0.8 mm (0.031 in)

Tyres

Size:								
Front	...	...	...	...	...	3.00S18—4PR	3.00S18—4PR	3.25S19—4PR
Rear	...	...	...	...	...	3.50S18—4PR	3.50S18—4PR	130/90—16 67S
Pressures:								
Front	...	...	...	...	...	25 psi (1.75 kg cm^2)	25 psi (1.75 kg cm^2)	25 psi (1.75 kg cm^2)
Rear — solo	...	...	...	...	...	28 psi (2.00 kg cm^2)	28 psi (2.00 kg cm^2)	21 psi (1.50 kg cm^2)
Rear — fully laden	...	...	...	...	...	36 psi (2.50 kg cm^2)	36 psi (2.50 kg cm^2)	25 psi (1.75 kg cm^2)

Brakes

								C1/C2	All other models
Type:									
Front	...	...	...	...	...	...	...	Drum	Disc
Rear	...	...	...	...	...	...	...	Drum	Drum

Front disc brake

All except C1/C2

Master cylinder:								
Inside diameter	...	...	...	...	...	...	...	14.000 — 14.063 mm (0.5512 — 0.5537 in)
Service limit	...	...	...	...	...	...	...	14.08 mm (0.5543 in)
Piston diameter	...	...	...	...	...	...	...	13.957 — 13.984 mm (0.5495 — 0.5506 in)
Service limit	...	...	...	...	...	...	...	13.90 mm (0.5472 in)
Primary cup diameter	...	...	...	...	...	...	...	14.2 — 14.6 mm (0.5591 — 0.5748 in)
Service limit	...	...	...	...	...	...	...	14.1 mm (0.5551 in)
Secondary cup diameter	...	...	...	...	...	...	...	14.65 — 15.15 mm (0.5768 — 0.5965 in)
Service limit	...	...	...	...	...	...	...	14.5 mm (0.5709 in)
Spring free length	...	...	...	...	...	...	...	42.8 — 46.8 mm (1.6850 — 1.8425 in)
Service limit	...	...	...	...	...	...	...	40.7 mm (1.6024 in)

								B1/B2	All other models
Caliper:									
Inside diameter	...	...	...	...	...	...	...	41.30 — 41.35 mm (1.6260 — 1.6279 in)	42.850 — 42.900 mm (1.6870 — 1.6890 in)
Service limit	...	...	...	...	...	...	...	41.60 mm (1.6378 in)	42.92 mm (1.6898 in)
Piston diameter	...	...	...	...	...	...	...	41.17 — 41.22 mm (1.6209 — 1.6228 in)	42.788 — 42.820 mm (1.6842 — 1.6858 in)
Service limit	...	...	...	...	...	...	...	40.90 mm (1.6102 in)	42.75 mm (1.6831 in)
Disc:									
Runout	...	...	...	...	...	...	...	Less than 0.15 mm (0.006 in)	Less than 0.15 mm (0.006 in)
Service limit	...	...	...	...	...	...	...	0.3 mm (0.012 in)	0.3 mm (0.012 in)
Thickness	...	...	...	...	...	...	...	6.9 — 7.1 mm (0.2717 — 0.2795 in)	4.8 — 5.1 mm (0.1890 — 0.2008 in)
Service limit	...	...	...	...	...	...	...	6.0 mm (0.2362 in)	4.5 mm (0.1772 in)

Front drum brake

C1/C2

Drum inside diameter	...	...	...	...	...	...	...	180.000 — 180.140 mm (7.087 — 7.092 in)
Service limit	...	...	...	...	...	...	...	180.75 mm (7.116 in)
Lining thickness	...	...	...	...	...	...	...	4.8 — 5.6 mm (0.189 — 0.220 in)
Service limit	...	...	...	...	...	...	...	2.5 mm (0.098 in)
Return spring free length	...	...	...	...	...	...	...	46.7 — 47.3 mm (1.839 — 1.862 in)
Service limit	...	...	...	...	...	...	...	48.5 mm (1.909 in)
Cam spindle diameter	...	...	...	...	...	...	...	14.957 — 14.984 mm (0.589 — 0.590 in)
Service limit	...	...	...	...	...	...	...	14.83 mm (0.584 in)
Spindle bearing bore ID	...	...	...	...	...	...	...	15.000 — 15.027 mm (0.591 — 0.592 in)
Service limit	...	...	...	...	...	...	...	15.18 mm (0.598 in)

Rear drum brake

All models

Drum inside diameter	...	...	...	...	...	...	...	160.000 — 160.160 mm (6.299 — 6.305 in)
Service limit	...	...	...	...	...	...	...	160.75 mm (6.329 in)
Lining thickness	...	...	...	...	...	...	...	4.0 — 4.5 mm (0.157 — 0.177 in)
Service limit	...	...	...	...	...	...	...	2.0 mm (0.08 in)
Return spring free length	...	...	...	...	...	...	...	47.5 — 48.5 mm (1.870 — 1.909 in)
Service limit	...	...	...	...	...	...	...	50.0 mm (1.969 in)
Cam spindle diameter	...	...	...	...	...	...	...	16.957 — 16.984 mm (0.668 — 0.669 in)
Service limit	...	...	...	...	...	...	...	16.83 mm (0.663 in)
Spindle bearing bore ID	...	...	...	...	...	...	...	17.000 — 17.027 mm (0.669 — 0.670 in)
Service limit	...	...	...	...	...	...	...	17.18 mm (0.676 in)

Specifications relating to Chapter 6

Battery

							B1/B2/G1/H1	C1/C2	B3/B4/G2/G3/H3
Make	...	...	...	...	...	...	Yuasa or Furukawa	Furukawa	Yuasa
Model	...	...	...	...	...	...	12N 12A — 4A — 1 or FB 12A — A	12N 5.5 — 4A	12N 12A — 4A — 1
Voltage	...	...	...	...	...	...	12V	12V	12V
Capacity	...	...	...	...	...	...	12Ah	5.5Ah	12Ah
Earth (ground)	...	...	...	...	...	...	Negative	Negative	Negative

Alternator

	B1/B2/C1/C2/H1	B3/B4/G2	G3/H3
Make	Nippon Denso	Not available	Nippon Denso
Model	5 — 037000 — 373	Not available	037000 — 1370
Charging voltage	About 14.5V @ 4000 rpm	About 14.5V @ 4000 rpm	About 14.5V @ 4000 rpm
Unregulated voltage	About 75V @ 4000 rpm	About 75V @ 4000 rpm	About 14.5V @ 4000 rpm
Stator resistance	0.26 — 0.38 ohm	0.36 — 0.38 ohm	0.26 — 0.38 ohm

Electronic regulator/rectifier

Make	Shindengen	Not available	Shindengen
Model	SH221 — 12	Not available	SH222 — 12B
Type	Open circuit	Short circuit	Short circuit

Starter motor

Make	Mitsuba
Model	SM — 223
Brush length	11.0 — 12.5 mm (0.4331 — 0.4921 in)
Service limit	6.0 mm (0.2362 in)
Commutator groove depth	0.5 — 0.8 mm (0.0197 — 0.0315 in)
Service limit	0.2 mm (0.008 in)

Bulbs

	UK models	US models
Voltage	12V	12V
Headlamp:		
B1/C1/H1	35/35W	50/35W sealed beam
All others	35/35W	50/40W sealed beam
Tail/stop lamp	5/21W	8/27W
Flashing indicator/running lamps	Not applicable	23/8W
Flashing indicators	21W	23W
Parking lamp	4W	Not applicable
Speedometer lamp	3.4W	3.4W
Tachometer lamp	3.4W	3.4W*
Neutral indicator lamp	3.4W	3.4W
Main beam warning	3.4W	3.4W
Indicator warning	3.4W	3.4W
Oil pressure warning	3.4W	3.4W*
Brake failure warning	3.4W	3.4W*

These items not fitted to C1/C2 models

Torque settings

	lbf-ft (ft-lb)	kgf m (kg-m)
Cylinder head cover bolts:		
8 mm	18.0	2.5
6 mm	7.2	1.0
Cylinder head nuts	29.0	4.0
Crankcase bolts:		
8 mm	18.0	2.5
6 mm	7.2	1.0
Main bearing cap bolts:		
10 mm	29.0	4.0
8 mm	18.0	2.5
Connecting rod cap nuts:		
400 models	17.5	2.4
440 models	27.0	3.7

Specifications

The following specifications relate to the 440 cc models bearing the suffixes A1, A2, B1, B2, C1, C2, D1, D2.

Specifications relating to Chapter 1
Engine

Type	Vertical parallel twin cylinder, SOHC, four-stroke
Bore	67.5
Stroke	62.0
Displacement	443 cc
Compression ratio	9.2 : 1
Max bhp:	
C1/C2	41 @ 8500 rpm
All others	40 @ 8500 rpm
Max torque	3.6 kgf m @ 7000 rpm

Pistons and bores

Oversizes	+0.5 and +1.0 mm (+0.020 and +0.040 in)
Piston diameter	67.30 mm (2.6496 in) minimum

Piston ring groove width service limit:

Top	1.33 mm (0.0524 in)
2nd	1.60 mm (0.0630 in)
Oil	2.61 mm (0.1028 in)

Ring thickness service limit:

Top	1.10 mm (0.0433 in)
2nd	1.40 mm (0.0551 in)

Ring to groove clearance service limit:

Top	0.18 mm (0.0071 in)
2nd	0.14 mm (0.0055 in)

Piston ring end gap (installed):

Service limit	0.7 mm (0.0276 in)
Gudgeon pin bore diameter service limit	15.08 mm (0.5937 in)
Gudgeon pin diameter service limit	14.96 mm (0.5890 in)
Small-end diameter service limit	15.05 mm (0.5925 in)
Gudgeon pin/piston clearance	0.005 − 0.016 mm (0.0002 − 0.0006 in)
Gudgeon pin/small-end clearance	0.003 − 0.019 mm (0.0001 − 0.0007 in)
Bore diameter	Less than 67.60 mm (2.6614 in)
Allowable difference between readings	0.05 mm (0.0020 in)
Piston diameter	

Cylinder head

Maximum warpage	0.05 mm (0.0020 in)
Combustion chamber volume	36.0 − 37.0 cc (1.27 − 1.30 imp fl oz, 1.22 − 1.25 US fl oz)

Valves

Valve seat angle	45°
Valve stem diameter service limit	6.90 mm (0.2717 in)
Valve guide bore diameter service limit	7.08 mm (0.2787 in)

Valve stem to guide clearance service limit:

Inlet	0.26 mm (0.0102 in)
Exhaust	0.25 mm (0.0098 in)
Valve seat width	0.5 − 1.0 mm (0.0197 − 0.0394 in)

Valve spring pressure service limit:

Inner at 22.2 mm	27.3 kg (60.19 lb)
Outer at 25.7 mm	51.4 kg (113.32 lb)
Valve spring warpage service limit	1.5 mm (0.06 in)

Valve clearances (engine cold)

Inlet and exhaust	0.17 − 0.22 mm (0.0067 − 0.0087 in)

Valve timing

Inlet opens	27° BTDC
Inlet closes	73° ABDC
Duration	280°
Exhaust opens	70° BBDC
Exhaust closes	30° ATDC
Duration	280°

Camshaft and drive

Lobe height service limit	38.25 mm (1.506 in)
Journal diameter service limit	24.93 mm (0.9815 in)
Journal to head clearance service limit	0.29 mm (0.0114 in)
Camshaft radial runout service limit	0.1 mm (0.0039 in)
Camshaft chain length (20 pin length under 5 kg/11 lb tension)	128.8 mm (5.0709 in)

Camshaft chain guide wear depth service limit:

Front	3.6 mm (0.1417 in)
Rear	4.5 mm (0.1772 in)
Camshaft tensioner spring free length service limit	40 mm (1.5748 in)

Crankshaft assembly

Big-end bearing radial play service limit	0.1 mm (0.0039 in)
Big-end bearing end float service limit	0.45 mm (0.0177 in)

Big-end eye internal diameter:

Unmarked	38.000 − 38.008 mm (1.4961 − 1.4964 in)
'O' marked	38.009 − 38.016 mm (1.4964 − 1.4967 in)

Crankshaft big-end journal diameter:

Unmarked	34.984 − 34.994 mm (1.3773 − 1.3777 in)
'O' marked	34.995 − 35.000 mm (1.3778 − 1.3780 in)
Service limit	34.97 mm (1.3768 in)

Big-end bearing shell thickness:
    Blue ... ...   1.485 − 1.490 mm (0.0585 − 0.0587 in)
    Black ... ...   1.480 − 1.485 mm (0.0583 − 0.0585 in)
    Brown ... ...   1.475 − 1.480 mm (0.0581 − 0.0583 in)
Big-end bearing to journal clearance service limit ... ...   0.1 mm (0.0039 in)
Connecting rod straightness (bend and twist) service limit ...   0.2 mm (0.0079 in)
Crankshaft centre journal runout service limit ... ...   0.05 mm (0.0020 in)
Main bearing clearance service limit ... ...   0.08 mm (0.0031 in)
Crankshaft main bearing journal diameter:
    '1' marked ... ...   35.992 − 36.000 mm (1.4170 − 1.4173 in)
    Unmarked ... ...   35.984 − 35.992 mm (1.4167 − 1.4170 in)
    Service limit ... ...   35.96 mm (1.4157 in)
Crankshaft main bearing bore diameter:
    'O' marked ... ...   39.000 − 39.008 mm (1.5354 − 1.5357 in)
    Unmarked ... ...   39.009 − 39.016 mm (1.5358 − 1.5361 in)
Crankshaft end float service limit ... ...   0.45 mm (0.0177 in)

Balancer mechanism

Balancer shaft diameter service limit ... ...   19.93 mm (0.7846 in)
Balancer shaft bore diameter service limit ... ...   20.08 mm (0.7905 in)
Balancer spring free length service limit ... ...   9.3 mm (0.3661 in)
Balancer chain length (20 pin length under 5 kg/11 lb tension)
service limit ... ...   162.4 mm (6.394 in)
Balancer chain guide wear limit:
    Upper ... ...   1.0 mm (0.04 in)
    Lower ... ...   1.25 mm (0.05 in)

Clutch

Number of plain plates   5
Number of friction plates   6
Number of springs   4
Friction plate thickness service limit ... ...   2.7 mm (0.106 in)
Plain plate warpage service limit ... ...   0.3 mm (0.012 in)
Friction plate tang/housing clearance service limit ... ...   0.7 mm (0.28 in)
Housing bore internal diameter service limit ... ...   25.03 mm (0.9854 in)
Mainshaft outside diameter service limit ... ...   24.94 mm (0.982 in)

Primary drive

Type ... ...   Hy-Vo chain
Make ... ...   Tsubakimoto
Size ... ...   3/8P − 5/8W
Number of links   74
Maximum free play ... ...   30 mm (1.18 in)
Primary chain guide thickness upper and lower, service limit ...   2.0 mm (0.08 in)

Gearbox

Type ... ...   Six-speed, constant mesh
Ratios:
    Bottom ... ...   2.54 : 1 (33/13T)
    2nd ... ...   1.75 : 1 (28/16T)
    3rd ... ...   1.32 : 1 (25/19T)
    4th ... ...   1.10 : 1 (23/21T)
    5th ... ...   0.96 : 1 (22/23T)
    6th ... ...   0.88 : 1 (21/24T)
Primary drive ratio ... ...   2.43 : 1 (56/23T)
Final drive ratio ... ...   3.00 : 1 (45/15T)
Overall drive ratio (top gear) ... ...   6.39 : 1

Specifications relating to Chapter 2

Fuel tank capacity

	A1/A2/D1/D2	B1/B2/C1/C2
Overall capacity	12 lit (2.64/3.17 Imp/US gal)	14 lit (3.08/3.70 Imp/US gal)
Reserve	2 lit (0.44/0.5 Imp/US gal)	1 lit (0.22/0.3 Imp/US gal)

Carburettors

Make	Keihin	Keihin
Model	CV36	CV36
Jet needle	NO2A	NO3A
Primary main jet:		
UK models	70	75
US models	62 (65, 1981 models)	68
Secondary main jet:		
UK models	85	88
US models	88	90

Pilot air jet	125	125
Primary air jet	130	130
Secondary air jet	50	50
Pilot jet	35	35
Fuel level	3 — 5 mm (0.12 — 0.20 in)	3 — 5 mm (0.12 — 0.20 in)

Engine lubrication system

Type	Pressure fed, wet sump
Capacity	2.9 lit (5.1/6.0 Imp/US pint)

Oil pump

Type	Trochoid
Inner to outer rotor clearance service limit	0.21 mm (0.0083 in)
Rotor end float service limit	0.15 mm (0.0059 in)
Outer rotor to body clearance service limit	0.25 mm (0.0098 in)
Oil pressure @ 4000 rpm/90°C	More than 2.0 kg cm^2 (28 psi)

Specifications relating to Chapter 3
Ignition system

	1980 models	1981 models
Type	Contact breaker	Electronic
Ignition timing:		
Retarded	10° BTDC @ 1200 rpm	10° BTDC @ 1200 rpm
Full advance	35° BTDC @ 3200 rpm	40° BTDC @ 3200 rpm
Advance begins at	Not available	1400 — 1600 rpm
Full advance at	Not available	3000 — 3400 rpm
Contact breaker gap	0.3 — 0.4 mm (0.012 — 0.016 in)	Not applicable
Dwell angle	185 — 200° (51 — 56%)	Not applicable

Ignition coil resistance

Primary windings	3.2 — 4.8 ohm	1.8 — 2.8 ohm
Secondary windings	10.4 — 15.6 K ohm	10.4 — 15.6 K ohm

Pick-up coil resistance

... ...	Not applicable	360 — 540 ohm

Spark plugs

Make	NGK or ND
Type	B7ES or W22ES-U
Reach	19 mm (¾ in)
Gap	0.7 — 0.8 mm (0.028 — 0.031 in)

Specifications relating to Chapter 4
Front suspension

Type	Oil-damped telescopic fork
Damping oil capacity per leg:	
Dry	150 cc
At oil changes	About 125 cc
Damping oil grade	SAE 5W 20 or fork oil
Oil level from top of stanchion*	
A and D models	475 ± 4 mm (18.7008 ± 0.1575 in)
B and C models	435 ± 4 mm (17.1260 ± 0.1575 in)
Fork spring type	Wire coil spring, dual rate
Free length service limit:	
A and D models	510 mm (20.0787 in)
B and C models	475 mm (18.7008 in)

Measure oil level with fork spring removed

Rear suspension

Type	Pivoted rear fork supported by oil — damped suspension units
Pivot sleeve diameter service limit	21.96 mm (0.8646 in)
Pivot shaft runout	Less than 0.14 mm (0.0055 in)
Service limit	0.7 mm (0.0276 in)

Suspension travel

Front	150 mm (5.9055 in)
Rear:	
A and D models	115 mm (4.5276 in)
B and C models	95 mm (3.7402 in)

Specifications relating to Chapter 5

Wheels

	A1/A2/D1/D2	C1/C2	B1/B2
Type ...	Cast alloy	Cast alloy	Steel rim, wire spoked
Rim size:			
Front ...	1.85 x 19	1.60 x 18	1.60 x 18
Rear ...	2.50 x 16	1.85 x 18	1.85 x 18
Maximum rim runout:			
Axial ...	0.5 mm (0.020 in)	0.5 mm (0.020 in)	2.0 mm (0.08 in)
Radial ...	0.8 mm (0.031 in)	0.8 mm (0.031 in)	2.0 mm (0.08 in)

Tyres

	A1/A2/D1/D2	C1/C2	B1/B2
Size:			
Front ...	3.25S19 — 4PR	3.00S18 — 4PR	3.00S18 — 4PR
Rear ...	130/90 — 16 67S	3.50S18 — 4PR	3.50S18 — 4PR

Pressures:	A1/A2/D1/D2	All other models
Front ...	1.75 kg cm^2 (25 psi)	1.75 kg cm^2 (25 psi)
Rear — solo ...	1.50 kg cm^2 (21 psi)	2.00 kg cm^2 (28 psi)
Rear — fully laden ...	1.75 kg cm^2 (25 psi)	2.50 kg cm^2 (36 psi)

Brakes

Type:	B1/B2	All other models
Front ...	Drum	Disc
Rear ...	Drum	Drum

Front disc brake

All except B1/B2

Master cylinder:	
Inside diameter ...	14.000 — 14.063 mm (0.5512 — 0.5537 in)
Service limit ...	14.08 mm (0.5543 in)
Piston diameter ...	13.957 — 13.984 mm (0.5495 — 0.5506 in)
Service limit ...	13.90 mm (0.5472 in)
Primary cup diameter ...	14.2 — 14.6 mm (0.5591 — 0.5748 in)
Service limit ...	14.1 mm (0.5551 in)
Secondary cup diameter ...	14.65 — 15.15 mm (0.5768 — 0.5965 in)
Service limit ...	14.5 mm (0.5709 in)
Spring free length ...	42.8 — 46.8 mm (1.6850 — 1.8425 in)
Service limit ...	40.7 mm (1.6024 in)
Caliper:	
Inside diameter ...	42.850 — 42.900 mm (1.6870 — 1.6890 in)
Service limit ...	42.92 mm (1.6898 in)
Piston diameter ...	42.788 — 42.820 mm (1.6842 — 1.6858 in)
Service limit ...	42.75 mm (1.6831 in)
Disc:	
Runout ...	Less than 0.15 mm (0.006 in)
Service limit ...	0.3 mm (0.012 in)
Thickness ...	4.8 — 5.1 mm (0.1890 — 0.2008 in)
Service limit ...	4.5 mm (0.1772 in)

Front drum brake

B1/B2

Drum inside diameter ...	180.000 — 180.140 mm (7.087 — 7.092 in)
Service limit ...	180.75 mm (7.116 in)
Lining thickness ...	4.8 — 5.6 mm (0.189 — 0.220 in)
Service limit ...	2.5 mm (0.098 in)
Return spring free length ...	46.7 — 47.3 mm (1.839 — 1.862 in)
Service limit ...	48.5 mm (1.909 in)
Cam spindle diameter ...	14.957 — 14.984 mm (0.589 — 0.590 in)
Service limit ...	14.83 mm (0.584 in)
Spindle bearing bore ID ...	15.000 — 15.027 mm (0.591 — 0.592 in)
Service limit ...	15.18 mm (0.598 in)

Rear drum brake

All models

Drum inside diameter ...	160.000 — 160.160 mm (6.299 — 6.305 in)
Service limit ...	160.75 mm (6.329 in)
Lining thickness ...	4.0 — 4.5 mm (0.157 — 0.177 in)
Service limit ...	2.0 mm (0.08 in)
Return spring free length ...	47.5 — 48.5 mm (1.870 — 1.909 in)
Service limit ...	50.0 mm (1.969 in)
Cam spindle diameter ...	16.957 — 16.984 mm (0.668 — 0.669 in)
Service limit ...	16.83 mm (0.663 in)
Spindle bearing bore ID ...	17.000 — 17.027 mm (0.669 — 0.670 in)
Service limit ...	17.18 mm (0.676 in)

Specifications relating to Chapter 6

Battery

Make ...	Furukawa —
Model ...	FB12A-A
Voltage ...	12V
Capacity ...	12Ah
Earth (ground) ...	Negative

Alternator

Make ...	Nippon Denso
Model ...	037000 − 1370
Charging voltage ...	About 14.5V @ 4000 rpm
Unregulated voltage ...	About 75V @ 4000 rpm
Stator resistance ...	0.26 − 0.38 ohm

Regulator/rectifier

Make ...	Shindengen
Model ...	SH222-12B
Type ...	Electronic, short circuit

Starter motor

Make ...	Mitsuba
Model ...	SM-8203
Brush length ...	11.0 − 12.5 mm (0.4331 − 0.4921 in)
Service limit ...	6.0 mm (0.2362 in)
Commutator groove depth ...	0.5 − 0.8 mm (0.0197 − 0.0315 in)
Service limit ...	0.2 mm (0.008 in)

Bulbs

	UK models	US models
Voltage ...	12V	12V
Headlamp:		
C1 ...	35/35W	50/40W
All others ...	35/35W	50/35W
Tail/stop lamp ...	5/21W	8/27W
Flashing indicator/running lamps ...	Not applicable	23/8W, B1/B2 only
Flashing indicators ...	21W	23W
Parking lamp ...	3.4W	Not applicable
Speedometer lamp ...	3.4W	3.4W
Tachometer lamp ...	3.4W	3.4W
Neutral indicator lamp ...	3.4W	3.4W
Main beam warning ...	3.4W	3.4W
Indicator warning ...	3.4W	3.4W
Oil pressure warning ...	3.4W	3.4W
Brake failure warning ...	4W	3.4W

---

1 Introduction

The preceding Chapters relate to the Kawasaki KZ400 models (known as Z400 in the UK) from their introduction in 1974 to 1976. This update Chapter covers the subsequent KZ400 models produced between 1977 and 1981, and the KZ440 variants of 1980 and 1981.

As is the case with most Japanese manufacturers, Kawasaki have chosen to modify and change the model range with bewildering frequency over the years, and this has resulted in some nineteen different model suffixes appearing in the period covered in this Chapter. Unfortunately, these suffixes do not follow any particular pattern and, therefore, model recognition is rather complicated. In most instances, changes between different models are largely cosmetic, as are those between similar models of different years, but a number of more significant modifications have been incorporated. The following describes the models produced in each year, giving the frame number for identification purposes and listing any major identifying changes.

1977

KZ400 D4   Frame No K4-065101 on
KZ400 S3   Frame No K4S-18101 on

These represent the 1977 versions of the previous D and S models, the former being the standard model, whilst the latter was the economy version. The only major change was the adoption of diaphragm-type constant depression carburettors in place of the previous piston-type instruments.

1978

KZ400 B1   Frame No K4-077801 on

This was the standard model for 1978 and was identified by its two into two exhaust system, electric starter and six-speed gearbox. On this and all subsequent models, valve clearance adjustment was by screw and locknut. It featured a single hydraulic disc brake on the front whilst the rear wheel housed a single leading shoe drum brake.

KZ400 C1   Frame No K4S-24701

The C1 was essentially the same as the previous year's S3 model, despite the sudden change of suffix. It can be distinguished from the B1 model by its two into one exhaust system. Two drum brakes were fitted and the electric starter was omitted. The C1 had a five-speed gearbox. This was the last of the 'economy' versions available in the USA, the standard model becoming the base model of the range for the next year's production.

1979

KZ400 B2   Frame No K4-099501 on

Essentially the same as the B1, but with a different colour scheme and new decals.

KZ400 C2   Frame No not available
Essentially the same as the C1, but with different carburettors and cosmetic changes.

KZ400 G1   Frame No K4-099501 on
This was the first of the Custom models (not to be confused with the later LTD machines which follow the current trend in chopper-styled machines) and was essentially a cosmetically reworked B2 model. It featured cast wheels and a modified single piston brake caliper which slid rather than pivoted to align with the disc.

KZ400 H1   Frame No KZ400H-000101 on
The H1 was the first of the LTD models and was equipped with a stepped dual seat and high pull-back handlebars. It was fitted with a drilled front disc and sintered metal brake pads.

1980
KZ400 B3   Frame No K4-115001 on
This was the 1980 version of the previous year's B2. A redesigned paint and decal scheme was included. Major changes were the adoption of the new front caliper as fitted to the G1, a new automatic chain tensioner and the disappearance of the kickstart lever. There were also less obvious changes in the electrical system.

KZ400 G2   Frame No K4-115001 on
Similar to the G1, this model also lost its kickstart lever and acquired an automatic cam chain tensioner.

KZ440 A1   Frame No KZ440A-000001 on
Generally similar to the 1979 KZ400-H1 but with 443 cc engine, LTD styling, cast wheels and chain drive.

KZ440 B1   Frame No KZ440B-000001 on
This was the 443 cc version of the KZ400 B2.

KZ440 C1   Frame No KZ440C-000001 on
Custom version of the above models.

KZ440 D1   Frame No KZ440D-000001 on
Generally similar to the KZ440A1, but with toothed belt final drive instead of chain.

1981
KZ400 B4   Frame No K4-116801 on
1981 version of the B3, no significant changes.

KZ400 G3   Frame No K4-116801 on
1981 'Custom' model. CDI Ignition system now fitted, plus detail cosmetic changes.

KZ400 H3   Frame No KZ400H-0.17201
1981 LTD model, now with CDI ignition.

KZ440 A2   Frame No KZ440A-022501
As 1980 model. Fitted with CDI system and self-cancelling indicators.

KZ440 B2   Frame No KZ440B-007801
As 1980 B1 model, but with CDI ignition system and cosmetic changes.

KZ440 C2   Frame No KZ440C-003301
As C1. CDI and cosmetic changes.

KZ440 D2   Frame No KZ440D-002101
The 1981 version of the belt-drive LTD. Fitted with CDI and automatically cancelling indicators, plus cosmetic changes.

---

2 Automatic camshaft chain tensioner: removal and refitting

---

1 All KZ400 models from 1980 onwards, plus all KZ440 machines are equipped with a fully automatic camshaft chain tensioner which requires no maintenance, models prior to this having employed the adjustable type shown in Fig. 1.1. The automatic tensioner consists of a spring-loaded plunger which bears upon the tensioner blade. The plunger housing has a tapered section which faces towards the cylinder barrel and which contains a spring-loaded retainer. The retainer holds a number of steel balls, the assembly being held against the narrow portion of the taper and the plunger by the spring.

2 As the chain begins to wear, the developing slack is taken up by the plunger moving inwards, the retainer assembly having no

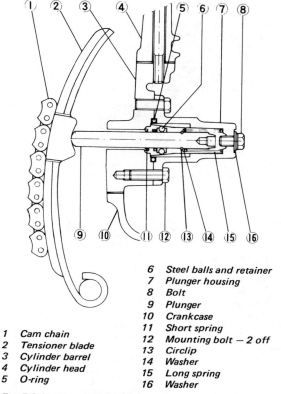

	6	Steel balls and retainer
	7	Plunger housing
	8	Bolt
	9	Plunger
	10	Crankcase
1	Cam chain	11	Short spring
2	Tensioner blade	12	Mounting bolt — 2 off
3	Cylinder barrel	13	Circlip
4	Cylinder head	14	Washer
5	O-ring	15	Long spring
	16	Washer

Fig. 7.0 Sectioned view of automatic cam chain tensioner

influence on its movement in this direction. If, however, the chain attempts to push the plunger back into the body, the steel balls are caught between the plunger and housing taper, effectively locking them. Fig. 7.0 shows the tensioner assembly in section.

3 Should removal of the tensioner assembly from the machine become necessary it should be noted that the plunger will extend fully as the mounting bolts are removed. On no account should they be partly removed and then retightened. Once disturbed, it is essential that the tensioner is removed completely and the mechanism reset prior to installation. The assembly can be lifted away once its two securing bolts have been released. Once the tensioner has been removed do not rotate the crankshaft.

4 Once the tensioner assembly has been released from the engine unit the plunger can be displaced and the long spring and plain washer removed, as can the short spring and the retainer which are fitted from the opposite end. The body and the tensioner components should be cleaned carefully to remove any traces of dirt. It is essential that the assembly is kept spotlessly clean, because even a small particle of dirt could jam the mechanism.

5 Rebuild the assembly by reversing the dismantling order, lubricating the various components with engine oil. Push the plunger into the tensioner body and, holding it in this position, fit and secure the lockbolt to retain it in the compressed position. It should be noted that the original lock bolt is 14 mm (0.55 in) long. If a new bolt is to be fitted for any reason it must not exceed this length or there will be a risk of damage to the cam chain.

6 Fit the balls, retainer and the short spring over the plunger end, and fit a new O-ring to the recess in the tensioner body. Offer up the tensioner assembly and fit the two retaining bolts, tightening them evenly and firmly. Once securely in position, slacken the lock bolt by three or four full turns to release the plunger which will automatically adopt the correct position for

the necessary chain tension setting. The lock bolt should now be screwed home in the housing and tightened to 1.0 kgf in (87 in f lb). Note that in all other respects the tensioner arrangement is the same as that described for the earlier models, and reference should be made to Section 30 of Chapter 1 for further information.

3 Setting the valve timing: all models 1978 onwards

1 From 1978 onwards the camshaft sprocket marks were modified and a revised setting procedure adopted. As an aid to identification of the affected models, note that the earlier type had bonded rubber pads on the face of the camshaft sprocket. The later versions, to which this section applies, have plain steel sprockets.

2 If the camshaft has been removed, clean it thoroughly before installation, paying particular attention to the oil passages which should be blown clear with compressed air. Where appropriate, refit the pressed steel oil well in its recess in the head, noting that the arrow must face forwards and that a non-hardening locking fluid should be applied to the screws.

3 Lubricate the camshaft and journals with engine oil, then feed the camshaft through the chain loop from the right-hand side. Note that the notched end of the camshaft must be positioned on the right-hand side of the head. Fit the sprocket with the embossed arrow mark visible from the right.

4 Using a 17 mm spanner on the crankshaft hexagon, turn the crankshaft anti-clockwise until the "T" mark on the automatic timing unit aligns exactly with the index mark on the crankcase. These can be viewed through the hole provided in the contact breaker baseplate. When turning the crankshaft the cam chain must be held taut to prevent it 'bunching' around the crankshaft sprocket.

5 With the crankshaft set at TDC as described above, fit the sprocket into the chain loop ensuring that the arrow mark faces forward and lies parallel to the gasket face. Holding the sprocket in position, turn the camshaft until the notch in its end faces rearwards and the bolt holes are aligned. Apply a non-hardening locking compound to the sprocket bolts and install them, tightening them to 1.5 kgf/m (11.0 lbf/ft).

6 Fit the camshaft cap dowel pins, then refit the caps with the arrow marks facing forwards. Fit and tighten the retaining bolts in the sequence shown in the accompanying diagram, noting that the correct torque setting is 1.2 kgf/m (104 lbf/in). Refit and adjust the camshaft chain tensioner, referring to Section 2 of this Chapter or Section 47 of Chapter 1 for details.

7 The camshaft timing should now be checked and any adjustments made before proceding further. Turn the crankshaft anti-clockwise through two full turns and realign the arrow mark on the camshaft sprocket so that it faces forwards and lies parallel to the gasket face. Check that the "T" mark is aligned correctly. Once the timing is set correctly, check and adjust the valve clearances. Note that the tachometer drive gear must be removed from the cylinder head cover before this is fitted; damage may occur if this precaution is ignored.

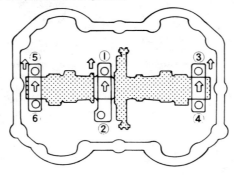

Fig. 7.1a Camshaft cap bolt tightening sequence

4 Valve clearance adjustment: all models 1978 on

1 From 1978 onwards the 400 and all 440 models were equipped with a modified arrangement for adjusting the valve clearances. The eccentric rocker shafts were omitted along with the inspection cover on each side of the cylinder head and the small inspection caps through which the clearance was measured. On the later machines, screw and locknut adjusters were fitted to the rocker arms and large inspection caps were incorporated in the cylinder head cover to give access to them.

2 The valve clearances should be checked with the engine cold, preferably after the machine has stood overnight. Remove the fuel tank to gain better access to the inspection caps. Remove all four caps and also the contact breaker/ignition pickup cover as appropriate. Using a 17 mm socket or ring spanner, turn the crankshaft anti-clockwise whilst watching the right-hand inlet valve. When the valve has opened and just closed, watch the timing plate closely. Continue turning the crankshaft slowly until the "T" mark appears in the window. Align the mark with the index mark on the crankcase. The right-hand inlet and exhaust valves can now be checked.

3 Using feeler gauges, measure the gap between the top of the valve and the adjuster screw. For both inlet and exhaust valves this should be 0.17 - 0.22 mm (0.0067 - 0.0087 in). If adjustment is necessary, slacken the locknut and turn the adjuster screw to give the required clearance. When set correctly, a 0.20 mm (0.008 in) feeler gauge should be a light sliding fit between the valve and adjuster screw. Hold the screw in position and tighten the locknut to 1.5 kgf/m (11.0 lbf/ft). Check that the clearance is still correct, then check the remaining right-hand valve in the same manner.

4 When the right-hand valves have been checked and reset, turn the crankshaft through one complete revolution and align the "T" mark once again. The left-hand inlet and exhaust valves can now be checked and adjusted as described above. When adjustment has been completed, refit the contact breaker/ignition pickup cover and fit the inspection caps, using new O-rings as required. Refit the fuel tank.

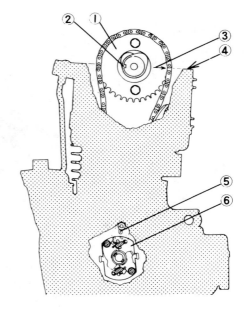

Fig. 7.1b Valve timing alignment marks

1 Camshaft sprockets	4 Cylinder head gasket face
2 Notch	5 Timing mark
3 Arrow mark	6 ATU

5 Pistons and rings: 1979 KZ400 G1

1 The piston rings, and consequently the pistons, used on the above model differ from the previous type and are thus not interchangeable. The top ring is of plain section with chamfered edges and is similar to the previous type. The second ring is of tapered section with plain edges, but does not have the rebate on its lower surface. The earlier one-piece oil ring is replaced by a three-piece arrangement composed of two plain rails with a steel expander.

2 When fitting the rings, note the 'N' marking etched on the upper face of the top and second rings. It is important that this faces upward and that the two rings are not interchanged. When assembling the oil control ring, note that the rails can be fitted either way up, but their ends must be positioned about 30° away from the joint in the expander.

6 Pistons and rings: KZ400 models

1 These are of similar design to the late (1979 on) 400 models and the remarks and descriptions in the previous Section can be applied. The only exception is the top ring of the 1981 model, some of which do not have the 'N' marking to denote the top surface. When new, these can be fitted either way up, but when a used ring is to be refitted it should be positioned the same way up as it was prior to removal. To facilitate this, mark the upper face with a spirit-based felt marker during removal.

7 Crankshaft overhaul: 1978-79 KZ400 models

1 The procedure for removing and overhauling the crankshaft assembly is broadly similar to that described in Chapter 1 of this manual, but in the case of the above models the following points should be noted.

Connecting rod and big-end bearing

2 The connecting rod assembly can vary in weight and it is important that any replacement connecting rod is of a similar weight to the component it replaces, otherwise imbalance and engine vibration will result. To this end, the machined face across the connecting rod and big-end cap is marked with an electro-etched weight coding letter. Always ensure that the new component has an identical letter code. The letter also serves to ensure that the big-end cap is fitted the right way round.

3 When fitting a new connecting rod or a replacement crankshaft it is vital that the parts are matched on a selective fit basis. To this end the connecting rod and the crankshaft are either unmarked or carry an 'O' marking. This will be found on the machined face of the connecting rod with the corresponding crankshaft mark on the flywheel face adjacent to the relevant big-end journal. The latter should be checked by measuring the journal and if necessary stamping the appropriate mark on the crankshaft.

Crankshaft big-end journal diameter and size coding

Marking	Standard	Service Limit
No mark	34.984 ~ 34.994 mm	34.97 mm
◯	34.995 ~ 35.000 mm	

Connecting rod big-end diameter and size coding

Marking	Standard
No mark	38.000 ~ 38.008 mm
◯	38.009 ~ 38.016 mm

4 If the above measurements reveal that the crankshaft is below the service limit it must be renewed. It is not possible to obtain undersize bearing shells from Kawasaki, and crankshaft grinding is therefore not feasible. Assuming the crankshaft to be within the limits specified, mark the adjacent flywheel with the O mark where necessary. If the journal measurement is below the smallest nominal diameter but above the service limit it is permissible to use the thickest bearing shell (green).

5 Having established the relevant dimensions, the new bearing shells can be selected according to the tables given below.

Big-end bearing shell selection

Crank-shaft Marking \ Con-Rod Marking	◯	No mark
◯	Black PN 13034-051	Brown PN 13034-052
No mark	Green PN 13034-050	Black PN 13034-051

Big-end bearing shell thickness

Color	Thickness
Green	1.485 ~ 1.490 mm
Black	1.480 ~ 1.485 mm
Brown	1.475 ~ 1.480 mm

6 During normal overhauls the condition of the assembly can be checked by measuring the bearing to journal clearance using Plastigage. This is a method of measuring assembled clearances by checking the amount by which a thin plastic strip becomes compressed when the components are assembled and tightened to the appropriate torque figure. With the crankshaft removed, clean the journal and bearing, then cut a piece of Plastigage to the width of the journal. Place it on the journal in line with the crankshaft axis, then reassemble the connecting rod and tighten the big-end bolts to 2.4 kgf m (17.5 lbf ft). **Do not** turn the connecting rod in relation to the journal. The big-end cap can now be removed and the clearance read off by measuring the width of the compressed Plastigage against the scale provided. The amount of spread will indicate the diametrical clearance of the bearing. Plastigage is available from most motorcycle shops in the US, and in the UK is available from World Radio, 950 North Circular Road, Cricklewood, London N.W.2.

Big-end bearing to journal clearance

Nominal clearance	*Service limit*
0.040 – 0.069 mm	0.1 mm

Unless the crankshaft has worn below its service limit, excessive clearance can be compensated for by fitting the appropriate bearing shell.

7 If the engine is being rebuilt as the result of a major component failure, such as seizure or a dropped or bent valve, it is advisable to have the connecting rods checked for straightness and twisting. This is done by fitting plain arbors to the big-end and small-end of the rod, and measuring at points 50 mm each side of the centre line of the connecting rod. Most owners will not have the necessary facilities and should entrust the work to a Kawasaki service agent who will be able to make the necessary checks quickly and inexpensively. The necessary limits are given below.

Connecting rod bend and twist limits

Nominal	*Service limit*
Bend less than 0.10 mm	0.2 mm
Twist less than 0.15 mm	0.2 mm

Crankshaft main bearings

8 These are checked in much the same way as described for the big-end bearings. The clearances are measured by inserting a strip of Plastigage between each journal and bearing and then securing the main bearing cap bolts to 4.0 kgf m (29.0 lbf ft) for the 10 mm bolts and to 2.5 kgf m (18.0 lbf ft) in the case of the 8 mm bolts. Check the clearance against the following nominal and service limit figures.

Main bearing clearance

Nominal	Service limit
0.034 – 0.076 mm	0.11 mm

If the clearance proves to be excessive, measure the diameter of the journals with a micrometer. It will be necessary to renew the crankshaft if it is worn below the service limit, otherwise new bearing shells should succeed in restoring it to an acceptable clearance figure.

Main bearing journal diameter

Nominal	Service limit
35.984 – 36.000 mm	35.96 mm

9 The assembled crankshaft should be checked for end float using feeler gauges. The measurement is made between the crankshaft and the centre main bearing cap as shown in Fig. 7.2. It should be noted that the crankcase halves and main bearing cap are supplied as a matched set, and must be renewed as such if end float proves to be excessive.

Crankshaft end float

Nominal	Service limit
0.20 – 0.30 mm	0.45 mm

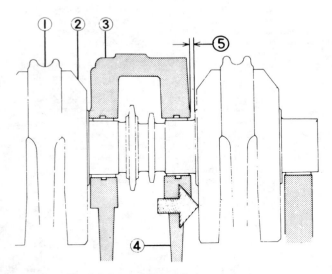

Fig. 7.2 Crankshaft end float measurement

1 Connecting rod	4 Crankcase
2 Crankshaft	5 End float
3 Main bearing cap	

8 Crankshaft overhaul: 1980-81 KZ400 models

1 For a detailed description of overhaul and examination procedures refer to Section 5 which covers the 1978-79 models. There are a number of dimensional and part changes, and these are shown below. See also Fig. 7.3 for details of size marking locations.

Big-end bearing shell selection table

Con-Rod Marking / Crankshaft Marking	O	No mark
O	Black P/N: 13034 –1026	Brown P/N: 13034 –1027
No mark	Green P/N: 13034 –1025	Black P/N: 13034 –1026

Note also that the size of the big-end cap bolts was increased from 7 mm to 8 mm, with a corresponding increase in the torque setting to 3.7 kgf m (27 lbf ft).

Main bearing shell selection table

Color	Thickness
Brown	1.490~1.494 mm
Black	1.494~1.498 mm
Blue	1.498~1.502 mm

Big-end bearing shell thickness

Crankcase Marking / Crankshaft Marking	O	No mark
1	Brown P/N: 13034 –1021	Black P/N: 13034 –1020
No mark	Black P/N: 13034 –1020	Blue P/N: 13034 –1019

Crankshaft main bearing/journal clearance

Service Limit	0.08 mm

Crankshaft main journal diameter

Marking	Standard	Service Limit
1	35.992~36.000 mm	35.96 mm
No mark	35.984~35.992 mm	

Crankshaft main bearing bore diameter.

Marking	Standard
O	39.000~39.008 mm
No mark	39.009~39.016 mm

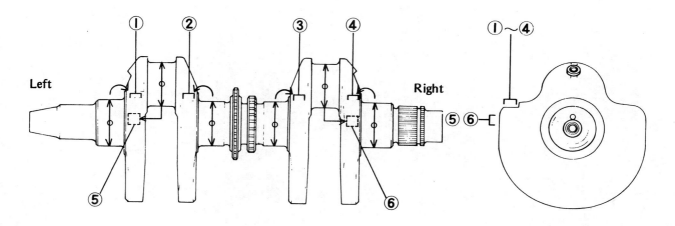

Fig. 7.3 Crankshaft size marking locations — 400 1980 — 81 models

1   '1' or no mark for no. 1 main journal size
2   '1' or no mark for no. 2 main journal size
3   '1' or no mark for no. 3 main journal size

4   '1' or no mark for no. 4 main journal size
5   '0' or no mark for left-hand big-end journal size
6   '0' or no mark for right-hand big-end journal size

9   Crankshaft overhaul: 1980-81 KZ440 models

1   The crankshaft overhaul procedure is the same as that described for the 1978-79 KZ400 models in Section 5, except where detailed below. The various tables relating to bearing shell selection and identification marks are also the same as those given in the above section unless different versions are shown here.

Big-end bearing shell selection

Crankshaft Marking \ Con-Rod Marking	O	No mark
O	Black P/N: 92028-1098	Brown P/N: 92028-1099
No mark	Blue P/N: 92028-1097	Black P/N: 92028-1098

Big-end bearing shell thickness

Color	Thickness
Blue	1.485 ~ 1.490 mm
Black	1.480 ~ 1.485 mm
Brown	1.475 ~ 1.480 mm

Crankshaft main bearing shell/journal clearance

Service Limit	0.08 mm

Crankshaft main bearing journal diameter

Marking	Standard	Service Limit
1	35.992 ~ 36.000 mm	35.96 mm
No Mark	35.984 ~ 35.992 mm	

Main bearing shell selection table

Crankshaft Marking \ Crankcase Marking	O	No mark
1	Brown P/N: 13034-1102	Black P/N: 13034-1101
No mark	Black P/N: 13034-1101	Blue P/N: 13034-1100

10 Gearbox assembly: modifications and overhaul

1   Models from the 1978 KZ400 B1 onward featured a 6-speed gearbox, the only exception being the C1 economy model of the same year, which retained the 5-speed arrangement. The gear assemblies are essentially similar, those of the 6-speed version having been slimmed down to allow the insertion of a double 3rd/4th gear pinion on each shaft, in place of the 3rd gear pinions of the earlier unit. The removal, overhaul and reassembly of each type is largely the same as described in Chapter 1 for the earlier 5-speed 400s. The following remarks can also be applied to all models from the KZ400 B1 onwards, including the 440 cc models.
2   The accompanying sectioned illustrations show the layout of the 5-speed and 6-speed gearboxes and provide a means of comparison. When removing the individual gears from either type, refer to the appropriate line drawing (Fig. 7.6 or Fig. 7.7) for details of washer and circlip location. The numbers quoted in the dismantling sequence refer to the above illustrations.

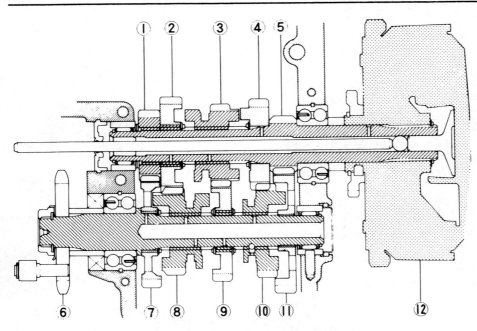

1 Mainshaft 2nd gear pinion
2 Mainshaft 5th gear pinion
3 Mainshaft 3rd gear pinion
4 Mainshaft 4th gear pinion
5 Mainshaft 1st gear pinion
6 Final drive sprocket
7 Layshaft 2nd gear pinion
8 Layshaft 5th gear pinion
9 Layshaft 3rd gear pinion
10 Layshaft 4th gear pinion
11 Layshaft 1st gear pinion
12 Clutch

Fig. 7.4 Sectioned view of five speed gearbox

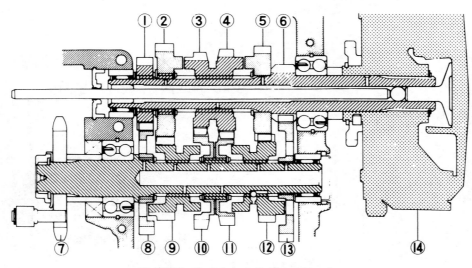

1 Mainshaft 2nd gear pinion
2 Mainshaft 6th gear pinion
3 Mainshaft 3rd gear pinion
4 Mainshaft 4th gear pinion
5 Mainshaft 5th gear pinion
6 Mainshaft 1st gear pinion
7 Final drive sprocket
8 Layshaft 2nd gear pinion
9 Layshaft 6th gear pinion
10 Layshaft 3rd gear pinion
11 Layshaft 4th gear pinion
12 Layshaft 5th gear pinion
13 Layshaft 1st gear pinion
14 Clutch

Fig. 7.5 Sectioned view of six speed gearbox

11 6-speed gearbox: dismantling and reassembly

1 Access to the gearbox shafts can be gained after the engine unit has been removed and the crankcase halves separated. Each shaft should be dismantled separately to avoid confusion or the interchanging of parts between shafts, and the work should be carried out in clinically clean conditions. Numbers shown in brackets refer to Fig. 7.7.

Mainshaft (drive shaft) assembly
2 Slide off the outer race of the needle roller bearing (3). Release the circlip (1), then remove the needle roller bearing (4), washers (5) and second gear pinion (6). Remove the second circlip (7) and splined washer (8). The 6th gear pinion (9) can now be slid off together with its bush (10) and splined washer (11).
3 Release the circlip (12) and remove the combined 3rd/4th gear pinion (13). Remove the circlip (14) and plain washer (15)

to free the 5th gear pinion (16). Dismantling is now complete apart from the removal of the clutch-side bearing (18). This is a press fit on the shaft and will require the use of a bearing extractor to remove and refit it. The extractor is unlikely to be required very frequently, and so it is probably easier to entrust this job to a motorcycle workshop than to purchase the tool required.
4 The gearbox components should be cleaned and checked for wear or damage as described in Section 34 of Chapter 1. Reassembly is a reversal of the dismantling sequence. The clutch-side ball bearing can be fitted with the aid of a press or can be tapped into place using a suitable tubular drift. Check that all circlips are secure and that the ends are positioned clear of the raised portion of the splines and away from the locating tangs of the washer(s).
5 Note that the mainshaft has lubrication holes which should coincide with similar holes in the 3rd/4th gear pinion and in the bush of the 6th gear. The assembled shaft can be installed as described in Chapter 1.

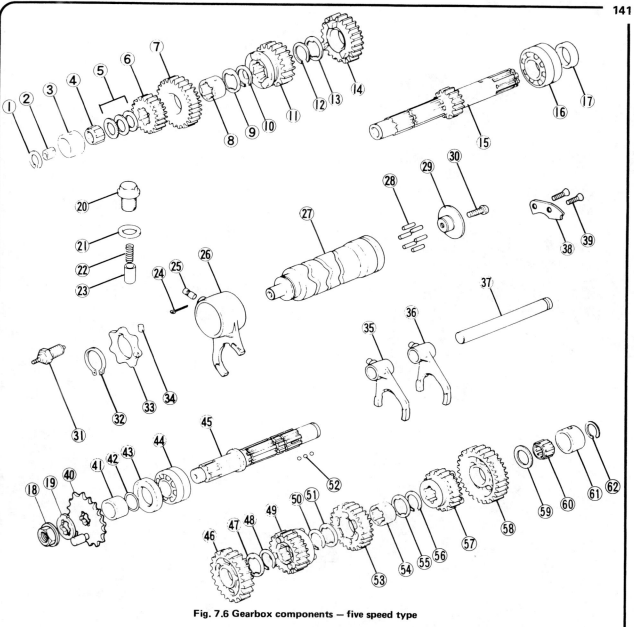

Fig. 7.6 Gearbox components — five speed type

1 Circlip	22 Spring	43 Oil seal
2 Bush	23 Detent plunger	44 Layshaft left-hand bearing
3 Needle roller bearing outer race	24 Split pin	45 Layshaft
4 Needle roller bearing	25 Locating pin	46 Layshaft 2nd gear pinion
5 Washers	26 3rd gear selector fork	47 Splined washer
6 Mainshaft 2nd gear pinion	27 Selector drum	48 Circlip
7 Mainshaft 5th gear pinion	28 Change pin — 6 off	49 Layshaft 5th gear pinion
8 Bush	29 Pin retaining plate	50 Circlip
9 Splined washer	30 Screw	51 Splined washer
10 Circlip	31 Neutral indicator switch	52 Neutral finder balls
11 Mainshaft 3rd gear pinion	32 Circlip	53 Layshaft 3rd gear pinion
12 Circlip	33 Quadrant	54 Bush
13 Splined washer	34 Locating pin	55 Splined washer
14 Mainshaft 4th gear pinion	35 5th gear selector fork	56 Circlip
15 Mainshaft	36 4th gear selector fork	57 Layshaft 5th gear pinion
16 Clutch — side bearing	37 Selector fork shaft	58 Layshaft 1st gear pinion
17 Collar	38 Drum guide plate	59 Washer
18 Nut	39 Screw — 2 off	60 Needle roller bearing
19 Tab washer	40 Final drive sprocket	61 Needle roller bearing outer race
20 Bolt	41 Spacer	62 Circlip
21 Washer	42 O-ring	

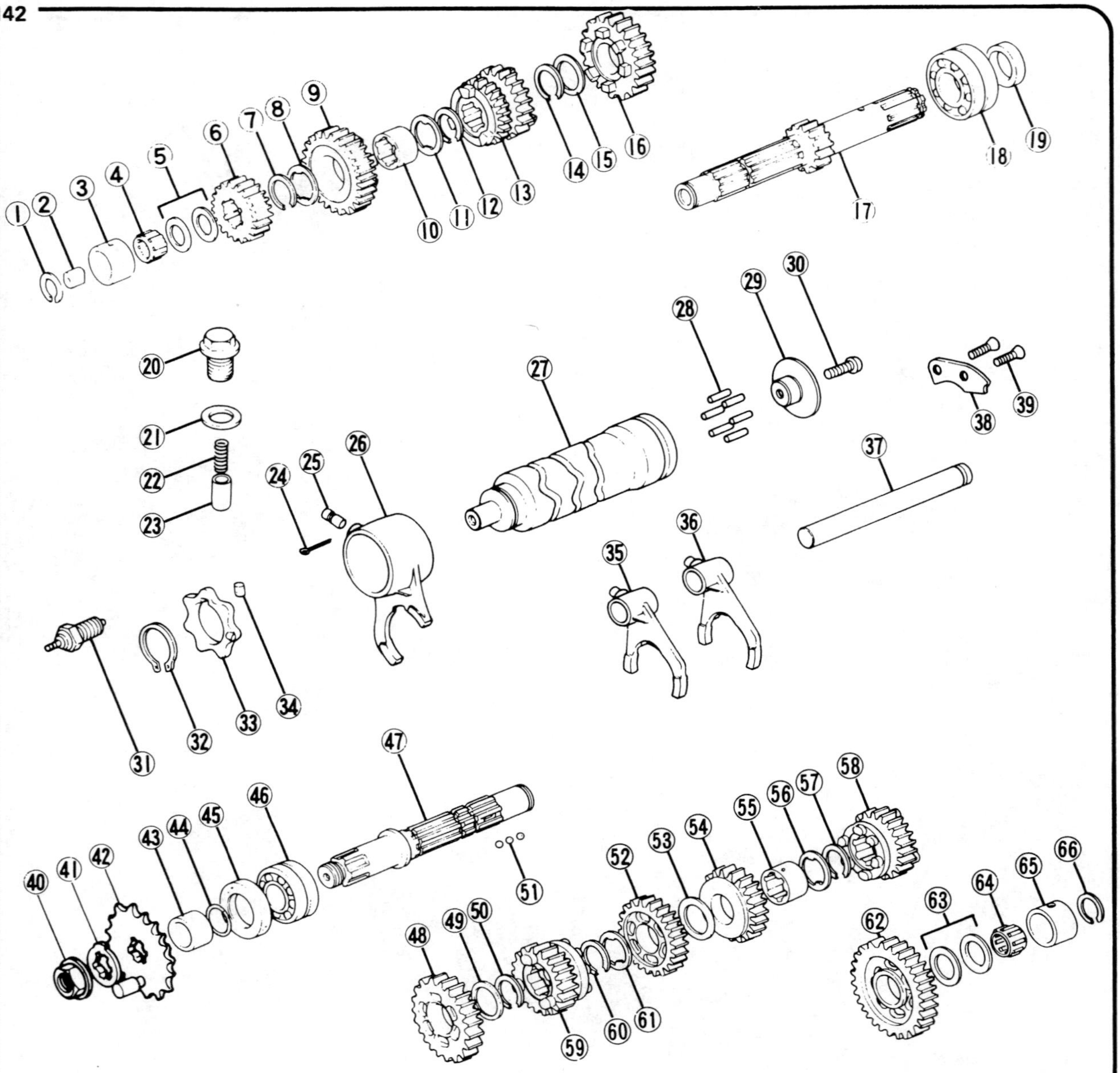

Fig. 7.7 Gearbox components — six speed type

1	Circlip	23	Detent plunger	45	Oil seal
2	Bush	24	Split pin	46	Layshaft left-hand bearing
3	Needle roller bearing outer race	25	Locating pin	47	Layshaft
4	Needle roller bearing	26	3rd and 4th gear selector fork	48	Layshaft 2nd gear pinion
5	Washers	27	Selector drum	49	Washer
6	Mainshaft 2nd gear pinion	28	Change pin — 6 off	50	Circlip
7	Circlip	29	Pin retaining plate	51	Neutral finder balls
8	Splined washer	30	Screw	52	Layshaft 3rd gear pinion
9	Mainshaft 6th gear pinion	31	Neutral indicator switch	53	Washer
10	Bush	32	Circlip	54	Layshaft 4th gear pinion
11	Splined washer	33	Quadrant	55	Bush
12	Circlip	34	Locating pin	56	Splined washer
13	Mainshaft 3rd and 4th gear pinion	35	6th gear selector fork	57	Circlip
14	Circlip	36	5th gear selector fork	58	Layshaft 5th gear pinion
15	Washer	37	Selector fork shaft	59	Layshaft 6th gear pinion
16	Mainshaft 5th gear pinion	38	Drum guide plate	60	Circlip
17	Mainshaft	39	Screw — 2 off	61	Splined washer
18	Clutch — side bearing	40	Nut	62	Layshaft 1st gear pinion
19	Collar	41	Tab washer	63	Washers
20	Bolt	42	Final drive sprocket	64	Needle roller bearing
21	Washer	43	Spacer	65	Needle roller bearing outer race
22	Spring	44	O-ring	66	Circlip

Layshaft (output shaft) assembly

6 Remove the needle roller bearing outer race (65), remove the circlip (66), bearing (64) and washer(s) (63). The 1st gear pinion (62) can now be removed. Hold the shaft vertically by the 3rd gear pinion (52) and spin the shaft so that the neutral finder balls are flung clear of their groove. This will release the 5th gear pinion (58) which can now be slid off. Take care not to lose the three steel balls (51). The remaining circlips washers and gears can be removed in sequence. The left hand bearing (46) can be removed with a bearing extractor, if necessary.

7 Reassemble by reversing the dismantling sequence noting that the 6th gear pinion and 3rd/4th gear pinion each have oil holes. Both gears are splined onto the layshaft and it is essential that the oil holes align with those of the shaft. Failure to observe the above can lead to lubrication failure in service, with catastrophic results.

8 Note that all circlips should be renewed as a precaution. It is essential that they locate firmly, and a clip which has been removed will have stretched and thus will be a loose fit. It is a false economy to re-use the old clips, given the amount of dismantling work involved in rectifying the damage that would result from a clip becoming displaced in service. To avoid stretching the new circlips open them **just** enough to fit over the shaft, and slide them into position using a length of tubing. If the factory transmission circlip driver (part number 57001-380) is available instead, so much the better, but a suitable length of tubing will do the job just as well. Note Fig. 7.8 which shows the correct positioning of circlips and splined washers in relation to each other and the shaft.

9 When fitting the layshaft 5th gear pinion to six-speed models (4th gear pinion on five-speed machines) do not omit to fit the three steel balls which form the neutral locator mechanism. These must be free to move and on no account should they be greased.

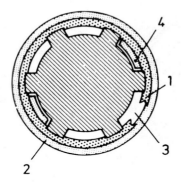

Fig. 7.8 Correct position of circlips and splined washers in relation to gearbox shafts reassembly

1 *Circlip*   3 *Shaft groove*
2 *Splined washer*   4 *Tooth of splined washer*

---

12 Neutral locator: operating principle

---

1 The later 400 cc models and all 440 cc machines feature a simple mechanical system which facilitates the selection of neutral when the machine is stationary. The output shaft (layshaft) carries a machined groove which corresponds with the centre of the 5th gear pinion (6-speed gearbox) or 4th gear pinion (5-speed gearbox) when the gearbox is in neutral. A corresponding channel around the bore of the pinion carries three steel balls.

2 When the machine is stationary and the output shaft is not turning one or more of the balls will drop down under gravity forming a limiter on the amount of side travel available. The grooves are arranged so that 1st gear may be selected with ease, but any attempt to shift past neutral into 2nd will be prevented by the ball. This ensures that when the gearchange pedal is lifted out of first neutral is always selected.

3 When the machine moves off and the output shaft begins to rotate, the balls are thrown outwards by centrifugal force and will remain inside the groove in the pinion until the machine is stationary again. In this position they do not impede the selection of 2nd or the remaining gears.

4 The neutral locator is simple in construction and operation, and does not require any specific attention. The only likely problem is that the balls may tend to stick in very old engines, or in those in which regular oil changes have been neglected and have allowed sludge to build up on the internal surfaces. Access to the steel balls and the location grooves will require separation of the crankcase halves and dismantling of the output shaft (layshaft) cluster. It follows that the mechanism should be cleaned and checked whenever the gearbox is overhauled.

---

13 Gear selector mechanism: modifications

---

1 An improved version of the gear selector mechanism is fitted to the later 400 cc models and all 440 cc machines. It was found on the earlier versions that there could be a tendency to 'overselect' when rapid gearchanges were executed. This was caused by the inertia of the selector drum overcoming the limiting effect of the detent plunger assembly, so that the drum rotated past the next gear position. Although this was not a common difficulty with the 5-speed gearbox, the greater precision demanded by the 6-speed cluster required positive control of overselection and a modified selector claw was introduced on all models.

2 The new claw arrangement features an 'overshift limiter'. This device is in effect a second claw running from a common pivot on the selector shaft quadrant and engaging the selection pins on the top edge of the selector drum. The accompanying illustration (Fig. 7.9) describes its operation.

3 If gear selection problems are experienced with the new mechanism, check the following points, having removed the clutch to gain access to the relevant parts. Examine the selector claw and the overshift limiter for signs of wear or damage. Wear in the former, if severe, could mean that the drum is not rotated fully into the next gear position, whilst in the case of the limiter, serious wear could permit overshifting. The small tension spring (pawl spring) which connects the two should be measured and renewed if it has stretched beyond the service limit. Its length can be checked by placing it over the internal jaws of a vernier caliper which should then be opened until it takes up any free play but not placing the spring under tension.

Pawl spring free length   18.0 mm (0.709 in)
Service limit   19.0 mm (0.748 in)

4 The detent plunger spring should also be checked for free length. Any noticeable compression will indicate loss of pressure which will allow the gearbox to jump out of gear in use. If gear selection problems have been evident it may be worth renewing both springs as a precautionary measure, even if they are within the prescribed service limits.

Detent spring free length 32.3 mm (1.272 in)
Service limit   31.0 mm (1.220 in)

Note that the detent plunger assembly should be locked in position using one of the proprietary thread locking compounds such as Loctite or Torqueseal. If the assembly loosens in service, selection problems are inevitable.

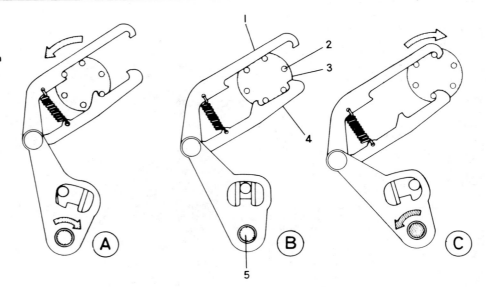

Fig. 7.9 Modified selector claw with overshift limiter

1 *Overshift limiter*
2 *Selector pin*
3 *Selector drum*
4 *Selector claw*
5 *Gearchange shaft*

In A a lower gear is being selected. The selector claw pushes on the adjacent pin, turning the drum to select the next lowest gear. The overshift limiter catches the opposing pin at the correct point, preventing the drum from rotating past the gear position and into a false neutral. B shows the selector claw and the overshift limiter in their rest positions, the selected gear being held by the detent plunger. In C an upward gearchange is being made.

14 Layshaft (output shaft) 2nd gear bush: 1980 models

1 The bush which carries the layshaft (output shaft) second gear has been modified on the above models. Instead of being pressed onto the shaft the bush is now a sliding fit. This does not materially affect dismantling or overhaul, but it is important that the bush is fitted correctly if it has been removed. It will be noted that the bush has an oil drilling and an internal groove on one side, and this must be fitted towards the locating shoulder so that it matches the oilway in the layshaft. If this precaution is not observed the lubrication supply to the bush will be blocked and will probably result in seizure.

15 Caburettors: general information

1 The 1977 KZ400 D4 and S3 models featured diaphragm CD carburettors in place of the previous piston type CD instruments. All subsequent models have employed various carburettors of the diaphragm type, there being some modifications regarding jet sizes and settings over the years. The principle of operation is essentially the same as the earlier type, except for the diaphragm arrangement. In the case of the piston type, the throttle valve formed part of the larger diameter piston which was housed in a close fitting chamber. The area above the piston was connected by a passage to the engine side of the carburettor. When a high depression exists around this port opening this is transmitted to the upper part of the chamber. This allows atmospheric pressure to open the valve until pressure is equalised, the resulting piston position being dependent on the engine requirements. The diaphragm types operate in much the same way, but the adoption of the diaphragm means that the instrument can be made considerably less bulky.

16 Carburettors: dismantling and reassembly

Dismantling
1 Carburettor removal is a fairly straightforward operation which will require the removal of the fuel tank, side panels and tool tray to provide access. The bolts which secure the upper brackets of the air cleaner assembly should be removed, thus allowing the assembly to be pushed back to clear the carburettors. Slacken the worm-drive clips which retain the instruments to the air cleaner stubs and the intake adaptors. Pull the air cleaner casing back to disengage the rubber stubs from the rear of the carburettors. The instruments can now be manoeuvred clear of the engine and withdrawn from the right-hand side. Slacken the throttle cable adjuster(s) and free the cable(s) from the pulley.

2 Unless attention to the connecting linkage is required the carburettors can be left attached to the mounting brackets. Always dismantle, overhaul and rebuild one instrument at a time to preclude any chance of parts being interchanged between the two carburettors. Remove the four float bowl retaining screws and lift the bowl away taking care not to damage the O-ring which seals it.

3 Using a screwdriver, remove the secondary main jet which screws into the projecting needle jet holder, followed by the hexagon-headed needle jet holder and the needle jet. From the adjacent projection, remove the primary main jet and the main jet bleed pipe which is retained by it. The pilot jet can be removed after the rubber blanking plug which covers it has been pulled off. The float assembly and valve needle can be released by displacing the float pivot pin with a short length of stiff wire. Lift the float away, then remove the float needle for safe keeping. Note that in cases where the needle jet proves reluctant to emerge from its bore it may prove necessary to remove the diaphragm and vacuum piston assembly. The needle jet can then be removed with the aid of a thin screwdriver or rod.

4 The diaphragm cover is secured by four screws. The cover will lift away once these have been removed, but take care during removal to ensure that the diaphragm is not damaged. It will be noted that the edge of the diaghragm incorporates a small locating lip which must engage in the corresponding recess during assembly. Carefully peel the edge of the diaghragm away from the carburettor top, then remove it together with the vacuum piston and jet needle. If necessary, the jet needle can be freed by releasing the circlip which retains it and its holder in the base of the vacuum piston.

Reassembly
5 When refitting the vacuum piston/diaphragm assembly it is best to ensure that the needle jet and holder are firmly in position

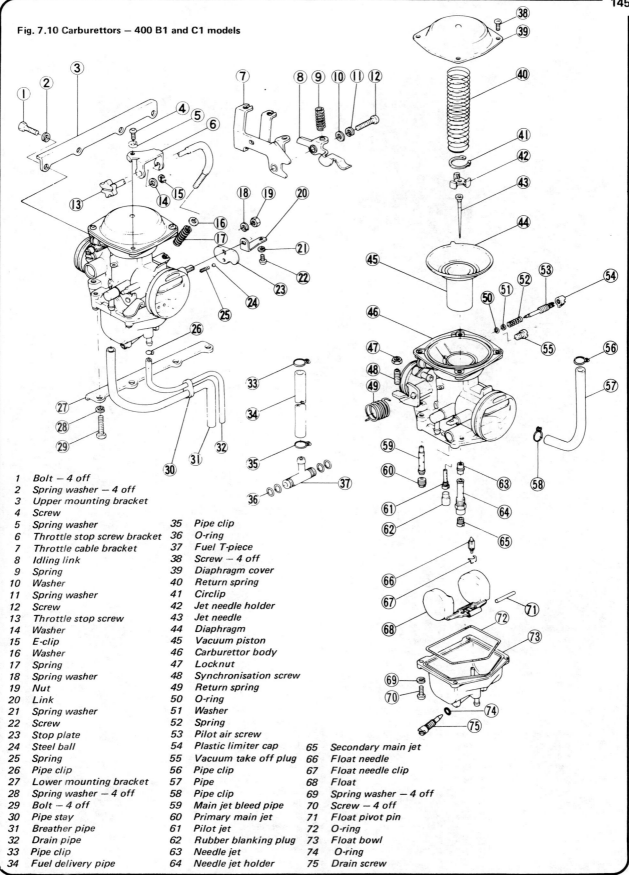

Fig. 7.10 Carburettors — 400 B1 and C1 models

1	Bolt — 4 off		
2	Spring washer — 4 off		
3	Upper mounting bracket		
4	Screw		
5	Spring washer	35	Pipe clip
6	Throttle stop screw bracket	36	O-ring
7	Throttle cable bracket	37	Fuel T-piece
8	Idling link	38	Screw — 4 off
9	Spring	39	Diaphragm cover
10	Washer	40	Return spring
11	Spring washer	41	Circlip
12	Screw	42	Jet needle holder
13	Throttle stop screw	43	Jet needle
14	Washer	44	Diaphragm
15	E-clip	45	Vacuum piston
16	Washer	46	Carburettor body
17	Spring	47	Locknut
18	Spring washer	48	Synchronisation screw
19	Nut	49	Return spring
20	Link	50	O-ring
21	Spring washer	51	Washer
22	Screw	52	Spring
23	Stop plate	53	Pilot air screw
24	Steel ball	54	Plastic limiter cap	65	Secondary main jet
25	Spring	55	Vacuum take off plug	66	Float needle
26	Pipe clip	56	Pipe clip	67	Float needle clip
27	Lower mounting bracket	57	Pipe	68	Float
28	Spring washer — 4 off	58	Pipe clip	69	Spring washer — 4 off
29	Bolt — 4 off	59	Main jet bleed pipe	70	Screw — 4 off
30	Pipe stay	60	Primary main jet	71	Float pivot pin
31	Breather pipe	61	Pilot jet	72	O-ring
32	Drain pipe	62	Rubber blanking plug	73	Float bowl
33	Pipe clip	63	Needle jet	74	O-ring
34	Fuel delivery pipe	64	Needle jet holder	75	Drain screw

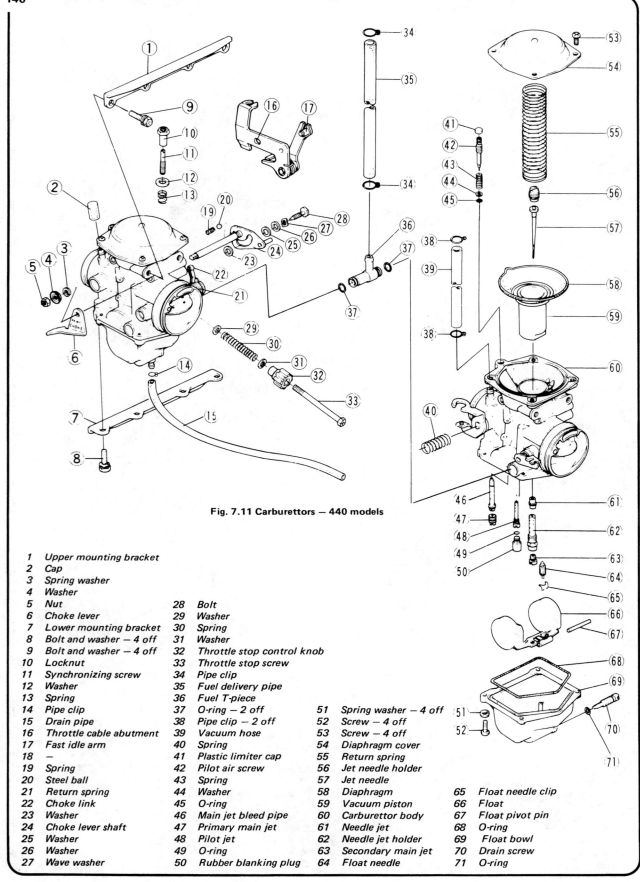

Fig. 7.11 Carburettors – 440 models

1	Upper mounting bracket		
2	Cap		
3	Spring washer		
4	Washer		
5	Nut	28	Bolt
6	Choke lever	29	Washer
7	Lower mounting bracket	30	Spring
8	Bolt and washer – 4 off	31	Washer
9	Bolt and washer – 4 off	32	Throttle stop control knob
10	Locknut	33	Throttle stop screw
11	Synchronizing screw	34	Pipe clip
12	Washer	35	Fuel delivery pipe
13	Spring	36	Fuel T-piece
14	Pipe clip	37	O-ring – 2 off
15	Drain pipe	38	Pipe clip – 2 off
16	Throttle cable abutment	39	Vacuum hose
17	Fast idle arm	40	Spring
18	–	41	Plastic limiter cap
19	Spring	42	Pilot air screw
20	Steel ball	43	Spring
21	Return spring	44	Washer
22	Choke link	45	O-ring
23	Washer	46	Main jet bleed pipe
24	Choke lever shaft	47	Primary main jet
25	Washer	48	Pilot jet
26	Washer	49	O-ring
27	Wave washer	50	Rubber blanking plug

51	Spring washer – 4 off	65	Float needle clip
52	Screw – 4 off	66	Float
53	Screw – 4 off	67	Float pivot pin
54	Diaphragm cover	68	O-ring
55	Return spring	69	Float bowl
56	Jet needle holder	70	Drain screw
57	Jet needle	71	O-ring
58	Diaphragm		
59	Vacuum piston		
60	Carburettor body		
61	Needle jet		
62	Needle jet holder		
63	Secondary main jet		
64	Float needle		

first. Lower the piston into its bore and check that it moves freely. Arrange the diaphragm so that the locating lip is engaged in its cutout, then press the diaphragm edge evenly into its recess. Place the return spring in the centre of the piston, and use a finger via the main bore of the carburettor to lift the it in this position, offer up the diaphragm cover and press it firmly down on the edge of the diaphragm. Release the piston and fit the retaining screws, holding the cover firmly until they are secure. This procedure will obviate any risk of the diaphragm becoming creased and thus allowing air leaks to develop.

6 Fit the various jets, taking care not to overtighten them. The jets and the carburettor body are rather soft and are easily damaged. Refit the float assembly ensuring that the float needle is located properly on the float tang. Check that the O-ring which seals the float bowl is undamaged and that the pilot jet plug is in place, then refit and secure the float bowl.

Separating the carburettors

7 It will only be necessary to separate the two instruments on rare occasions when specific attention to the throttle and choke linkages or to the fuel T-piece is required. Start by removing the single screw which retains the choke link. The screws which secure the instruments to the upper and lower mounting brackets should now be released and the brackets lifted away. As the carburettors are pulled apart the fuel T-piece and the throttle linkage spring will be freed. If it is wished to dismantle the throttle cable bracket assembly, refer to the accompanying line drawing for details of the relative position of the component parts.

8 The carburettors can be joined by reversing the separation sequence. Note that the fuel T-piece should be fitted to the left-hand carburettor, and ensure that the throttle linkage spring is correctly positioned so that it engages the throttle link and the pulley. Once assembled it will be necessary to check and adjust the carburettor synchronisation as described in Section 18.

17 Carburettors: examination and renovation

1 The procedure for checking the carburettor components for wear is essentially similar to that described in Chapter 2, Section 6, with the obvious exception of the diaphragm assembly. This must be in perfect condition if the carburettor is to function correctly, and any cracks or splits in the diaphragm will necessitate its renewal. In practice the diaphragm should last for a long time without giving rise to problems, but should renewal become necessary it should be noted that the diaphragm and vacuum piston can only be purchased as an assembly. It is not considered practical to repair a damaged diaphragm, because any attempt at patching will reduce its elasticity. A new assembly is the only solution.

18 Carburettors: synchronisation

1 It is important that the carburettors are set up so that each one provides exactly the same amount of air and fuel to each cylinder. If the instruments are out of synchronisation one cylinder will be working harder than the other and this will produce poor fuel consumption, roughness and impaired performance.

2 If the carburettors have been removed and overhauled initial synchronisation should be carried out prior to refitting them to the engine. The object is to set the synchronising screw which is incorporated in the throttle butterfly linkage so that both butterfly valves move in synchronisation at all throttle settings. To accomplish this look down into the main bore of the carburettors and adjust the synchronising screw so that each butterfly valve is open by the same amount. Now open the throttle and view the throttle butterflies edge on. If correctly adjusted they should lie parallel. The carburettors can now

be refitted, but do not secure the synchronising screw locknut at this stage.

3 Accurate synchronisation requires fine adjustment of the synchronising screw with the engine running. To this end a pair of vacuum gauges of the dial or mercury manometer type will be required, together with the necessary adaptors which can be obtained from a Kawasaki Service Agent. During this operation the engine must be run with the fuel tank removed, so a length of fuel pipe will be required to arrange a temporary fuel supply.

4 Remove the fuel tank and place it near to the machine and above carburettor height. Connect the temporary fuel pipe extension to the carburettors and fuel tap. Remove the vacuum take-off plugs which are fitted to the engine side of each instrument, immediately below the pilot screws. Note that on later models the vacuum take-off takes the form of a built in stub which is normally covered by a small synthetic rubber cap. On these models no adaptor is required, the vacuum gauge pipes should push straight onto the take-off stubs. Where necessary the adaptors should be screwed into place, then fit the vacuum gauge pipes. The free end of the vacuum hose to the fuel tap should be plugged during this operation, and the tap should be set to the 'PRI' position.

5 Set the vacuum gauge damper valves to the fully closed position and start the engine, which should be allowed to reach normal working temperature before adjustment begins. Let the engine idle and open the damper valves until needle flutter (or column movement) reaches but does not exceed 3 cm Hg. At normal idle speed the gauges should show a reading of about 21 — 27 cm Hg although this is not vitally important. What is essential is that the two readings are within 3 cm Hg of each other, and where necessary the synchronising screw should be set to obtain readings within this limit. Kawasaki dealers can supply a special tool to make adjustment easier, but this can be improvised using a box spanner or a suitable socket and extension. Whichever method is chosen, re-check the synchronisation after the adjuster locknut has been secured.

6 Where a vacuum gauge set is not available, it is possible to set the carburettor synchronisation by feeling the exhaust pressure from each cylinder. It should be stressed that this method is far from accurate, but it will suffice in an emergency until the check can be made properly. Start the engine and let it idle, then place one hand about an inch from the end of each silencer. If the carburettors are out of synchronisation, the exhaust pulses from one cylinder will feel much stronger and more regular than the other, which will tend to fire spasmodically and may backfire slightly. Adjust the screw until even exhaust pulses can be felt on both cylinders. When synchronisation is complete check the idle mixture and speed settings as described in Chapter 2, Section 7.

19 Throttle cable adjustment

The throttle control on most models consists of a twist-grip control operating via an opening cable and a closing cable and assisted by a light return spring. On certain 440 models, however, a single cable arrangement may be found. The adjustment procedure for each is given below.

Twin cable models

1 With this arrangement it is important to set the cables to give the specified amount of free play, otherwise erratic throttle response will make the machine unpleasant and rather difficult to ride, particularly at low speeds in the lower gears. Start by checking the free play by turning the twistgrip from its rest position until the free play in the opening cable is **just** taken up. If a reference mark is made on the edge of the flanged end of the twistgrip rubber, 2 — 3 mm free play should be obtained.

2 To check the closing cable setting, turn the throttle twistgrip hard against its stop whilst observing the cable anchor bracket at the carburettor end. This should be pushed downwards by 1 — 2 mm if the cable is adjusted correctly.

3 If adjustment is necessary to either cable, it should be noted that an adjuster is fitted to both ends of each one. It is preferable to start by setting the adjusters at the twistgrip end to the fully closed position, and then to make any necessary alterations via the carburettor-mounted adjusters. Note that the front adjuster (at the carburettor and at the twistgrip) controls the opening cable, and the rear adjusters the closing cable.

Single cable models

4 In the case of machines fitted with a single throttle cable the throttle butterfly is opened by the cable and closed by a return spring. Check that when the twistgrip is operated there is 2 – 3 mm free movement at the twistgrip rubber flange. As with the twin cable models, two adjusters are provided. Again, it is best to screw the handlebar end adjuster fully home and set the initial clearance at the carburettor end. Subsequent adjustment can then be made at the more accessible upper adjuster.

20 Carburettors: checking the fuel level

All models up to 1978

1 Variations in the level of the fuel contained in the float bowl will have a marked effect on the overall mixture strength at various engine speeds. If the carburettors have been dismantled and overhauled, or if flooding, poor fuel consumption or generally erratic running have been noted, the fuel level should be checked.

2 Obtain either the official Kawasaki fuel level gauge or improvise one using a length of fuel pipe with a plastic or glass tube fitted at one end. It will be necessary to contrive some method of connecting the hose to the drain plug hole. The correct tool uses a banjo union, but for the home-made alternative a suitable screw can be modified to act as an adaptor. Obtain a long screw of the same size as the drain plug, then carefully drill a small hole along its length. Cut off the screw head and saw a screwdriver slot in the end. The resulting threaded tubular sleeve can

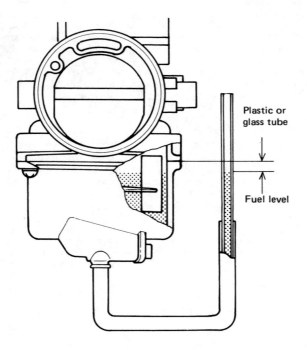

Fig. 7.12 Fuel level measurement

now be fitted into the drain screw orifice and the pipe connected to it.

3 In the case of the later 400 and all 440 models, a modified drain screw arrangement is employed, and this makes the above procedure unnecessary. With this type of instrument the drain screw is slackened to allow the fuel in the float bowl to discharge through a drain hose. To check the fuel level it is necessary only to attach a suitable length of clear plastic or glass tubing to the end of the drain hose.

4 Hold the pipe in a U-shape so that the clear section is against the side of the float bowl. Turn on the fuel supply, using the priming position in the case of vacuum fuel taps, and note the height of the fuel in relation to the float bowl gasket face.

Fuel level below gasket face

1977 UZ400 D4 and S3	2.0—4.0 mm	(0.08—0.16 in)
All KZ400 models 1978—81	1.5—3.5 mm	(0.06—0.14 in)
All KZ440 models 1980—81	1.5—3.5 mm	(0.06—0.14 in)

If the fuel level is found to be outside the range given adjustment should be made to the float height by bending the float needle actuating tang on the floats.

21 Carburettors: idle speed and pilot screw adjustment

1 Before any adjustment is undertaken it should be noted that care must be taken to avoid infringement of any local laws relating to unburnt hydrocarbon emissions. In the US in particular it may be illegal to alter any of the carburettor settings where these have been made 'tamper-proof'. Most of the later 400 models are equipped with plastic limiter caps on the pilot screw heads. These allow very limited movement of the screws. The US versions of the KZ440 have pilot screws which are pre-set during assembly and are then covered by small blanking plugs. Whilst the removal of these devices to permit adjustment presents no great problem, the owner must first ascertain whether local laws will permit this action.

Limiter cap removal

2 The plastic limiter caps fitted to the later KZ400 models and non-US KZ440s allow less than one turn of the pilot screw. Whilst this is usually adequate for fine adjustment of the pilot mixture it may prove necessary to remove the caps for full adjustment after the carburettors have been overhauled. The caps are pushed onto the splined heads of the pilot screws and may be dislodged using a small screwdriver. After adjustment is complete, fit the caps with the tang in the midway position to facilitate subsequent fine adjustment to be made.

'Tamper-proof' pilot screws — US KZ440 models

3 As mentioned, the pilot screws on these models are set at the factory and are then sealed by pressing a small blanking plug into the recess above the pilot screw head. The plug can be removed by using a punch or a similar pointed tool to distort the plug sufficiently to allow it to be prised out. A less barbaric method would be to use a very small drill to provide a pilot hole in the plug. A self-tapping screw or a small eze-out can then be screwed into the plug and used to pull it out of its recess. When adjustment has been made, a new plug should be tapped squarely into the recess, using a suitable semi-hardening bonding agent to seal it.

4 Pilot screw location on the KZ440 carburettors is immediately adjacent to the vacuum chamber cover, the screw passing vertically down into the body. On all other models the screw is horizontal, passing into the engine side of the main bore, next to the vacuum take-off plug. If the screws have been removed or disturbed, they should be set at the following nominal settings before work commences. In each case, the figure quoted

is in turns out; that is, the screw is turned inwards until it seats lightly (**do not over-tighten**) and then unscrewed by the prescribed number of turns and part turns.

Pilot screw nominal settings/idle speed

1977		
KZ400 D4, S3	1½ ± 3/8	1000 − 1200 rpm
1978		
KZ400 B1	1¼ ± ½	1000 − 1200 rpm
KZ400 C1	1¼ ± ½	*
1979		
KZ400 B2, G1	1¼ ± ½	1000 − 1200 rpm
KZ400 C2	1¼ ± ½	*
1980		
KZ400 B3, G2	1¼ ± ½	1000 − 1200 rpm
KZ440 A1, B1, C1, D1	1¾	1100 − 1300 rpm
1981		
KZ400 B4, G3, H1, H3	2¼	1000 − 1200 rpm
KZ440 A2, B2, C2, D2	1¾	1100 − 1300 rpm

* Adjust to lowest regular idle speed

Note that in the case of US models equipped with the plugged pilot screws, no nominal setting is available, but as a rough guide set the screws about 1¾ turns out if they have been disturbed and the original settings not noted.

5 Start the engine and allow it to reach its normal operating temperature, preferably by riding the machine for a few miles. Using the large knurled throttle stop control set the idle speed at the prescribed setting. On machines with no tachometer the idle speed should be set to the lowest reliable tick-over rate. The pilot screws should now be unscrewed by an equal amount in ¼ turn stages until the engine runs at the lowest idle speed possible without becoming hesitant or misfiring. Open and close the throttle a few times and check that the engine settles at a reliable tick-over. Check the idle speed, and if necessary reset it using the throttle stop control.

6 A more accurate method of setting the pilot mixture strength involves the use of a device known as the Colortune 500. This is basically a special test plug which temporarily replaces the standard spark plug. It has a heat-resistant glass core in place of the usual ceramic insulator, through which the combustion flame can be observed. By following the manufacturer's instructions the mixture strength can be set with great accuracy irrespective of the nominal pilot screw settings. The Colortune 500 is widely available from accessory shops in the UK and US.

7 If it proves impossible to obtain satisfactory idle performance it should be noted that many other factors contribute to regular running at all speeds. It is essential that the carburettors are correctly synchronised and that the ignition timing, valve clearances and general engine condition are within limits. Also note that worn or damaged carburettors preclude accurate adjustment.

22 Cleaning the air filter element: all models 1977 − 80

1 A modified air filter arrangement will be found on the later 400 cc models and on the 440 cc machines up to 1980. To gain access to the element unlock and lift the dualseat and then release the tool tray by unscrewing its single retaining screw. The tool tray doubles as the air filter housing lid, and the element can be removed once the lid has been lifted away.
2 The element can be cleaned in the same way as described for the earlier type, using compressed air to dislodge accumulated dust. Alternatively a non greasy solvent can be used to clean either type. Kerosene (paraffin) should be avoided since it will leave an oily residue that will quickly clog the element, and low flash-point solvents such as petrol (gasoline) are best avoided in view of the fire risk. If available, a high flash-point solvent

such as trichloroethane should be used in well ventilated conditions. Wash the element thoroughly then allow it to dry naturally or blow it dry from the inside using compressed air. Note that the efficiency of the element is reduced each time it is cleaned, and it should always be renewed after five cleanings as a matter of course. Also, if the element is found to be damaged or contaminated with oil it should be renewed.

23 Cleaning the air filter element: 1981 models

1 The above models employ a filter element which takes the form of a foam band mounted on a metal supporting frame. The element can be removed for cleaning by lifting the dualseat and removing the air filter housing lid, the latter being retained by two screws. Lift the filter out of the housing and remove the foam band by unhooking it from the small tangs at each end. Clean the foam by washing it in a high flash-point solvent such as paraffin (kerosene) then squeeze out any residual solvent and allow it to dry. The foam should now be soaked in clean engine oil. Wrap it in a clean rag and squeeze out any excess oil before fitting it to the support frame.

24 Vacuum fuel tap: examination and renovation

1 Various types of vacuum operated fuel taps have been fitted to the later 400 cc models and to all 440 cc machines. The types differ only in obvious detail, such as the location of the vacuum pipe stub and whether or not a drain screw is fitted. The variations do not affect the operation of the tap or the way in which it is overhauled.
2 The tap has three positions, these being on, reserve and prime. The settings are marked on the tap as 'On', 'Res' and 'Pri' respectively. In the first two positions the tap will allow fuel to flow to the carburettors only when the engine is running. A diaphragm and plunger contained in the tap are connected to the inlet manifold. When the engine is running the resulting depression acts on the diaphragm, opening the plunger and allowing fuel to flow through the tap. As soon as the engine stops the diaphragm moves back to the closed position and shuts off the supply, thus the tap lever may be left in the 'On' or 'Res' positions with no risk of flooding. The 'Pri' position allows fuel to flow through the tap with the engine off. As the marking suggests, this allows the carburettors to be primed when the machine has run out of fuel, and also facilitates draining of the fuel tank.
3 If it proves necessary to remove the fuel tap it will first be necessary to drain the tank. This can be done via the small drain plug in the underside of the tap where one is fitted, or alternatively by placing the petrol pipe in a suitable drain can. The tap should be set at the 'Pri' position to drain it. Some residual fuel will remain in the tank, so it is best to remove the tank from the machine and to place it on its side on some soft rag so that the fuel runs away from the tap area. The tank is secured by rubber mountings at the front and by a rubber strap or a single fixing bolt at the rear.
4 Remove the two bolts which secure the fuel tap flange to the underside of the tank. The tap can now be removed, taking care not to damage the O-ring or the filter gauze. Overhaul of the tap is similar to that described for the manual type in Section 3 of Chapter 2 with the obvious exception of the diaphragm assembly. This can be removed after the four cover retaining screws have been released. Lift away the cover and remove the return spring. Lift one corner of the diaphragm and carefully work around it until it is free from the tap body, then lift the assembly away. The diaphragm assembly should be checked for signs of cracks or holes and renewed if found to be defective. Reassemble by reversing the dismantling order taking care that the diaphragm

is perfectly flat when the cover is refitted. Do not use any jointing compound on the tap components, but do renew any O-rings which appear flattened or damaged.

25 Electronic ignition system: KZ400 G3 and H3, KZ440 all 1981 models

All 1981 models except the KZ400 B4 utilise an electronic ignition system in place of the contact breaker system fitted to the previous models. This has the advantage of having no mechanical wearing parts, and thus regular checking and cleaning of contact breaker points is eliminated. The heart of the system is the pick-up assembly which consists of a permanent magnet coil mounted on a baseplate, and a rotor or reluctor which is mounted on the end of the crankshaft. As the reluctor rotates, a small peak passes close to the pick-up coil and in doing so induces a small current in its windings. This pulse provides a trigger input for the ignition amplifier or IC (integrated circuit) ignitor.

The pick-up has the added advantage of providing a far more stable and accurate high tension pulse. As the peak of the reluctor approaches the pick-up coil the induced voltage rises to the point where it triggers a Darlington power transistor in the IC ignitor, supplying a low tension feed to the primary windings of the ignition coil. After further rotation the voltage peak in the pick-up coil dies abruptly, cutting off the low tension supply. This in turn induces a high tension pulse in the ignition coil

secondary windings and produces a spark at the plug electrodes. The angle of crankshaft rotation during which the low tension supply is on is known as the dwell angle.

Unlike contact breaker systems where the dwell angle is constant, that of the electronic system increases as engine speed rises, because the point at which the power transistor is triggered becomes more advanced. The increased dwell angle allows longer for the electro-magnetic field to build in the ignition coil primary windings. The induced pulse in the secondary windings is consequently stronger and more accurate.

26 Electronic ignition system: fault diagnosis

1 Most faults in the electronic ignition system can be traced to bad connections, or less frequently, failure of the IC ignitor, coil or pick-up assembly. It should be noted that once set there is no reason for the system to go out of adjustment, so the incidence of ignition faults will be low. Do not forget that the ignition and kill switches can contribute to ignition malfunctions and should be included in any checks on wiring connections.
2 Reference should be made to Fig. 7.14. This is a flow chart which outlines the sequence of fault diagnosis, the various tests being described below. Note that each test is numbered in the flow chart, the description of the procedure carrying the appropriate test number.

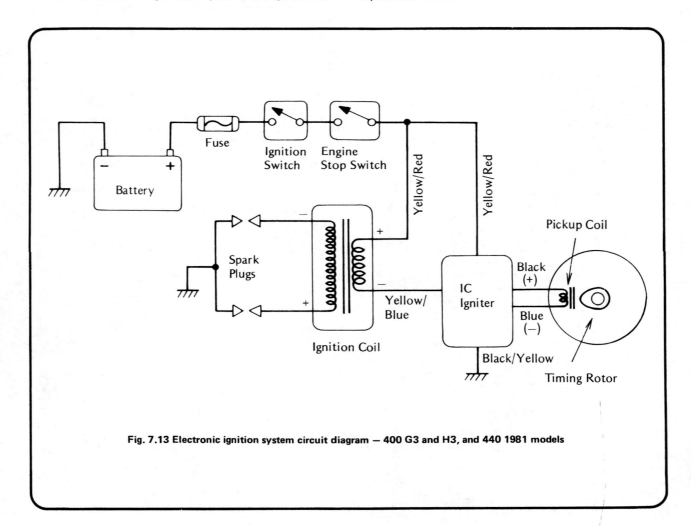

Fig. 7.13 Electronic ignition system circuit diagram — 400 G3 and H3, and 440 1981 models

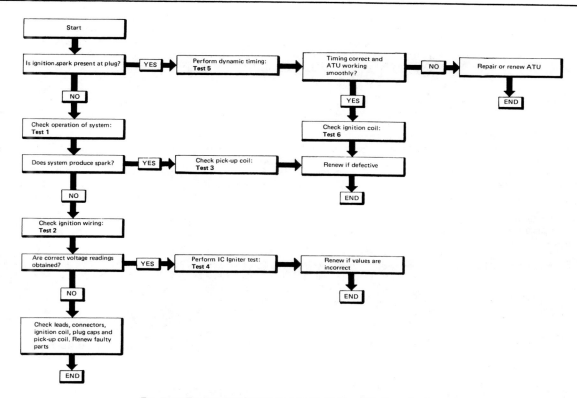

Fig. 7.14 Electronic ignition system fault diagnosis flow chart

27 Electronic ignition system: testing

Test 1 Checking the ignition system operation

1   This test requires the use of a separate 6 or 12 volt motorcycle battery in addition to that fitted to the machine. Kawasaki recommend the use of an electrotester to provide a pre-set 7 mm electrode gap. In view of the fact that this device will probably not be available it is recommended that a similar piece of equipment be fabricated using an insulated stand of wood, and four electrodes of stiff wire or fashioned from nails. The opposing ends of the electrodes, across which the spark will jump, should be sharpened, and the outer ends of the two electrodes to which the HT voltage is to be applied should be ground down so that the sparking plug caps are a push fit. The accompanying figure shows the general arrangement.

2   Remove the fuel tank, then trace and separate the two-pin connector between the IC ignitor and the pick-up coil leads. The second battery must be connected to the IC ignitor as shown in Fig. 7.16. Note that the blue lead is connected to the battery negative (−) terminal and the black lead to the positive (+) terminal. The switch shown in the circuit is not vital; in practice the test circuit can be made and broken by joining and separating the black lead to the battery positive terminal.

3   Connect the test apparatus so that the plug caps are connected to one side of the electrodes, and connect the other side of the electrodes to a good earth point on the engine. Check that the electrode gaps do not exceed 7 mm. If intermittent earthing occurs or if the spark gap is too great to allow the spark to jump (in normal operation) damage to the electronic ignition may result. Turn the ignition switch on.

4   The test is conducted by applying voltage from the second battery to the IC ignitor for a few seconds, then disconnecting the supply. This energises the low tension windings in the ignition coil, and a spark should be produced at both plugs when the supply is disconnected. If no spark occurs, investigate the system wiring as in **test 2**. If the plugs spark properly, the fault must lie in the pick-up coil, which can be checked as described in **test 3**. **Important note:** do not connect the second battery for more than 30 seconds, otherwise the ignition coil and ignitior may overheat and be damaged.

Test 2 Checking the ignition system wiring

5   With the fuel tank removed for access and with all ignition system connections made, carry out the following tests using a multimeter on the appropriate volts dc ranges. In each test the negative (−) meter probe is connected to earth (ground). The ignition switch must be on but the engine should not be started. The positive (+) meter probe connections can be made by inserting the probe from the back of the connector.

Wiring connection tests

Meter Range	Connections*	Reading
25V DC	Meter (+) → Yellow/Red or Yellow/Blue	Battery voltage
10V DC	Meter (+) → Black	0.5 ~ 1.0 V
	Meter (+) → Blue	0.8 ~ 3.0 V

* : Connect the meter (−) lead to ground.

6 If the readings obtained do not agree with the above, check the ignition system wiring connections, the ignition coil, high tension leads and plug caps and the pick-up coil. Renew any defective parts. If the readings obtained agree with the table, the fault probably lies in the IC ignitor unit, see test 4.

Test 3 Checking the ignition pick-up coil

7 Remove the fuel tank and separate the two-pin connector between the pick-up coil and the ignitor unit. Set the multimeter to the ohms x 100 scale, and connect one probe lead to the black pick-up lead, and the remaining probe lead to the blue pick-up lead. At room temperature (with the engine cold) a reading of 360 − 540 ohms should be indicated. If a fault exists it is likely that a very high reading (open circuit) or very low reading (short circuit) will be indicated. If faulty, the pick-up coil should be renewed; it is not possible to repair it.

Test 4 Checking the IC ignitor

8 Trace and disconnect the 2-pin and 3-pin connectors from the IC ignitor. The resistance checks are made with the unit isolated from the rest of the system. It should be noted that the readings shown in the table below are those which should be obtained using a Kawasaki Tester (multimeter), part number 57001-983. The manufacturer points out that there may be some variation when using other multimeters, but despite this a reasonable indication of the unit's condition should be obtained.

IC ignitor resistance tests

Meter Range	Connections		Reading*
x 100 Ω	Meter (+) → Yellow/Red Meter (−) → Black/Yellow		0.3~1.2 kΩ
	Meter (+) → Black/Yellow Meter (−) → Yellow/Red		1~3 kΩ
	Meter (+) → Yellow/Blue Meter (−) → Black/Yellow		200~700 Ω
x 1 kΩ	Meter (+) → Black/Yellow Meter (−) → Yellow/Blue		∞
	Meter (+) → Blue Meter (−) → Black		30~130 kΩ
	Meter (+) → Black Meter (−) → Blue		20~70 kΩ

28 Ignition timing: checking

1 This test requires the use of a stroboscopic timing lamp (strobe), preferably of the battery or mains powered xenon tube type. The cheaper neon tube versions may be used but give a less distinct image. The strobe is connected to the ignition system in accordance with the manufacturer's instructions. Note that where a battery powered xenon tube lamp is used it is better to use a separate battery than to connect it to the battery on the machine. This avoids the risk of spurious pulses in the electrical system triggering the lamp. The test is best performed outside in the shade or in a darkened but well ventilated garage, and it may prove helpful to highlight the fixed index mark and the timing marks with white paint.

2 Start the engine and allow it to idle. The strobe should be aimed at the timing marks, where it will make them appear to 'freeze' at the point at which the plugs spark. If the ignition is set correctly, the 'F' mark will be aligned with the fixed index mark. Next raise the engine speed to 4000 rpm, noting that this can be approximated on machines not fitted with a tachometer. Alternatively, if a Gunson Tachostrobe is available, the built-in rpm indicator can be used to obtain the specified engine speed. Note that as the engine speed rises the timing marks will appear to move as the automatic timing unit operates. At the fully advanced position the fixed mark should coincide with two parallel lines on the ATU backplate, these indicating that the unit has moved to its fullest extent. Check that the ATU advances smoothly and progressively.

3 If there appear to be timing problems it will be necessary to dismantle and overhaul the timing unit (ATU), relubricating it where it is not badly worn. Accurate timing will be unobtainable where the unit is badly worn, and excessive play will necessitate renewal. There is no provision for adjustment of the timing, this being considered unnecessary under normal circumstances.

29 Ignition coil: testing

1 The coil can best be tested by an auto-electrical specialist or by a Kawasaki Service Agent, using an electro tester to check the arcing distance. A sound coil should produce a reliable spark up to a distance of 7 mm (0.28 in). Failing this, check the primary and secondary winding resistances using a multimeter.

2 Remove the fuel tank to gain access to the coil, then disconnect the yellow/blue and the yellow/red low tension leads from the coil terminals. Set the multimeter on the ohms x 1 scale and measure the primary winding resistance by placing a probe on each of the exposed low tension terminals. A coil in good condition should indicate a resistance of 1.8 − 2.8 ohms. Check for internal shorting by placing one probe on a sound earth (ground) point and the other to each terminal in turn with the meter set on kilo ohms (ohms x 1000). Anything other than infinite resistance indicates that the primary windings have shorted and that the coil must be renewed.

3 Leave the meter set on the kilo ohms position and measure the secondary winding resistance by placing a probe lead on each of the high tension connections in the plug caps. A reading of 10.4 − 15.6 kilo ohms should be obtained. If the coil does not conform to the above tests, try renewing the plug caps. Failing this, have the coil checked on an electro tester and renew it as required.

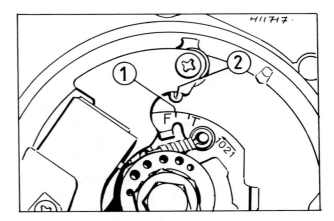

Fig. 7.15 Ignition timing alignment mark on ATU

1 'F' mark on ATU
2 Index mark on casing

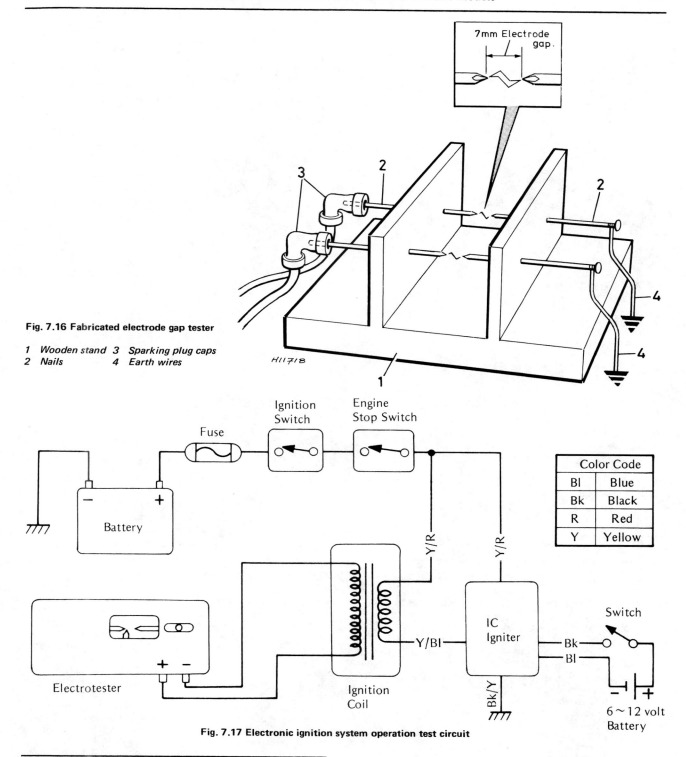

Fig. 7.16 Fabricated electrode gap tester

1 Wooden stand   3 Sparking plug caps
2 Nails   4 Earth wires

Color Code	
Bl	Blue
Bk	Black
R	Red
Y	Yellow

Fig. 7.17 Electronic ignition system operation test circuit

30 Needle roller swinging arm bearings: maintenance

1 All models from 1978 onwards featured needle roller bearings in place of the plain bushes fitted to the earlier models. These will give very good service if they are kept well lubricated, but in the event that the rollers become dry they will soon seize up and wear. To prevent their untimely demise they should be lubricated at regular intervals — every 6000 miles (10 000 km) or yearly, whichever comes sooner. To do this properly the swinging arm should be removed from the machine (see Chapter 4, Section 9) and the bearings degreased and examined for wear or corrosion. If in good condition, pack each bearing with grease and reassemble. Any good quality grease will suffice if lubrication is done on a regular basis, or one of the water repellent types can be used to prevent water finding its way into the bearings. When the time comes for renewal, the procedure is largely the same as that described for the bushed type.

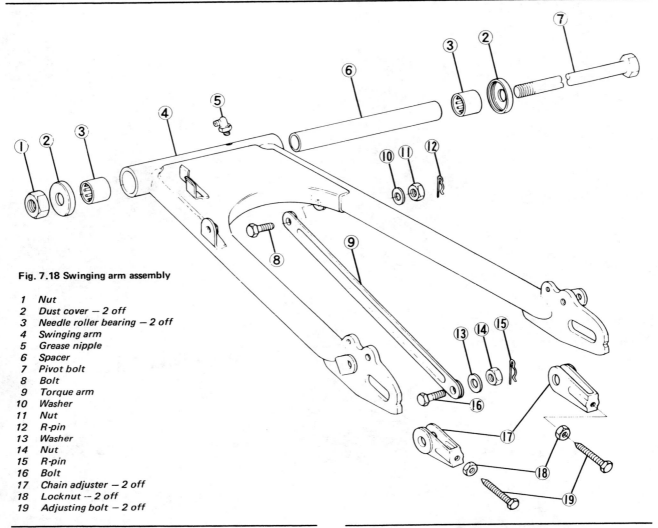

Fig. 7.18 Swinging arm assembly

1   Nut
2   Dust cover — 2 off
3   Needle roller bearing — 2 off
4   Swinging arm
5   Grease nipple
6   Spacer
7   Pivot bolt
8   Bolt
9   Torque arm
10 Washer
11 Nut
12 R-pin
13 Washer
14 Nut
15 R-pin
16 Bolt
17 Chain adjuster — 2 off
18 Locknut — 2 off
19 Adjusting bolt — 2 off

31 Front disc brake: modifications to the caliper unit

1   All disc brake machines up to 1977 employed a single-piston caliper containing one fixed pad and one moving pad. To facilitate compensation for pad wear, the caliper was mounted on the fork leg by means of a support bracket to which it was retained by two pins. The caliper body was allowed to slide in relation to the support bracket and was thus self-aligning in relation to the disc. This caliper is covered in Chapter 5 of this manual.

2   In 1978, a modified single-piston caliper was introduced on the KZ400 B1 and also appeared on the 1979 KZ400 B2. Essentially similar in principle, the caliper did not slide on pins as in the earlier type, but was arranged to pivot on a circular section of the support bracket. It is covered in this Chapter and is referred to as the 1978 type.

3   1979 saw the introduction of yet another type of single-piston caliper, this time a sliding body type carried by a large, flat mounting bracket. This caliper is covered in this Chapter and is referred to as the 1979 type. It was subsequently adopted on all other 400 and 440 models except those mentioned below.

4   The 1981 KZ440 C2, featured another type of sliding single-piston caliper in which a more complex mounting bracket was arranged to carry the disc pads. It is covered in this Chapter and is described as the 1981 type. At the time of writing, no other models had incorporated this variation, although it is likely that it will be adopted throughout the range during the next year or two.

32 Front disc brake caliper: general description — 1978 type

1   The KZ400 B1 and B2 models featured a new front brake caliper in which the single piston caliper body is supported on and located by a fork mounted pivot. This takes the form of a bracket with a round section bar projecting rearwards and down from the fork leg, just above the edge of the disc. The main caliper body is retained to this mounting by a circlip and a lock washer, with grease seals at each end. When the brake lever is operated, the caliper body is pushed into the correct position by the single piston, this movement bringing both pads into contact with the disc surface. The major difference between this arrangement and the previous type is that the caliper body pivots rather than slides into alignment with the disc.

2   Throughout the sections related to caliper assembly reference is made to the use of PBC (Poly Butyl Cuprysil) grease, which Kawasaki recommends for assembly lubrication. If this grease is not available, any specially formulated extreme-temperature, water-resistant brake assembly grease may be used.

33 Front disc brake: pad renewal — 1978 type

1   Slacken and remove the two caliper mounting bolts, noting the plain and locking washer fitted beneath the head of each one. Lift the caliper assembly clear of the fork leg and brake disc. It is not necessary to disconnect the hydraulic hose, but

do not allow the caliper to hang from it. A temporary wire hook can be employed to avoid straining the hose.

2 Working from the caliper opening, the fixed pad (pad B) can be pushed inwards and lifted away. The moving pad (pad A) can now be displaced into the space left, and can be removed in a similar manner. The shims can now be slid off the pad backing plate to release the anti-rattle springs.

3 The design of the caliper is such that pad wear will be very uneven, the thinner fixed pad (B) showing the most noticeable wear. Wear will be evident by the angled face of both pads which is a result of the caliper's pivoting action. A small notch in pad B is positioned at the point of most pronounced wear, and when the friction material has worn to the bottom of the notch, **both** pads will require renewal. On no account should the pads be renewed singly. Although the moving pad A will appear relatively unworn, it will have bedded into an angle which matches its companion, and thus will not align properly if pad B alone is renewed.

4 Before fitting new pads the caliper should be cleaned to remove all traces of road dirt, and more importantly any grease or oil. If the assembly has been contaminated it is vital that the source of the problem is located and remedied to avoid ruining a new set of pads. The best method of removing grease or oil is to use an aerosol degreasing fluid, such as Ultraclene which can usually be obtained from electrical suppliers as contact cleaner. Any trichlorethylene-based cleaning solvent is suitable for this purpose. Small oil spots on otherwise sound pads may be removed in this fashion, but severe contamination can only be remedied by renewing the pads.

5 When fitting new pads, ensure that the anti-rattle springs and shims are fitted correctly. Refer to Fig. 7.19 for details of pad, shim and spring positions. Each of the shims has a base groove which is noticeably larger than the other, and it is to this that the anti-rattle spring must be fitted. Assemble the pads, springs and shims as follows. Identify pad A, noting that it is the thicker of the two, and does not have the notched edge which indicates

pad wear. It will be noted that the pad has one long edge, and the similar long edge on the shim, and the anti-rattle spring must be fitted to it. The correct shim for pad A is asymmetrical about its vertical axis. Fit the spring in its larger groove and slide the shim onto the pad backing plate.

6 Pad B can be easily identified by its wear notch and it is always noticeably thinner than its companion. Its shim is symmetrical and is roughly H-shaped. It and the pad have longer edges at one end, and these should match and contain the anti-rattle spring when assembled.

7 Before the new pads can be installed it will be necessary to push the piston back into the caliper as far as possible to obtain sufficient clearance. Fit a length of tubing to the caliper bleed nipple and place the open end in a jar. Slacken the bleed nipple, then push the piston inwards. As it moves into the caliper bore fluid will be expelled from the bleed valve and into the jar. Tighten the bleed nipple to prevent air being drawn back into the system, then remove the tube and jar. Take great care not to allow hydraulic fluid to come into contact with any plastic or painted parts of the machine.

8 Fit pad A to the piston side of the caliper, ensuring that the shim tangs engage correctly. Pad B can now be slid into its recess, and the caliper fitted over the disc. Insert the mounting bolts ensuring that the plain and spring washers are in place. Tighten the caliper mounting bolts to 4.0 kgf m (29 lbf ft) using a torque wrench.

9 It is a sound precaution to bleed the hydraulic system in case any air entered the caliper when the bleed nipple was opened. Details of this operation will be found in Chapter 5, Section 3. Before the machine is ridden it is essential to operate the brake lever a few times until the pads and piston assume their normal operating position. This may lower the fluid level in the reservoir, which should be topped up as required using *only* new hydraulic fluid having an SAE J1703 or DOT 3 rating. No other fluid or oil should be used under any circumstance.

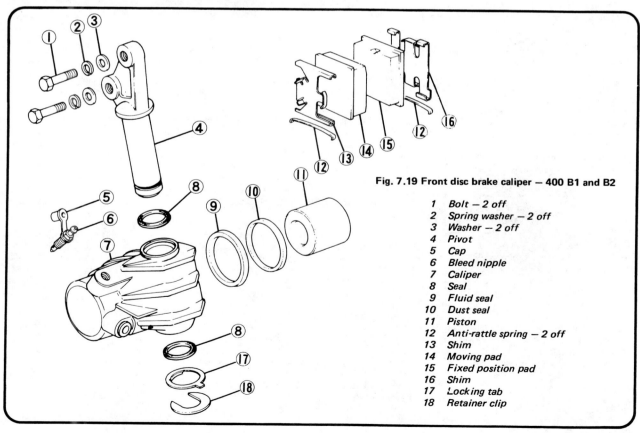

Fig. 7.19 Front disc brake caliper — 400 B1 and B2

1   Bolt — 2 off
2   Spring washer — 2 off
3   Washer — 2 off
4   Pivot
5   Cap
6   Bleed nipple
7   Caliper
8   Seal
9   Fluid seal
10 Dust seal
11 Piston
12 Anti-rattle spring — 2 off
13 Shim
14 Moving pad
15 Fixed position pad
16 Shim
17 Locking tab
18 Retainer clip

34 Front disc brake caliper overhaul — 1978 type

1 Commence dismantling by releasing the caliper assembly from the fork leg and removing the pads as described in Section 31. Unless compressed air is available it will be necessary to use the hydraulic system to displace the piston from the caliper. Wrap the caliper in rag to catch any jets of fluid as the piston emerges, and take care not to hold the caliper in such a way that fingers could be trapped by the piston. Gently squeeze the brake lever repeatedly until a sudden lack of resistance indicates that the piston has emerged. Remove the rag and hold the caliper over a drain tray, then pump the lever until the fluid in the system has been expelled. Wipe off any residual fluid to avoid it coming into contact with the paintwork.

2 Remove the banjo bolt from the caliper and free the hydraulic hose and union. The banjo bolt and sealing washers can be refitted to prevent their loss. To complete dismantling, remove the piston then carefully prise the dust seal and piston seal from their grooves in the caliper body. Take care not to score the caliper bore during this operation.

3 Straighten the locking tab at the lower end of the caliper pivot shaft and remove the C-shaped retainer and tab washer. The pivot shaft/bracket unit can now be removed from the caliper body and the seals displaced. If necessary, the bleed nipple can be unscrewed for inspection.

4 It is essential that the caliper components are kept clinically clean at all times. Every trace of road dirt should be removed, particularly from the caliper bore which must be absolutely free from any sort of contamination. Use only hydraulic fluid, ethyl alcohol or isopropyl alcohol for cleaning purposes. On no account should any other solvent or cleaning agent be used because it will attack and damage the seals, even when present in minute quantities. Oil, petrol (gasoline) or any related product will rapidly destroy new seals.

5 The seals should be renewed as a matter of course whenever the caliper is dismantled. Once disturbed any minor scratch in the seal surface will be inclined to allow leakage. Another important factor is that the piston seal acts as a return spring medium, pulling the piston and pads clear of the disc surface when the brake lever is released. As the seal ages and becomes less elastic there may be a tendency for the brake to drag.

6 The caliper bore and the piston must be clean and entirely free from corrosion or scoring. The piston surface is the more important of the two in this respect, and even small score marks will cause leakage problems. Very light corrosion on the *outside* of the piston seal groove in the bore may be removed with fine abrasive paper, but damage in any other area will necessitate renewal of the affected parts. If facilities are available, measure the caliper bore diameter and the piston diameter.

	Nominal	Service limit
Caliper bore diameter	41.30 — 41.35 mm	41.6 mm
	(1.6260 — 1.6279 in)	(1.6378 in)
Piston diameter	41.17 — 41.22 mm	40.9 mm
	(1.6209 — 1.6228 in)	(1.6102 in)

7 Examine the caliper pivot bore and the support bracket shank upon which it is mounted. The two parts should move freely but without undue free play. Excessive wear in this area can lead to judder when the brake is operated, and if severe, will necessitate renewal of the caliper or the bracket or both. A seal is fitted at each end of the pivot bore. These prevent road dirt from entering the bore, and provide a friction medium to damp any side to side chatter which might otherwise cause problems. These friction seals should be renewed whenever the caliper is overhauled or if judder is apparent.

8 Reassembly is carried out by reversing the dismantling sequence, noting the following points. Check that all internal parts are absolutely clean, then lubricate the piston, seals and bore with brake fluid. Fit the piston seal and dust seal into their respective grooves in the body, then fit the piston, taking great care not to damage the seal faces. Assemble the caliper bracket using new friction seals and coat the sliding surfaces with grease. Kawasaki recommends the use of PBC (Poly Butyl Cuprysil) grease. Assemble the bracket and fit the lock washer and retainer, bending up the locking tab to retain the assembly. If all is well the caliper should move smoothly but stiffly with no discernible free play. Refit the caliper and fit the pads. It will be necessary to fill and bleed the hydraulic system as described in section 45. Note the following torque wrench settings.

Caliper torque wrench settings.

	kgf m	lbf ft
Caliper mounting bolts	4.0	29.0
Brake hose banjo bolt	3.0	22.0
Bleed valve	0.8	69 lbf in

35 Front disc brake: master cylinder overhaul — 1978 type

1 The master cylinder fitted to the above model differs in detail only from the earlier type. The screw cap on the fluid reservoir is replaced by a flat lid with four retaining screws as an anti-tamper measure. Internally, the only significant difference is that the circlip which retained the piston assembly on the earlier version has been replaced by a moulded plastic liner which is clipped into position by two locating lugs. To dismantle the assembly depress the lugs with a small electrical screwdriver, then withdraw the liner. For overhaul details refer to Fig. 7.20 and Section 5 of Chapter 5.

36 Front disc brake: examining the disc and hoses — 1978 type —

1 The brake disc should be checked for wear or damage as described in Chapter 5, Section 4, noting that the warpage and thickness limits are as follows:

Disc warpage
Nominal	Less than 0.15 mm (0.0059 in)
Service limit	0.3 mm (0.0118 in)

Disc thickness
Nominal	6.9 — 7.1 mm (0.272 — 0.280 in)
Service limit	6.0 mm (0.236 in)

Check the hoses, pipes and fitting for signs of wear, cracking or corrosion, and renew any that look dubious or have shown signs of leaking.

37 Front disc brake: torque settings — 1978 type

The following torque settings should be observed when overhauling the disc brake components. The manufacturer recommends that those items marked with an asterisk should be re-torqued at 6000 mile/10 000 km intervals. To do this slacken off the nut or bolt about ½ a turn and then torque to the correct value.

	kgf m	lbf ft	lbf in
Bleed valve	0.80	—	69.0
Brake lever pivot	0.60	—	52.0
* Caliper mounting bolts	4.00	29.0	—
Disc mounting bolts	4.00	29.0	—
Banjo union bolts	3.00	22.0	—
Front brake lamp switch	2.80	20.0	—
* Master cylinder clamp	0.80	—	69.0
3-way union	0.80	—	69.00

Fig. 7.20 Front disc brake master cylinder — 1978 type

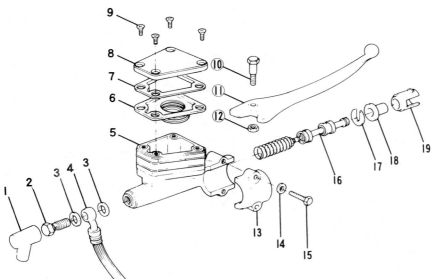

1   Rubber cover
2   Banjo union bolt
3   Washer — 2 off
4   Hydraulic hose
5   Master cylinder reservoir
6   Diaphragm
7   Diaphragm plate
8   Reservoir top
9   Screw — 4 off
10 Pivot bolt
11 Brake lever
12 Nut
13 Handlebar clamp
14 Washer — 2 off
15 Bolt — 2 off
16 Piston and spring
17 Piston retaining plate
18 Dust seal
19 Plastic liner

38 Front disc brake: pad renewal — 1979 type

1   The method required for pad renewal is essentially similar to that described for the 1978 type, but with a number of differences in procedure. Start by removing the caliper mounting bolts and lifting the caliper clear of the disc and front fork leg. The fixed pad (pad B) is retained by a single screw which passes through a retaining plate. Both the pad and the plate can be displaced once the screw has been released. The moving pad (pad A) can now be removed by sliding the caliper mounting bracket across to allow the pad to be displaced.

2   When fitting new pads, attach a clear plastic tube to the bleed valve, slackening it by one or two turns. The piston can then be pushed back into the caliper to make room for the new pads and the valve re-tightened before the tube is renewed. Check that the pads are located properly and use a non-hardening locking fluid on the screw that retains pad B. Refit the caliper to the fork leg and tighten the mounting bolts to 4.0 kgf m (29 lbf ft). Bleed the brake system as described in Section 45, and check that the brake operates efficiently.

39 Front disc brake: caliper overhaul — 1979 type

1   Remove the caliper from the fork leg and free the pads as described in Section 33. The general overhaul procedure is similar to that described in Section 34, and the same method of piston removal can be employed. The following aspects of the procedure differ from that described for the previous type. Reference should also be made to Fig. 7.21 for details of the caliper components.

2   Slacken and remove the caliper holder bolts, nuts and spacers, slackening each one gradually and evenly to avoid damaging the dust seals. The caliper holder can now be pulled clear and the dust seals and O-rings removed. It is important to ensure that the caliper is free to slide on the plain shanks of the holder bolts, and the latter should be lubricated with PBC grease during reassembly. Note that the piston dust seal must locate in the groove formed by the seal stop in the caliper body.

40 Disc brake torque settings: 1979 type

The following torque settings apply to all models using the 1979 type disc brake arrangement.

	kgf m	lbf ft	lbf in
Bleed valve	0.85	—	74.0
Brake lever pivot bolt	0.30	—	26.0
Brake lever pivot bolt locknut	0.60	—	52.0
* Caliper holder nuts	2.60	19.0	—
Caliper mounting bolts	4.00	29.0	—
Disc mounting bolts	3.30	24.0	—
Banjo bolts	3.00	22.0	—
* Master cylinder clamp bolts	0.90	—	78.0

Note that items marked with an asterisk should be re-torqued every 6000 miles (10 000 km). To do this slacken off the nut or bolt about ½ a turn and then torque to the correct value.

41 Front disc brake: pad renewal — 1981 type

1   Yet another revised caliper unit was introduced on the 1981 KZ440 C2 model. The caliper mounting bracket is a robust casting in a horseshoe shape and is bolted directly to the fork lower leg. The ends of the mounting bracket incorporate two sliding pins to which the caliper is secured by two bolts. The bolts pass lengthwise into the sliding pins, and the caliper is thus securely located but able to slide in relation to the disc to permit alignment of the disc pads. Caliper travel is limited by the disc itself.

2   This design is unusual in that the pads are located by the caliper mounting bracket, the caliper itself fitting over the assembly. To remove the pads, slacken the two bolts which secure the caliper body to the mounting pins. With the bolts removed the caliper unit can be lifted clear, leaving the disc

pads attached to the mounting bracket. The pads can now be lifted away, noting that the tangs on the pad ends bear upon small pressed steel sliders. These may drop free when the pads are removed, and they should be retained for re-use.

3   Check the pads for wear in the normal way, rejecting them if damaged or cracked, or if they have become badly contaminated with oil or grease. Small oil spots can be removed with a high flash-point solvent such as white spirit (Stoddart Solvent). Measure the amount of pad material left before the stepped portion is reached. If on either pad there is 1 mm or less they must be renewed as a pair.

4   Before fitting the new pads clean the inside of the caliper unit and the mounting bracket. Check that the sliders are in position on the bracket and if necessary bend the locating tabs inwards to retain them. A very light film of PBC grease may be

applied to the sliders, but take care that there is no excess to find its way onto the pad surfaces. Examine the caliper to ensure that there are no signs of leakage and that the anti-rattle spring is in position. Fit a drain tube on the bleed valve and then slacken it just enough to allow the piston to be pushed back into the caliper. Tighten the bleed valve immediately and remove the drain tube. Check that the sliding holder shafts are free to move. It is a good idea to remove them and the dust seals for cleaning. Reassemble using a coating of PBC (Poly Butyl Cuprysil) grease on the shafts. Offer up the caliper, ensuring that the holder shafts are aligned properly. Fit the holder bolts and tighten to 1.8 kgf m (13.0 lbf ft). Operate the front brake lever several times to adjust the piston and pads to their correct position. If there was any suspicion of air having entered the caliper, bleed the system as described in Section 45.

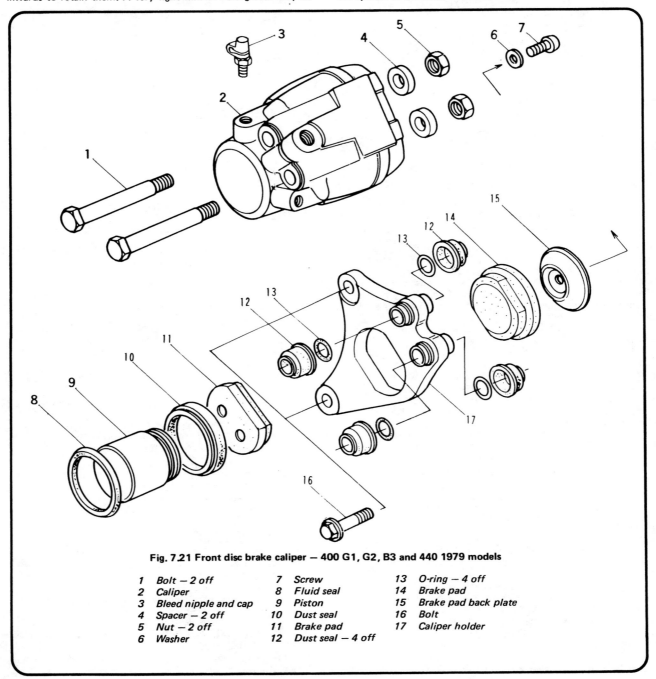

Fig. 7.21 Front disc brake caliper — 400 G1, G2, B3 and 440 1979 models

1	Bolt — 2 off	7	Screw	13	O-ring — 4 off
2	Caliper	8	Fluid seal	14	Brake pad
3	Bleed nipple and cap	9	Piston	15	Brake pad back plate
4	Spacer — 2 off	10	Dust seal	16	Bolt
5	Nut — 2 off	11	Brake pad	17	Caliper holder
6	Washer	12	Dust seal — 4 off		

Fig. 7.22 Front disc brake caliper — 1981 400 and 440 models

1   *Bleed nipple*
2   *Cap*
3   *Caliper*
4   *Sliding pin*
5   *Dust seal — 2 off*
6   *Bolt*
7   *Mounting bracket*
8   *Pressed steel slider — 2 off*

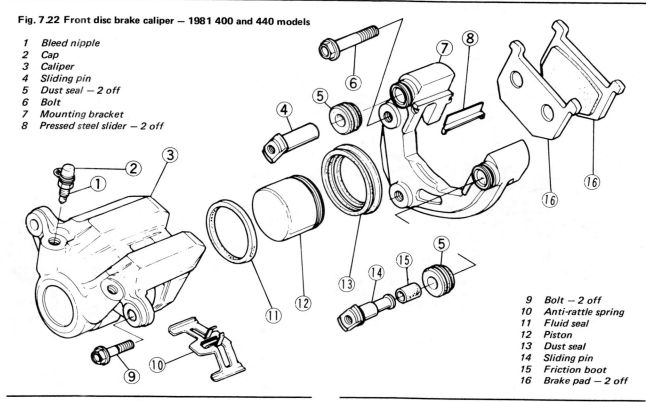

9   *Bolt — 2 off*
10   *Anti-rattle spring*
11   *Fluid seal*
12   *Piston*
13   *Dust seal*
14   *Sliding pin*
15   *Friction boot*
16   *Brake pad — 2 off*

42 Front disc brake: caliper overhaul — 1981 type

1   The overhaul procedure is generally similar to that outlined in Section 34, with a few obvious changes due to the different design of the caliper. Start by removing the caliper and pads as described in Section 33, then displace the piston by wrapping rag around the caliper and pumping it out using the front brake lever. The remarks relating to examination and renovation of the earlier units can be applied.
2   Remove and clean the caliper holder shafts and seals, and check them and the caliper holder bores for wear or corrosion. Any defect in these components will impair braking efficiency and must be rectified by renewing the damaged parts. Assemble the shafts using liberal amounts of PBC grease to provide lubrication and prevent the subsequent ingress of water. It is worthwhile fitting new friction boots and dust seals as a precautionary measure.

43 Front disc brake: torque settings — 1981 type

The following torque settings are applicable to all models using the 1981 type braking system. The caliper mounting bolts should be re-torqued at 6000 mile/10 000 km intervals.

	kgf m	lbf ft	lbf in
Bleed valve	0.80	—	69.0
Brake lever pivot	0.30	—	26.0
Brake lever pivot locknut	0.60	—	52.0
Caliper holder shaft bolts	1.80	13.0	—
Caliper mounting bolts	4.00	29.0	—
Disc mounting Allen bolts	2.30	16.5	—
Banjo bolts	3.00	22.0	—
Master cylinder clamp bolts	0.90	—	78.0

44 Front disc brake: topping up and changing the hydraulic fluid

1   Irrespective of the type of caliper or master cylinder, it is essential on all hydraulic systems that the fluid is kept at the prescribed level in the master cylinder reservoir. In the case of the early screw-cap types the correct fluid level is indicated by a level line scribed around the inside of the body. Later models make use of a translucent reservoir body in which upper and lower fluid level limits were marked. The fluid level could be seen through the reservoir body. The latest models have a solid black reservoir, but incorporate a small sight glass to facilitate quick checks on the fluid level.
2   In normal circumstances the fluid level will fall very slowly due to the gradual wear of the pads, and although the level should be checked regularly, it will rarely be necessary to add fluid. If the fluid level drops suddenly and significantly it should be taken as a warning that a leak has developed and must be investigated and rectified before the machine is ridden again. Never take chances with the braking system. Although total failure of the seals is unusual it is to be avoided for obvious reasons.
3   The choice of hydraulic fluid is of great importance. The hydraulic system is designed to use a specific type of fluid and the use of any other type of hydraulic fluid or oil will destroy the master cylinder and caliper seals. Ordinary engine oils and petroleum based compounds must never be allowed to come into contact with any of the brake parts. The correct fluid will be supplied in a can marked SAE J1703 (UK standard) or DOT 3 (US standard). Most of the common universal types conform to these standards, but check carefully before using.
4   After the reservoir top has been removed, lift out the diaphragm which covers the fluid. The diaphragm serves to allow fluid movement whilst excluding contact with the air. This is because hydraulic fluids of this type are hygroscopic. This means that they will attract and absorb moisture from the air, and in doing so their performance is impaired. During heavy use the caliper and brake disc can become surprisingly hot, and it is

essential that the fluid can withstand this temperature without boiling. The fluid temperature can reach 150°C at times, and whilst new fluid can easily withstand this, its boiling point drops dramatically after it has absorbed a very small amount of water. For example, its boiling point falls below the 150°C (300°F) level with just a 2.5% water content.

5   This is why it is important to change the hydraulic fluid on a two yearly basis, or whenever contamination is suspected. For the same reason, the washer cylinder reservoir and any cans of hydraulic fluid must be kept sealed to avoid contact with water vapour.

6   To change the hydraulic fluid, obtain a length of plastic tubing which will fit firmly over the caliper bleed nipple, and place the free end in a jar. Remove the reservoir cap or cover and slacken the bleed nipple. Operate the front brake lever repeatedly until all of the fluid has been expelled. If sediment is present in the fluid the system should be flushed through with new fluid to minimise future seal wear.

7   Top up the reservoir and commence filling the system by pumping the brake lever. Squeeze the lever, then before it is released, close the bleed valve to prevent air from being drawn back into the system. Release the lever, open the bleed valve again and repeat this cycle until fluid starts to emerge from the bleed valve. Do not forget to keep the level of fluid in the reservoir above the minimum mark. It will now be necessary to bleed any residual air from the system as described in the following Section.

45 Bleeding the hydraulic system

1   It is essential that the hydraulic system is kept completely free of air. This is because air is extremely elastic and is easily compressed, thus any air in the system will absorb energy instead of transmitting full braking effort to the disc pads. The result is that the brake will feel spongy in operation and it will be impossible to brake hard. Bleeding the system will remove any air bubbles, and this must be carried out whenever any part of the system has been disconnected.

2   If the fluid has been drained, start by refilling it as described in the preceding Section, then check that the fluid level in the reservoir is at its maximum level. The reservoir must be checked frequently during the bleeding operation; if the fluid level falls too low during bleeding more air will be admitted to the system and the whole operation will have to be repeated. Before the bleeding operation commences, check that there is no air trapped in the reservoir side of the master cylinder by squeezing the brake lever a few times. Any air will emerge as bubbles in the fluid.

3   Obtain a length of clear plastic tubing that is a tight push fit over the end of the bleed nipple. Fit the tube and place the free end in a glass jar or a similar container. Bleeding is carried out in the following sequence:

a) Apply the front brake, and hold it on.
b) Slacken the bleed valve until the brake lever moves back to its stop, then quickly close the valve.
c) Release the brake lever, then repeat the procedure from stage a).

4   During the bleeding operation, air will be seen as bubbles emerging from the bleed valve and moving along the tube. Bleeding should continue until all traces of air bubbles have ceased, not forgetting to top up the reservoir as required. When the operation has been completed, check that the bleed valve is fully tightened to 0.80 kgf m (69 lbf in). Remove the plastic tubing and wipe up any residual fluid. Top up the reservoir and refit the lid. **Note:** hydraulic fluid will attack paint finishes or plastic. Take care not to spill or splash the fluid on these parts and remove any accidental splashes **immediately** and wash down with warm water and detergent.

46 Cast wheels: general information

1   Many of the later model variations feature cast alloy wheels in place of the traditional steel rim and wire spoked types. These are of conventional tubed design and as such pose no special problem when removal and replacement becomes necessary. A slightly modified approach to examination and renovation is called for.

2   Carefully check the complete wheel for cracks and chipping. particularly at the spoke roots and the edge of the rim. As a general rule a damaged wheel must be renewed as cracks will cause stress points which may lead to sudden failure under heavy load. Small nicks may be radiused carefully with a fine file and emery paper (No. 600 — No. 1000) to relieve the stress. If there is any doubt as to the condition of a wheel, advice should be sought from a Kawasaki repair specialist.

3   Each wheel is covered with a coating of lacquer, to prevent corrosion. If damage occurs to the wheel and the lacquer finish is penetrated, the bared aluminium alloy will soon start to corrode. A whitish grey oxide will form over the damaged area, which in itself is a protective coating. This deposit however, should be removed carefully as soon as possible and a new protective coating of lacquer applied.

4   Check the lateral run out at the rim by spinning the wheel and placing a fixed pointer close to the rim edge. If the maximum run out is greater than 0.5 mm, Kawasaki recommend that the wheel be renewed. This is, however, a counsel of perfection; a run out somewhat greater than this can probably be accommodated without noticeable effect on steering. No means is available for straightening a warped wheel without resorting to the expense of having the wheel skimmed on all faces. If warpage was caused by impact during an accident, the safest measure is to renew the wheel complete. Worn wheel bearings may cause rim run out. These should be checked before the suspect wheel is renewed.

5   The procedure for changing tyres is generally similar to that applied to wire spoked wheels, but additional care must be taken to avoid damaging the rather soft alloy rims. Insert a tyre lever close to the valve and lever the edge of the tyre over the outside of the wheel rim. Very little force should be necessary; if resistance is encountered it is probably due to the fact that the tyre beads have not entered the well of the wheel rim all the way round the tyre. Should the initial problem persist, lubrication of the tyre bead and the inside edge and lip of the rim will facilitate removal. Use a recommended lubricant, a dilute solution of washing-up liquid or french chalk. Lubrication is usually recommended as an aid to tyre fitting but its use is equally desirable during removal. The risk of lever damage to wheel rims can be minimised by the use of proprietary plastic rim protectors placed over the rim flange at the point where the tyre levers are inserted. Suitable rim protectors may be fabricated very easily from short lengths (4 — 6 inches) of thick-walled nylon petrol pipe which have been split down one side using a sharp knife. The use of rim protectors should be adopted whenever levers are used and, therefore, when the risk of damage is likely.

47 Belt drive system: general description

1   The KZ440 D1 and D2 (LTD) models are equipped with a toothed belt arrangement in place of the more common final drive chain. The belt is constructed from a polyurethane compound, reinforced with Kevlar tensile cord and with a nylon fabric facing. Similar arrangements have been used for camshaft drives on car engines for many years, and have been supplied as accessory parts for Harley-Davidson and Triumph primary and secondary drives.

2   The belt arrangement is claimed to be quieter and smoother in operation and can be expected to last at least as long as a conventional chain. A more tangible advantage is that the belt

should require less adjustment than a chain and does not require lubrication. It is less likely to cause damage to the machine or rider in the event of breakage, but it cannot be repaired. The only precaution against being stranded with a broken belt is to inspect it regularly and to renew it as soon as serious wear or damage become apparent. If long trips are planned, a spare belt should be carried, and for emergency purposes a worn but unbroken belt will suffice. In normal use the belt should prove at least as reliable as a chain drive system.

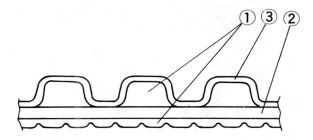

Fig. 7.23 Final drive toothed belt construction — 440 D model

1   Polyurethane compound　　*3   Nylon fabric facing*
2   Kevlar tensile cord

48 Belt drive system: examination and maintenance

1   The belt condition and adjustment should be checked at 3000 mile (5000 km) intervals or more frequently in particularly adverse conditions. The belt is strong and reasonably resistant to wear, but it will be appreciated that accumulations of abrasive dirt on the belt teeth or pulleys will shorten the life of both. It is good practice to clean the belt and pulleys whenever the machine is cleaned. This is not a difficult task and, unlike chains, does not involve large quantities of dirty grease.
2   Examine the belt teeth carefully, noting that the belt must be renewed if the nylon facing has worn through to the black polyurethane compound. If the belt and pulleys are in good condition the belt tension should be checked as described below. If renewal or further examination is required, refer to the next Section for full details.
3   Belt tension is as important as chain tension on the other models. If the belt is allowed to run with excessive slack it will wear more quickly and will tend to jump over the pulley teeth during acceleration. Conversely, an over-tight belt will become strained and will tend to overstress the gearbox and rear wheel bearings.
4   Belt tension is checked with the aid of a special tool which is included in the machine's tool kit. The tool consists of a cylindrical body which houses a spring-loaded plunger. The plunger has two engraved lines which indicate maximum and minimum belt tension settings. To check the tension place the machine on its centre stand and place the tool between the upper, toothed, face of the lower belt run and the underside of the swinging arm. The base of the tool should face downwards. Check the position of the lines on the plunger in relation to the upper face of the body. If the belt tension is such that the plunger is compressed to the range between the lines, it can be considered correct. If this is not the case, remove the tool and proceed as follows.
5   Remove the R-pin from the rear brake torque arm stud and slacken the retaining nut. Slacken the wheel spindle drawbolt locknuts. Remove the split pin which retains the wheel spindle nut, then slacken the nut. Turn each drawbolt by an equal amount to tighten or slacken the belt. Check the new setting with the tool and when correct secure the drawbolt locknuts. Make sure that the rear wheel is correctly aligned (see Chapter 5 Section 15) then secure the wheel spindle nut and fit its split

pin. Tighten the torque arm nut and refit the R-pin. Note the following torque settings:

	kgf m	lbf ft
Wheel spindle nut	7.5	54.0
Torque arm nut	3.3	24.0

Check, and where necessary adjust, the rear brake setting and the brake switch setting.

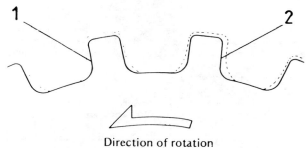

Direction of rotation

Fig. 7.24 Final drive toothed belt wear limits — 440 D model

1   Example of worn tooth on engine pulley
2   Example of worn tooth on rear wheel pulley

49 Belt drive system: renewing the belt

1   If the drive belt has shown signs of wear or damage, it will be necessary to remove the rear wheel and swinging arm before belt renewal can be accomplished. Place the machine on its centre stand and release the rear brake rod, torque arm and wheel spindle nut. Slacken off the wheel spindle drawbolts, pivoting them clear of the swinging arm fork end. Support the weight of the wheel and withdraw the wheel spindle; the chain adjusters and wheel spacer will drop free. Disengage the belt from the pulley wheel and lift the wheel clear of the machine.
2   Slacken and remove the swinging arm pivot shaft nut and remove the suspension lower mounting bolts. Support the swinging arm and withdraw the pivot shaft. An end cap is fitted to each end of the pivot tube, and these probably will drop free as the fork is withdrawn. The caps should be retrieved and placed with the fork to await reassembly. Remove the gearbox pulley cover and withdraw the clutch pushrod from its bore. The belt can now be disengaged from the pulley and removed.
3   Before a new belt is fitted, clean and examine the two pulleys. If either is badly worn or damaged both should be renewed together with the drive belt. It should be noted that worn pulleys will wear out a new drive belt quite quickly. Pulley wear can be measured across the tooth faces using a vernier caliper. The service limits are as follows.

Service limits: belt drive pulleys

Gearbox pulley	95.0 mm (3.74 in)
Rear wheel pulley	264.0 mm (10.39 in)

4   Reassemble by reversing the dismantling sequence. Note that the clutch pushrod has a waisted section at one end, and this must be positioned to face outwards. Check that the swinging arm pivot bearings are greased and that the end caps are in position. When fitting the rear wheel, check alignment and belt tension before securing the wheel spindle nut. Note the following torque settings.

	kgf m	lbf ft
Swinging arm pivot nut	9.0	65
Wheel spindle nut	7.5	54
Torque arm nut	3.3	24

50 Voltage regulator and rectifier: modifications

1 All models from 1978 onwards were fitted with a completely revised regulator/rectifier unit. The previous system, described in Chapter 6, Sections 5 and 6, utilised an electro-mechanical voltage regulator in conjunction with a separate full-wave rectifier, the two components serving to control the system voltage and to convert the alternator output to direct current (dc) respectively. The later system employs a single sealed unit which is entirely electronic in operation. There are no contacts or moving parts in the unit and thus adjustment is not necessary. In practice the unit will work accurately unless an internal component fails, in which case it must be renewed as a unit. No repair is possible because the unit is of sealed construction. Two basic systems are employed and are described separately in the following Sections.

51 Regulator/rectifier unit: operation and testing — 1978 -- 79 models

1 The voltage regulation system of the above models is of the open-circuit type, as distinct from the later short-circuit type. This section covers all models not fitted with the electro-mechanical system up to and including the 1979 KZ400 B2 and G1. For all subsequent models refer to the following Section for details of the later system.

2 **Important note:** the regulator/rectifier unit can be seriously damaged if the following precautions are not observed.
a) Do not disconnect the regulator/rectifier unit with the ignition switched on. Always make sure that the switch is off and if possible isolate the battery. The same applies to reconnection.
b) Do not disconnect the battery leads with the engine running.

3 The regulator/rectifier is a sealed integrated circuit housed in a finned aluminium case to provide the necessary heat dissipation when the machine is in use. A total of four leads are connected to the unit. Two of these, both yellow, are the input from the alternator and carry unregulated alternating current (ac). The remaining leads, one red and one black, are the positive (+) and negative (−) output leads and feed regulated direct current (dc) into the battery and electrical system in accordance to its demands.

4 The internal construction and function of the unit is of purely academic interest since it is not possible to effect repairs if the unit malfunctions. In view of this, this section will concentrate on the testing procedures necessary to identify the fault. In the event of a complete or partial failure of the charging system, proceed as follows.

Alternator output test

5 With the engine at normal operating temperature, remove the gearbox sprocket cover and separate the alternator output connectors. Using a multimeter set on the 25V ac scale, connect the probe leads to the yellow output connectors, noting that polarity does not affect this test. Start the engine and note the output reading at 4000 rpm. This should be about 75 volts if the alternator is operating normally. If significantly less than this check the stator resistance. If the correct reading is obtained skip this test and move on to regulator/rectifier resistance test.

Alternator stator resistance test

6 Using a multimeter set on the ohms x 1 scale, check the resistance between the two alternator output leads. This should be about 0.26 -- 0.38 ohms. If there is a very high resistance, or no resistance, the stator can be considered faulty and will need to be renewed. Set the meter on the kilo ohms setting and measure the resistance between each of the yellow leads and earth (ground). If anything less than infinite resistance is shown

it is likely that the stator windings are shorted internally and this will again necessitate renewal of the complete assembly. If the resistance readings are correct but the alternator output is below the normal value, it is possible that the rotor magnets have become weak. This condition should be checked by an auto-electrician.

Regulator/rectifier resistance test

7 Check that the ignition switch is off, remove the right-hand side panel and separate the three-pin connector. Using a multimeter set on the appropriate scale check the various combinations of connections as shown below. If any pair of leads show a high or low reading in *both* directions, the unit can be considered defective and must be renewed. It should be noted that this test is not foolproof, and if problems persist despite the readings appearing to be correct check the unit by substituting one known to be in good condition, or seek professional help with the diagnosis.

Regulator/rectifier resistance tests

Meter	Connections	Reading
x 1 Ω	Meter (+) ↔ Yellow Lead Meter (−) ↔ Black Lead	less than 20Ω
x 1 kΩ	Meter (+) ↔ Black Lead Meter (−) ↔ Yellow Lead	more than 100 kΩ

52 Regulator/rectifier unit: operation and testing — 1980 — 81 models

1 The system covered in this Section applies to the KZ400 B3 and G2, and all KZ440 models. The voltage regulation system is changed to the short-circuit type with corresponding changes in the regulator/rectifier unit and test procedures. For detail covering the previous system refer to the preceding Section.

2 **Important note:** the regulator/rectifier unit can be seriously damaged if the following precautions are not observed.

a) Do not allow the battery connections to be reversed. If this happens, even briefly, the Zener diode may be destroyed.
b) Note that the unit cannot function properly unless the battery is fully charged. If faults develop, make sure that the battery is in good condition (reading above 12 volts) and that all of the associated terminals and connectors are secured and free from corrosion.

3 Make an initial test to check the overall condition of the charging system. Remove the left-hand side panel and connect the positive (+) probe of a multimeter to the battery positive lead and the negative (−) probe to the negative lead. With the meter set on the 0 − 25 volts dc scale. Start the engine and check the meter reading at various speeds with the lights off and then on. Note that on certain US models it will be necessary to detach the black/yellow lead from the headlamp unit to turn the lights off. At low engine speeds the meter should indicate something close to battery voltage, this figure increasing as the engine speed rises, but not exceeding 15 volts.

Alternator output voltage test

4 Remove the gearbox sprocket or pulley cover and disconnect the two yellow alternator output leads. Set the multimeter to the 250 volts ac scale and connect one probe lead to each of the output leads. Start the engine and note the voltage reading obtained at 4000 rpm. This should be about 75 volts. If the reading found is much lower than this check the stator resistance as follows, otherwise move on to the regulator/rectifier tests. Set the meter to the ohms x 1 range and connect one probe lead to each of the alternator output leads. A reading of 0.26 − 0.38

ohms should be obtained. Next, set the meter to the ohms x 1000 (kilo ohms) scale and check the resistance between each of the yellow leads in turn and the nearest sound earth (ground) point. A reading of less than infinity indicates a partial or short circuit and will require renewal of the stator.

Rectifier circuit testing

5   Refer to paragraph 7 of the previous Section. The resistance figures shown in the table can be applied as a rough guide, but there may be some variation with different meters.

Regulator circuit testing

6   The regulator circuitry can be checked using three 12 volt motorcycle (or car) batteries, and a test lamp made up from a bulbholder with probe lead attached. The bulb used must be rated at 3 — 6W. The test is performed with the unit removed from the machine. Note that the test results are not conclusive. It is possible that the results might indicate a sound unit, but there may still be an undetected fault. Note also that the bulb acts as a current limiter and must not be replaced by an ammeter.
7   Connect the batteries, test lamp and regulator/rectifier shown in Fig. 7.25 and note whether the test lamp comes on. Repeat the test, this time connecting the test lead to the other yellow output lead, again noting whether the lamp is illuminated. If the test lead to the brown regulator/rectifier lead is removed the lamp should go out, but should come on when 24 volts is applied to the brown and black terminals. **Note:** to avoid damage to the unit, do not apply more than 24 volts to it, and do not leave the test arrangement connected for more than a few seconds. If these conditions are not observed the unit may be damaged.

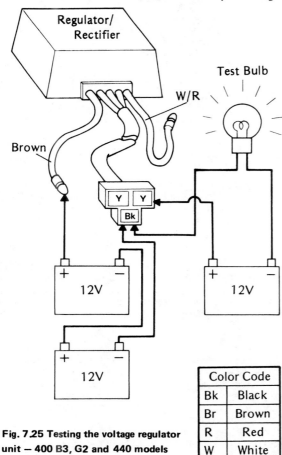

Fig. 7.25 Testing the voltage regulator unit — 400 B3, G2 and 440 models

Color Code	
Bk	Black
Br	Brown
R	Red
W	White
Y	Yellow

53 Brake light failure warning circuit: testing

1   Most models from the 1978 KZ400 B1 onward have incorporated a brake failure warning system. A switch unit mounted beneath the fuel tank controls a warning lamp incorporated in the tachometer face. When the front brake lever or rear brake pedal is depressed the brake light and the warning lamp both come on indicating that the circuit is operating normally. If, however, the warning lamp flashes when the brake is operated it indicates to the rider that the brake lamp filament has failed and requires renewal.
2   If the warning switch is suspected of being faulty it is best to check it by fitting it to a machine with a brake light and warning circuit known to be in good condition. Failing this check the entire circuit, following the wiring diagram at the end of the book, and making sure that it is in good order throughout. Having done this, remove the fuel tank and release the three pin connector from the warning switch. The brake light circuit can now be tested as shown in the table below. Note that the ignition switch must be turned off when making the resistance tests, otherwise the multimeter will be damaged. In all tests, the negative (—) meter probe should be connected to a sound earth (ground).

Brake light circuit tests

Meter	Connections†	Brake	Standard
Voltmeter 20V DC	Meter (+) ←→ Blue	Apply	Battery Voltage
		Releaze	0V
	Meter (+) ←→ Green/White	——	Battery Voltage
Ohmmeter x 1 Ω	Meter (+) ←→ Black/Yellow	——	0Ω

If the circuit shows the above readings it can be assumed that the fault lies in the warning switch unit which should be tested as described below.
3   Reconnect the warning switch and carry out the following tests. In all cases, the negative (—) meter probe should be connected to a sound earth (ground). The meter scale in all tests should be set to 0 — 20V dc.

Brake light failure warning switch tests

Meter	Connections†	Brake	Standard
20V DC	Meter (+) ←→ Blue	Apply	Battery Voltage
		Release	0V
	Meter (+) ←→ Green/White	Apply	about 0V
		Release	Battery Voltage

If the readings obtained do not match those shown above, the switch should be considered faulty and must be renewed.

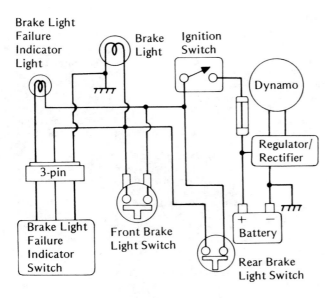

Fig. 7.26 Brake light failure warning circuit diagram

54 Indicator automatic cancelling system: 1981 KZ440 A2 and D2

1   A more sophisticated direction indicator system is fitted to the above models. It is designed to turn the indicators off after four seconds, plus the time required for the machine to cover fifty yards. This system will only switch off the indicators after both of the above conditions have been fulfilled, thus when overtaking on an open road the system will switch off quite quickly, whereas when waiting to turn at a road junction the indicators will continue to operate until the correct distance has been covered.

2   In addition to the normal indicator circuit components, the system incorporates a distance sensor in the speedometer and a control unit which includes the timing circuitry. When the indicators are operated, the control unit starts a count of four seconds, after which it begins to measure the number of pulses from the distance sensor. When both functions have elapsed the control unit triggers a solenoid which cancels the indicators. In the event of a malfunction, the following diagnosis and repair sequence should be undertaken.

Handlebar switch overhaul

3   Problems can arise in the switch through corrosion of the switch contacts. This condition can largely be avoided by spraying a silicone-based maintenance aerosol, such as WD40, into the switch on a regular basis. The fluid will displace any water and will lubricate the moving parts of the switch. To check the switch operation, remove the fuel tank and separate the white/ green lead at the connector plus the 6-pin and 3-pin connectors from the left-hand switch unit. Using a multimeter set on the highest resistance scale (ohms x 1000 or kilo ohms) measure the resistance between the various leads at the switch positions shown in the following tables. Zero resistance indicates that the circuit is complete (continuity) whilst resistance indicates insulation. Note that in the case of high, but not infinite, resistance a short circuit or dirty contact is indicated.

Manual/automatic switch connection test

4   The following test is made between leads at the three pin connector. I = Isolated, C = Continuity.

Switch position	Test connections	Reading
M	Brown to Yellow leads	I
A	Brown to Yellow leads	C

Indicator switch connection tests (made at 6-pin connector)

Switch position	Test connections	Reading
R	Grey to Orange	C
R	White/red to Blue/white	C
R	All others	I
N	Red/white to Earth (ground)	C
N	All others	I
L	Orange to Green	C
L	White/red to Blue/white	C
L	All others	I

Indicator circuit wiring tests

5   The negative (—) probe should be connected to earth and the positive (+) probe connected as shown below. All measurements are taken at the 6-pin connector behind the right-hand side panel. The multimeter should be set on the 0 — 25V dc scale.

Ignition switch	A/M switch	Indicator switch	+ probe to	Reading
ON	A	All positions	Yellow lead	Battery voltage
ON	A	All positions	Blue/white lead	Battery voltage
OFF	M	All positions	Yellow lead	0 volts
OFF	M	All positions	Blue/white lead	0 volts
ON	A	R or L	White/red lead	Battery voltage
OFF	M	N	White/red lead	0 volts

6   If the above tests show any discrepancy, check the wiring connections, the indicator switch unit, distance sensor and the control unit. The indicator switch can be dismantled for cleaning, but replacement parts are not available. If any part is beyond repair it will be necessary to purchase a new switch unit.—

Distance sensor test

7   Remove the headlamp unit and disconnect the red lead and the light green lead from the sensor in the speedometer head. Disconnect the lower end of the speedometer drive cable. Connect a multimeter set on the resistance scale to the two sensor leads, then turn the speedometer cable inner. If the sensor is functioning correctly the meter will indicate on and then off four times per revolution of the cable. If the sensor fails there is a choice of buying a new speedometer or remembering to turn the indicators off manually.

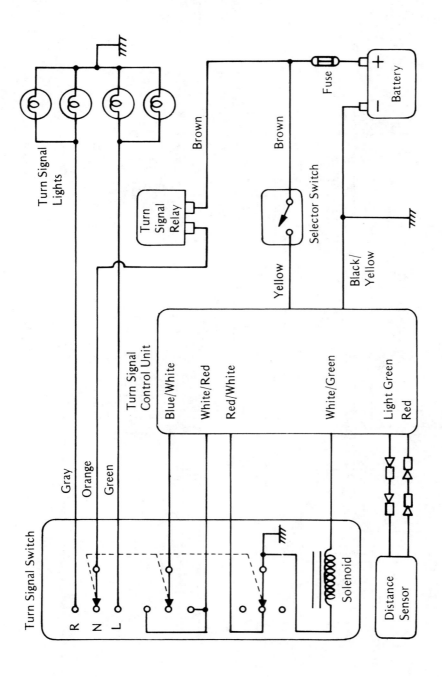

Fig. 7.27 Indicator automatic cancelling system circuit diagram

Wiring diagram – UK Z400 D4

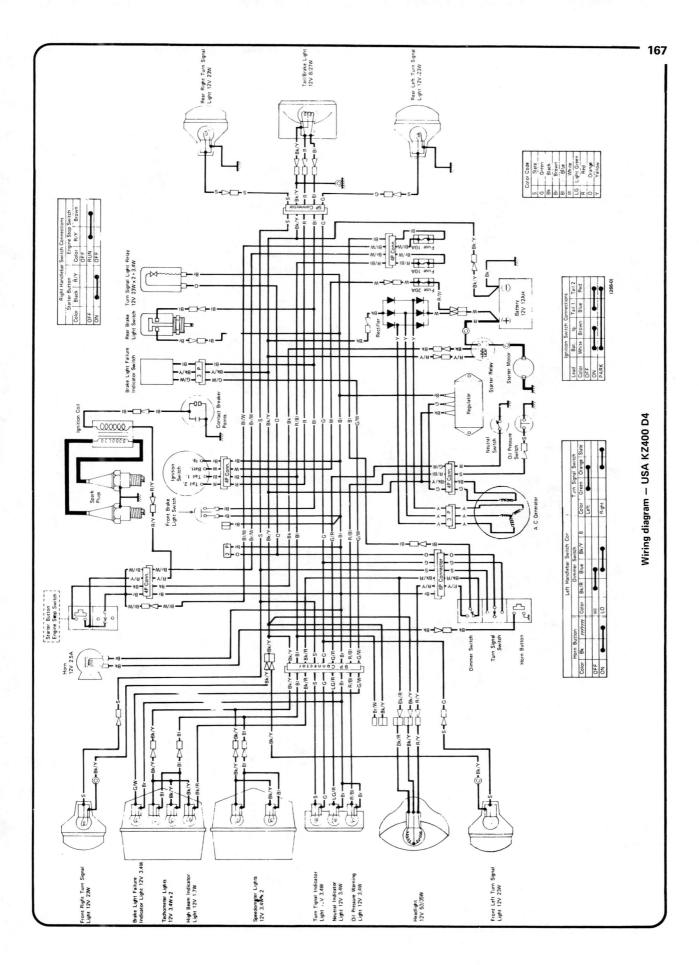

Wiring diagram – USA KZ400 D4

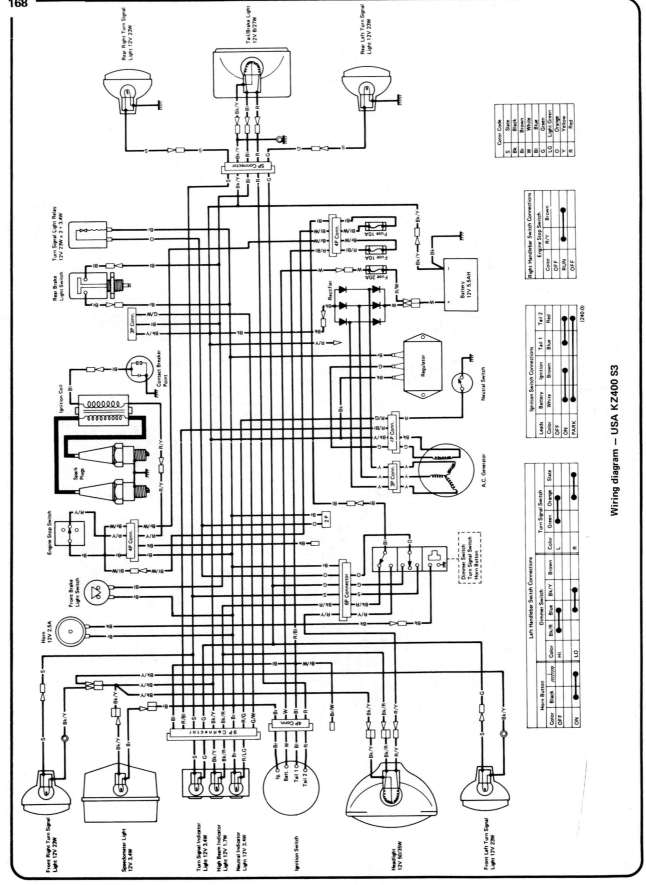

Wiring diagram – USA KZ400 S3

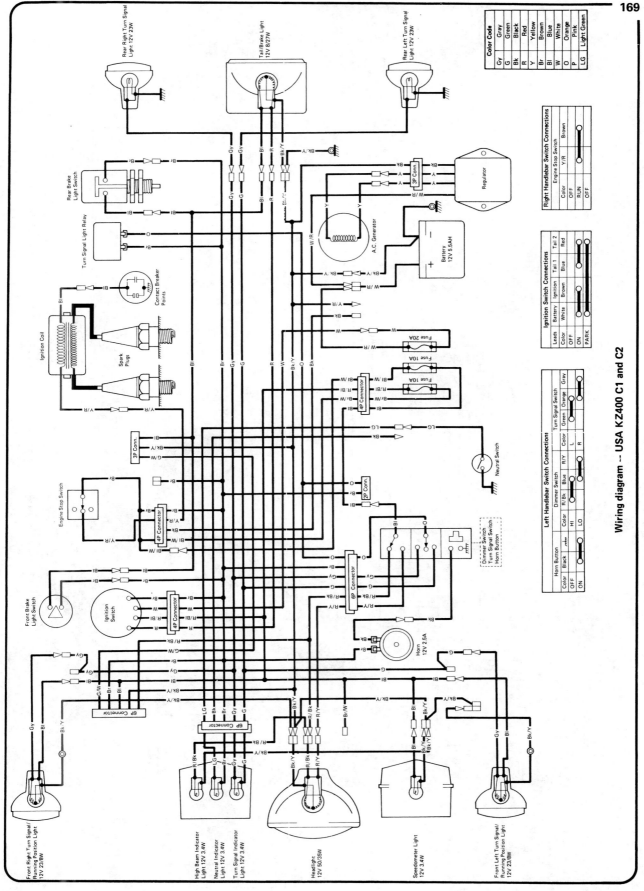

Wiring diagram -- USA KZ400 C1 and C2

Color Code

Gy	Gray	
G	Green	
Bk	Black	
R	Red	
Y	Yellow	
Br	Brown	
Bl	Blue	
W	White	
O	Orange	
P	Pink	
LG	Light Green	

Right Handlebar Switch Connections

Engine Stop Switch		
Color	Y/R	Brown
OFF		
RUN		
OFF		

Ignition Switch Connections

Leads	Battery	Ignition	Tail 1	Tail 2
Color	White	Brown	Blue	Red
OFF				
ON				
PARK				

Left Handlebar Switch Connections

Turn Signal Switch					
		Green	Orange	Gray	
Dimmer Switch					
	Color	R/Bk	Blue	R/Y	
	HI				
	LO				
	Color	L	R		
Horn Button					
	Color	Black			
	OFF				
	ON				

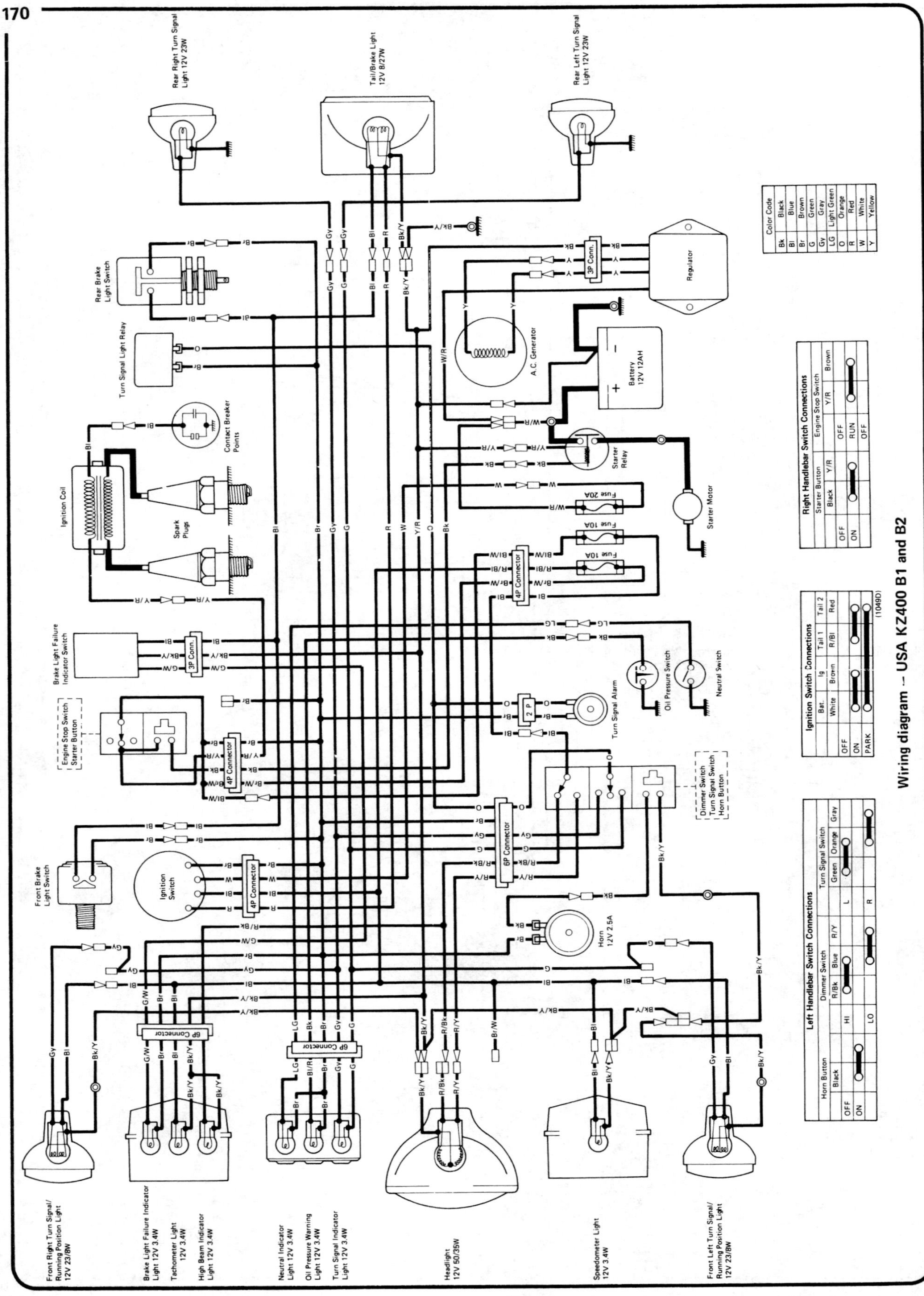

Rear Right Turn Signal Light 12V 23W

Tail/Brake Light 12V 8/27W

Rear Left Turn Signal Light 12V 23W

Rear Brake Light Switch

Turn Signal Light Relay

Contact Breaker Points

Ignition Coil

Spark Plugs

Brake Light Failure Indicator Switch

3P Conn.

Engine Stop Switch
Starter Button

4P Connector

Front Brake Light Switch

Ignition Switch

4P Connector

6P Connector

6P Connector

3P Conn.

Regulator

A.C. Generator

Battery 12V 12AH

Starter Relay

Starter Motor

Fuse 20A

Fuse 10A

Fuse 10A

4P Connector

Oil Pressure Switch

Neutral Switch

Turn Signal Alarm

Dimmer Switch
Turn Signal Switch
Horn Button

6P Connector

Horn 12V 2.5A

Front Right Turn Signal/ Running Position Light 12V 23/8W

Brake Light Failure Indicator Light 12V 3.4W

Tachometer Light 12V 3.4W

High Beam Indicator Light 12V 3.4W

Neutral Indicator Light 12V 3.4W

Oil Pressure Warning Light 12V 3.4W

Turn Signal Indicator Light 12V 3.4W

Headlight 12V 60/35W

Speedometer Light 12V 3.4W

Front Left Turn Signal/ Running Position Light 12V 23/8W

Wiring diagram -- USA KZ400 B1 and B2

Color Code	
Bk	Black
Bl	Blue
Br	Brown
G	Green
Gy	Gray
LG	Light Green
O	Orange
R	Red
W	White
Y	Yellow

Right Handlebar Switch Connections

Engine Stop Switch	Y/R	Brown
OFF		
RUN		
OFF		

Starter Button	Black	Y/R
OFF		
ON		

Ignition Switch Connections

	Bat.	Ig		Tail 1	Tail 2
	White	Brown	R/Bl	Red	
OFF					
ON					
PARK					

Left Handlebar Switch Connections

Turn Signal Switch	Green	Orange	Gray
		L	R

Dimmer Switch	R/Bk	Blue	R/Y
	HI		
	LO		

Horn Button	Black	
OFF		
ON		

(1049D)

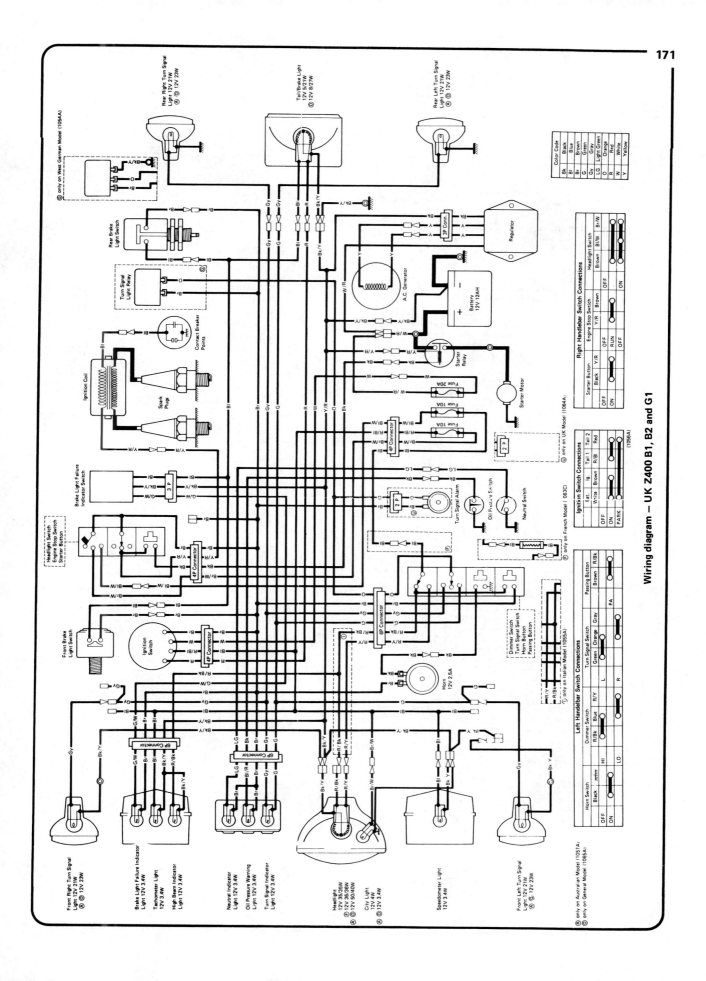

Wiring diagram – UK Z400 B1, B2 and G1

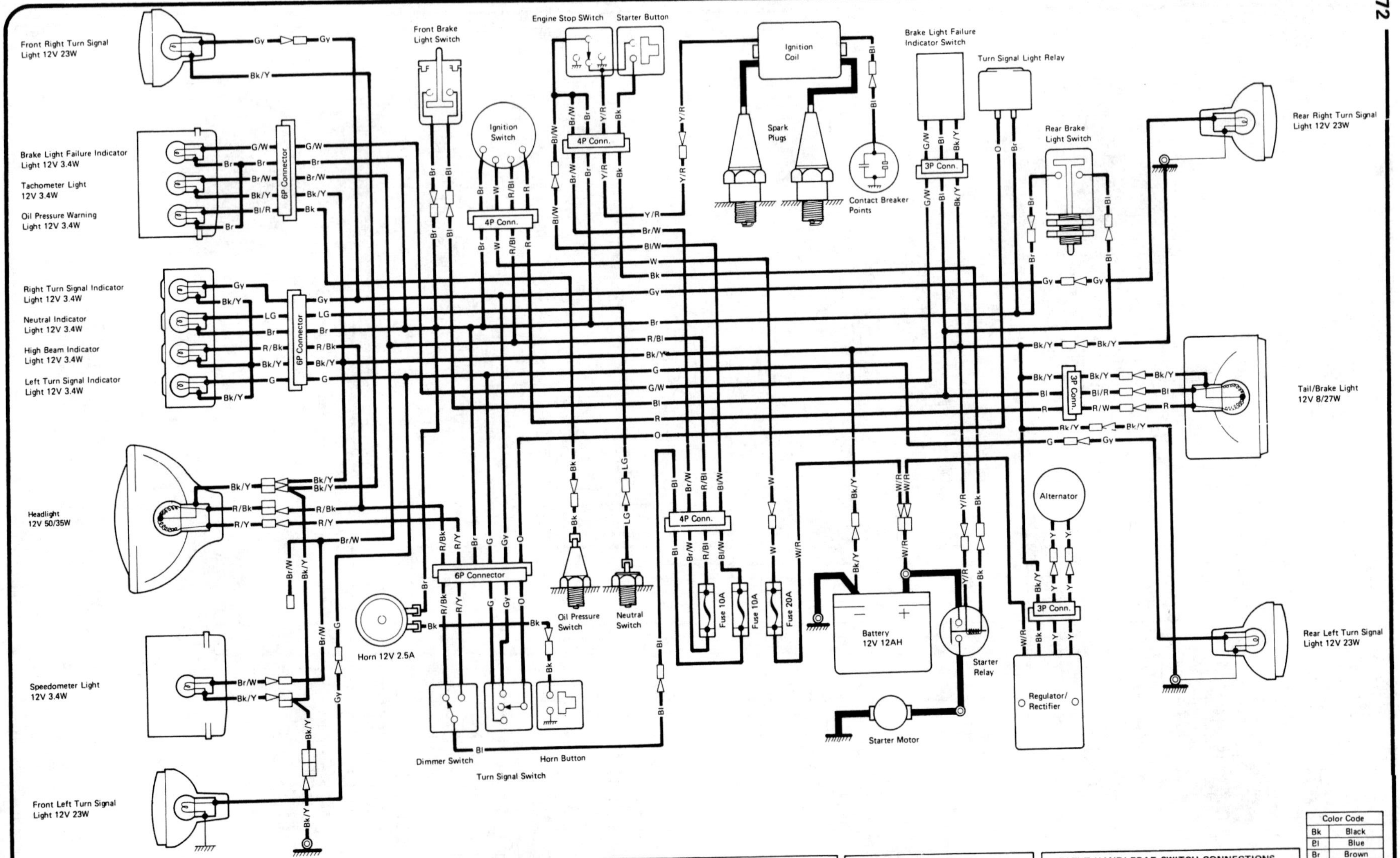

Rear Right Turn Signal Light 12V 23W

Tail/Brake Light 12V 8/27W

Rear Left Turn Signal Light 12V 23W

Color Code

Bk	Black
Bl	Blue
Br	Brown
G	Green
Gy	Gray
LG	Light Green
O	Orange
R	Red
W	White
Y	Yellow

RIGHT HANDLEBAR SWITCH CONNECTIONS

Engine Stop Switch

Color	Bk	Y/R	Br
OFF			
RUN			
OFF			

Starter Button

Color	Bk	Y/R
OFF		
ON		

(116 1C)

IGNITION SWITCH CONNECTIONS

	Battery	Ignition	Tail 1	Tail 2
Color	W	Br	R/Bl	R
OFF				
ON				
PARK				

LEFT HANDLEBAR SWITCH CONNECTIONS

Turn Signal Switch

Color	G	O	Gy
L			
R			

Dimmer Switch

Color	R/Bk	Bl	R/Y
HI			
LO			

Horn Button

Color	Bk	
OFF		
ON		

Rear Brake Light Switch

Turn Signal Light Relay

Brake Light Failure Indicator Switch

3P Conn.

Contact Breaker Points

Ignition Coil

Spark Plugs

Starter Button

Engine Stop Switch

Ignition Switch

4P Conn.

Front Brake Light Switch

Alternator

3P Conn.

Regulator/Rectifier

Starter Relay

Battery 12V 12AH

Starter Motor

Fuse 20A

Fuse 10A

Fuse 10A

4P Conn.

Neutral Switch

Oil Pressure Switch

Horn Button

Turn Signal Switch

Dimmer Switch

6P Connector

Horn 12V 2.5A

Front Right Turn Signal Light 12V 23W

Brake Light Failure Indicator Light 12V 3.4W

Tachometer Light 12V 3.4W

Oil Pressure Warning Light 12V 3.4W

Right Turn Signal Indicator Light 12V 3.4W

Neutral Indicator Light 12V 3.4W

High Beam Indicator Light 12V 3.4W

Left Turn Signal Indicator Light 12V 3.4W

6P Connector

6P Connector

Headlight 12V 50/35W

Speedometer Light 12V 3.4W

Front Left Turn Signal Light 12V 23W

Wiring diagram – USA KZ400 H1

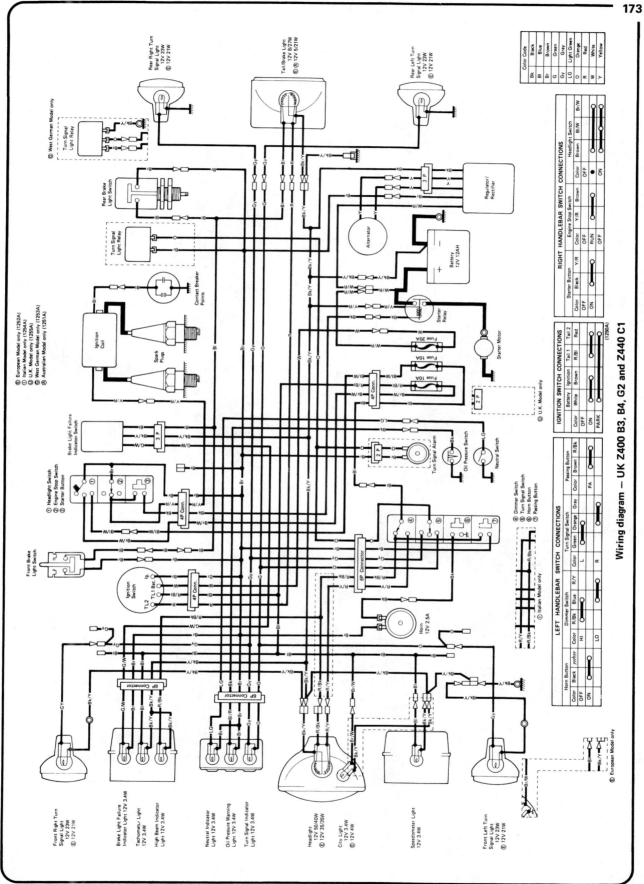

Wiring diagram — UK Z400 B3, B4, G2 and Z440 C1

Rear Right Turn Signal Light 12V 23W / 12V 21W

Tail/Brake Light 12V 8/27W / 12V 5/21W

Rear Left Turn Signal Light 12V 23W / 12V 21W

Turn Signal Light Relay

Battery

Turn Signal Light Relay

Rear Brake Light Switch

Brake Light Failure Indicator Switch

Turn Signal Light Relay

IC Igniter

Pickup Coil

Fuse 10A
Fuse 10A
Fuse 20A

Ignition Coil

Spark Plugs

Battery 12V 12AH

Horn 12V 2.5W x 2

Starter Relay

Starter Motor

Regulator/Rectifier

Alternator

Neutral Switch

Oil Pressure Switch

Right Handlebar Switch
Starter Button
Engine Stop
Headlight Switch

Ignition Switch

Front Brake Light Switch

Left Handlebar Switches
① Passing Button
② Dimmer Switch
③ Turn Signal Switch
④ Horn Button

Turn Signal Alarm

Horn 12V 2.5A

Front Right Turn Signal Light 12V 23W / 12V 21W

Tachometer Light 12V 3.4W

Brake Light Failure Indicator Light 12V 3.4W

High Beam Indicator Light 12V 3.4W

Oil Pressure Warning Light 12V 3.4W

Neutral Indicator Light 12V 3.4W

Turn Signal Indicator Light 12V 3.4W

Headlight 12V 50/40W / 12V 35/35W / 12V 36/36W / 12V 45/45W

City Light 12V 4W

Speedometer Light 12V 3.4W

Front Left Turn Signal Light 12V 23W / 12V 21W

European model (1382A) Norwegian model
① European model except Norwegian model
② West German model (1383A)
③ U.K. model (1383A)
④ Norwegian model (1383B)
⑤ French model (1383A)
⑥ Austrian model (1382A)

Color Code

Bl	Black
Bu	Blue
Br	Brown
G	Green
Gr	Grey
LG	Light Green
O	Orange
R	Red
W	White
Y	Yellow

RIGHT HANDLEBAR SWITCH CONNECTIONS

Headlight Switch	Color	Bl/W	Bl/Y
	OFF		
	ON		

Engine Stop Switch	Color	Y/R	
	OFF		
	RUN		

Starter Button	Color	Black	
	Push		

IGNITION SWITCH CONNECTIONS

	Tail 1	Tail 2
Battery Color	White	Red
OFF		
ON		
P(PARK)		(1382A)

LEFT HANDLEBAR SWITCH CONNECTIONS

Turn Signal Switch	Color	Bl/Y	Orange	Grey
	L			
	R			

Dimmer Switch	Color	Red	Blue
	HI		
	LO		

Passing Button	Color	Brown
	Push	

Horn Button	Color	Black
	Push	

Wiring diagram – UK Z400 G3

Rear Right Turn Signal Light 12V 21W

Tail/Brake Light 12V 5/21W

Rear Left Turn Signal Light 12V 21W

Color Code
B	Black
Bl	Blue
Br	Brown
G	Green
Gy	Gray
LG	Light Green
O	Orange
R	Red
W	White
Y	Yellow

Rear Brake Light Switch

Turn Signal Light Relay

Fuse 10A
Fuse 10A
Fuse 20A

Brake Light Failure Indicator Switch

IC Igniter

Pickup Coil

Battery 12V 12Ah

Starter Relay

Starter Motor

Ignition Coil

Spark Plugs

Regulator/Rectifier

Alternator

Neutral Switch

Oil Pressure Switch

Starter Button Engine Stop Switch Lighting Switch

Ignition Switch

Front Brake Light Switch

Passing Button Dimmer Switch Turn Signal Switch Horn Button

Horn 12V 2.5A

French Model / Other than French Model

6P Connector

RIGHT HANDLEBAR SWITCH CONNECTIONS

Horn Button
Color	Black	B/W
OFF		
ON		

Dimmer Switch
Color	R/Bl	Blue	R/Bk
HI			
LO			

Turn Signal Switch
Color	Green	Orange	Gray
L			
R			

Passing Button
Color	Brown	R/Bk
PA		

IGNITION SWITCH CONNECTIONS

Color	Battery White	Ignition Brown	Tail 1 R/Bl	Tail 2 Red
OFF				
ON				
LOCK				
PARK				

LEFT HANDLEBAR SWITCH CONNECTIONS

Starter Button
Color	Black	Y/R
OFF		
ON		

Engine Stop Switch
Color	Y/R	Brown
OFF		
RUN		

Lighting Switch
Color	Brown	B/W
OFF		
ON		

Wiring diagram – UK Z400 H3

Front Right Turn Signal Light 12V 21W

Tachometer Light 12V 3.4W
Brake Light Failure Indicator 12V 3.4W
Oil Pressure Warning Light 12V 3.4W

Right Turn Signal Indicator Light 12V 3.4W
High Beam Indicator 12V 3.4W
Neutral Indicator Light 12V 3.4W
Left Turn Signal Indicator 12V 3.4W

Headlight 12V 45/40W

City Light 12V 4W

Speedometer Light 12V 3.4W

Front Left Turn Signal Light 12V 21W

Rear Right Turn Signal
Light 12V 21W

Tail/Brake Light
12V 5/21W

Rear Left Turn Signal
Light 12V 21W

Color Code	
Bk	Black
Bl	Blue
Br	Brown
G	Green
Gy	Gray
LG	Light Green
O	Orange
R	Red
W	White
Y	Yellow

Gy Bk/Y Bl Bk/Y Gy Bk/Y

West German Model only (1274A)
Turn Signal
Light Relay

Bk/Y Bk

3 P Y Y
Y Y

Regulator/
Rectifier

Br W/R

Rear Brake
Light Switch

Gy G Bk/Y

3 P

Bk/Y

Y

Alternator

W/R Bk/Y

W/R

R

Battery
12V 12AH

Bk/Y

Turn Signal
Light Relay

Y/R

Bk

Contact Breaker
Points

Ignition
Coil

Spark
Plugs

W/R Fuse 20A

Starter
Motor

Bl/W Bl
R/Bl Fuse 10A
Br/W Fuse 10A

4P Conn.

Y/R

Bk

Oil Pressure Switch

LG

Neutral Switch

Brake Light Failure
Indicator Switch

Bk/Y Bl

3 P

Y/R Bl Gy Br LG G/W R/Bl R W Bk/Y O Br/W Bl/W

① Headlight Switch
② Engine Stop Switch
③ Starter Button

Br/W Y/R
Bl/R Bk

4P Conn.

6P Connector

R/Bk

④ Dimmer Switch
⑤ Turn Signal Switch
⑥ Horn Button
⑦ Passing Button

Front Brake
Light Switch

Br

Ignition
Switch

R/Bl
R W

4P Conn.

R/Y

Horn
12V 2.5A

Br Bk

Italian Model only (1275A)

Gy G Gy

Bk/Y Br/W Bk/Y Gy

6P Connector

G/W Br/W Bl/R Bk/Y
Br Bk/Y

6P Connector

Gy R/Bk Br LG Bk/Y
Bk/Y

Bk/Y Bk/Y Br/W
R/Bk R/Y

Front Right Turn Signal
Light 12V 21W

Brake Light Failure
Indicator Light
12V 3.4W

Tachometer Light
12V 3.4W

Oil Pressure Warning
Light 12V 3.4W

Right Turn Signal
Indicator Light 12V 3.4W

High Beam Indicator
Light 12V 3.4W

Neutral Indicator
Light 12V 3.4W

Left Turn Signal
Indicator Light 12V 3.4W

Headlight
12V 35/35W

City Light
12V 3.4W

Speedometer Light
12V 3.4W

Front Left Turn Signal
Light 12V 21W

Wiring diagram — UK Z440 A1

(1273A)

RIGHT HANDLEBAR SWITCH CONNECTIONS

Headlight Switch		
Color	Bl/W	Br/W
OFF		
ON	●	

Engine Stop Switch		
Color	Y/R	Br/W
OFF		
RUN		
OFF		

Starter Button		
Color	Black	Y/R
OFF		
ON		

IGNITION SWITCH CONNECTIONS

	Battery	Ignition	Tail 1	Tail 2
Color	White	Brown	R/Bl	Red
OFF				
ON				
PARK				

LEFT HANDLEBAR SWITCH CONNECTIONS

Passing Button	
Color	R/Bk
	Brown
PA	

Turn Signal Switch		
Color	Orange	Gray
	Green	
L		
R		
R/Y	Blue	

Dimmer Switch	
Color	R/Bk
HI	
LO	

Horn Button	
Color	Black
OFF	
ON	

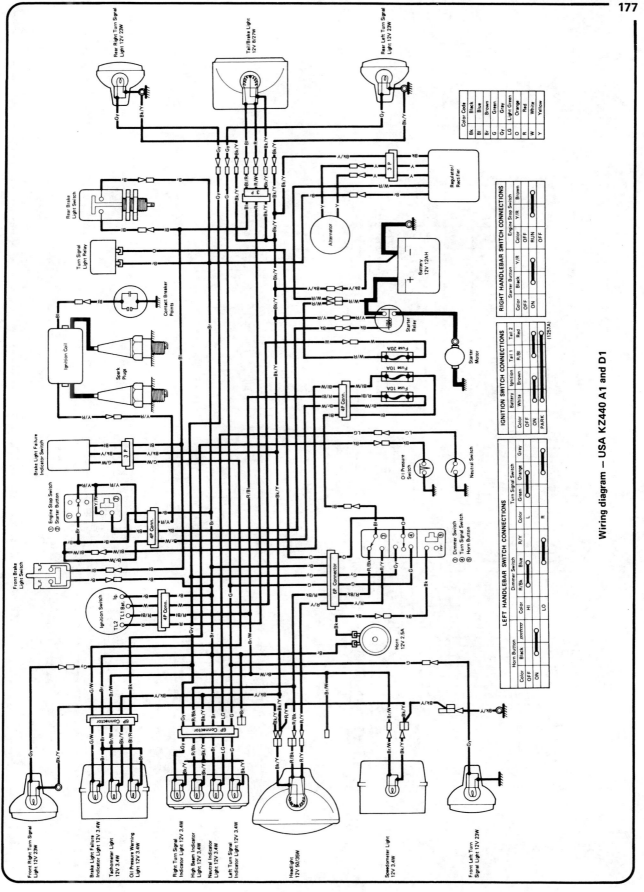

Wiring diagram – USA KZ440 A1 and D1

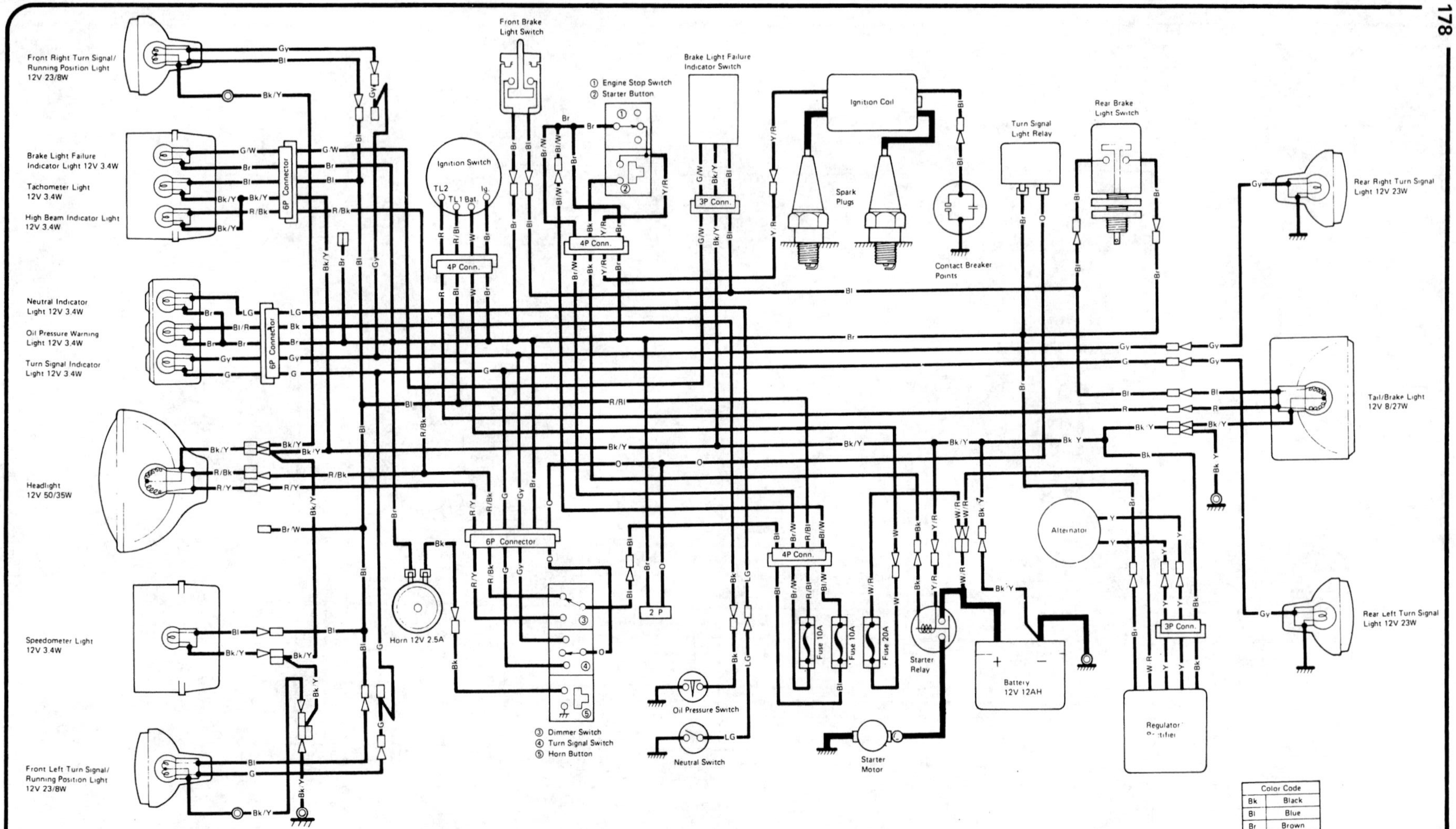

Wiring diagram – USA KZ440 B1

Rear Right Turn Signal Light 12V 23W

Tail/Brake Light 12V 8/27W

Rear Left Turn Signal Light 12V 23W

Rear Brake Light Switch

Turn Signal Light Relay

Contact Breaker Points

Ignition Coil

Spark Plugs

Brake Light Failure Indicator Switch

Engine Stop Switch
① Engine Stop Switch
② Starter Button

Front Brake Light Switch

Ignition Switch
TL2 TL1 Bat

Alternator

Battery 12V 12AH

Starter Relay

Starter Motor

Regulator Rectifier

3P Conn.

4P Conn.

Fuse 20A

Fuse 10A

Fuse 10A

Oil Pressure Switch

Neutral Switch

2 P

① Dimmer Switch
② Ignition Switch
③ Turn Signal Switch
④ Horn Button

6P Connector

Horn 12V 2.5A

Front Right Turn Signal/ Running Position Light 12V 23/8W

Brake Light Failure Indicator Light 12V 3.4W

Tachometer Light 12V 3.4W

High Beam Indicator Light 12V 3.4W

Neutral Indicator Light 12V 3.4W

Oil Pressure Warning Light 12V 3.4W

Turn Signal Indicator Light 12V 3.4W

Headlight 12V 50/35W

Speedometer Light 12V 3.4W

Front Left Turn Signal/ Running Position Light 12V 23/8W

6P Connector

6P Connector

Color Code	
Bk	Black
Bl	Blue
Br	Brown
G	Green
Gy	Gray
LG	Light Green
O	Orange
R	Red
W	White
Y	Yellow

LEFT HANDLEBAR SWITCH CONNECTIONS

Turn Signal Switch			
Color	L	Green	Gray
R			

Dimmer Switch		
Color	R/Bk	Blue
HI		
LO		

Horn Button		
Color	Black	
OFF		
ON		

IGNITION SWITCH CONNECTIONS

	Battery	Ignition	Tail 1	Tail 2	
Color	White	Brown	R/Bl	Red	
OFF					
ON					
PARK					

(1256A)

RIGHT HANDLEBAR SWITCH CONNECTIONS

Engine Stop Switch		
Color	Y/R	Brown
OFF		
RUN		
OFF		

Starter Button		
Color	Y/R	Black
OFF		
ON		

Wiring diagram — USA KZ440 A2 and D2

Wiring diagram — UK Z440 A2 and D2

Wiring diagram – USA KZ440 B2

Wiring diagram — UK Z440 C2

Safety first!

Professional motor mechanics are trained in safe working procedures. However enthusiastic you may be about getting on with the job in hand, do take the time to ensure that your safety is not put at risk. A moment's lack of attention can result in an accident, as can failure to observe certain elementary precautions.

There will always be new ways of having accidents, and the following points do not pretend to be a comprehensive list of all dangers; they are intended rather to make you aware of the risks and to encourage a safety-conscious approach to all work you carry out on your vehicle.

Essential DOs and DON'Ts

DON'T start the engine without first ascertaining that the transmission is in neutral.

DON'T suddenly remove the filler cap from a hot cooling system – cover it with a cloth and release the pressure gradually first, or you may get scalded by escaping coolant.

DON'T attempt to drain oil until you are sure it has cooled sufficiently to avoid scalding you.

DON'T grasp any part of the engine, exhaust or silencer without first ascertaining that it is sufficiently cool to avoid burning you.

DON'T allow brake fluid or antifreeze to contact the machine's paintwork or plastic components.

DON'T syphon toxic liquids such as fuel, brake fluid or antifreeze by mouth, or allow them to remain on your skin.

DON'T inhale dust – it may be injurious to health (see *Asbestos* heading).

DON'T allow any spilt oil or grease to remain on the floor – wipe it up straight away, before someone slips on it.

DON'T use ill-fitting spanners or other tools which may slip and cause injury.

DON'T attempt to lift a heavy component which may be beyond your capability – get assistance.

DON'T rush to finish a job, or take unverified short cuts.

DON'T allow children or animals in or around an unattended vehicle.

DON'T inflate a tyre to a pressure above the recommended maximum. Apart from overstressing the carcase and wheel rim, in extreme cases the tyre may blow off forcibly.

DO ensure that the machine is supported securely at all times. This is especially important when the machine is blocked up to aid wheel or fork removal.

DO take care when attempting to slacken a stubborn nut or bolt. It is generally better to pull on a spanner, rather than push, so that if slippage occurs you fall away from the machine rather than on to it.

DO wear eye protection when using power tools such as drill, sander, bench grinder etc.

DO use a barrier cream on your hands prior to undertaking dirty jobs – it will protect your skin from infection as well as making the dirt easier to remove afterwards; but make sure your hands aren't left slippery. Note that long-term contact with used engine oil can be a health hazard.

DO keep loose clothing (cuffs, tie etc) and long hair well out of the way of moving mechanical parts.

DO remove rings, wristwatch etc, before working on the vehicle – especially the electrical system.

DO keep your work area tidy – it is only too easy to fall over articles left lying around.

DO exercise caution when compressing springs for removal or installation. Ensure that the tension is applied and released in a controlled manner, using suitable tools which preclude the possibility of the spring escaping violently.

DO ensure that any lifting tackle used has a safe working load rating adequate for the job.

DO get someone to check periodically that all is well, when working alone on the vehicle.

DO carry out work in a logical sequence and check that everything is correctly assembled and tightened afterwards.

DO remember that your vehicle's safety affects that of yourself and others. If in doubt on any point, get specialist advice.

IF, in spite of following these precautions, you are unfortunate enough to injure yourself, seek medical attention as soon as possible.

Asbestos

Certain friction, insulating, sealing, and other products – such as brake linings, clutch linings, gaskets, etc – contain asbestos. *Extreme care must be taken to avoid inhalation of dust from such products since it is hazardous to health.* If in doubt, assume that they *do* contain asbestos.

Fire

Remember at all times that petrol (gasoline) is highly flammable. Never smoke, or have any kind of naked flame around, when working on the vehicle. But the risk does not end there – a spark caused by an electrical short-circuit, by two metal surfaces contacting each other, by careless use of tools, or even by static electricity built up in your body under certain conditions, can ignite petrol vapour, which in a confined space is highly explosive.

Always disconnect the battery earth (ground) terminal before working on any part of the fuel or electrical system, and never risk spilling fuel on to a hot engine or exhaust.

It is recommended that a fire extinguisher of a type suitable for fuel and electrical fires is kept handy in the garage or workplace at all times. Never try to extinguish a fuel or electrical fire with water.

Note: *Any reference to a 'torch' appearing in this manual should always be taken to mean a hand-held battery-operated electric lamp or flashlight. It does **not** mean a welding/gas torch or blowlamp.*

Fumes

Certain fumes are highly toxic and can quickly cause unconsciousness and even death if inhaled to any extent. Petrol (gasoline) vapour comes into this category, as do the vapours from certain solvents such as trichloroethylene. Any draining or pouring of such volatile fluids should be done in a well ventilated area.

When using cleaning fluids and solvents, read the instructions carefully. Never use materials from unmarked containers – they may give off poisonous vapours.

Never run the engine of a motor vehicle in an enclosed space such as a garage. Exhaust fumes contain carbon monoxide which is extremely poisonous; if you need to run the engine, always do so in the open air or at least have the rear of the vehicle outside the workplace.

The battery

Never cause a spark, or allow a naked light, near the vehicle's battery. It will normally be giving off a certain amount of hydrogen gas, which is highly explosive.

Always disconnect the battery earth (ground) terminal before working on the fuel or electrical systems.

If possible, loosen the filler plugs or cover when charging the battery from an external source. Do not charge at an excessive rate or the battery may burst.

Take care when topping up and when carrying the battery. The acid electrolyte, even when diluted, is very corrosive and should not be allowed to contact the eyes or skin.

If you ever need to prepare electrolyte yourself, always add the acid slowly to the water, and never the other way round. Protect against splashes by wearing rubber gloves and goggles.

Mains electricity and electrical equipment

When using an electric power tool, inspection light etc, always ensure that the appliance is correctly connected to its plug and that, where necessary, it is properly earthed (grounded). Do not use such appliances in damp conditions and, again, beware of creating a spark or applying excessive heat in the vicinity of fuel or fuel vapour. Also ensure that the appliances meet the relevant national safety standards.

Ignition HT voltage

A severe electric shock can result from touching certain parts of the ignition system, such as the HT leads, when the engine is running or being cranked, particularly if components are damp or the insulation is defective. Where an electronic ignition system is fitted, the HT voltage is much higher and could prove fatal.

Conversion factors

Length (distance)
Inches (in)	X	25.4	=	Millimetres (mm)	X	0.0394	= Inches (in)
Feet (ft)	X	0.305	=	Metres (m)	X	3.281	= Feet (ft)
Miles	X	1.609	=	Kilometres (km)	X	0.621	= Miles

Volume (capacity)
Cubic inches (cu in; in³)	X	16.387	=	Cubic centimetres (cc; cm³)	X	0.061	= Cubic inches (cu in; in³)
Imperial pints (Imp pt)	X	0.568	=	Litres (l)	X	1.76	= Imperial pints (Imp pt)
Imperial quarts (Imp qt)	X	1.137	=	Litres (l)	X	0.88	= Imperial quarts (Imp qt)
Imperial quarts (Imp qt)	X	1.201	=	US quarts (US qt)	X	0.833	= Imperial quarts (Imp qt)
US quarts (US qt)	X	0.946	=	Litres (l)	X	1.057	= US quarts (US qt)
Imperial gallons (Imp gal)	X	4.546	=	Litres (l)	X	0.22	= Imperial gallons (Imp gal)
Imperial gallons (Imp gal)	X	1.201	=	US gallons (US gal)	X	0.833	= Imperial gallons (Imp gal)
US gallons (US gal)	X	3.785	=	Litres (l)	X	0.264	= US gallons (US gal)

Mass (weight)
Ounces (oz)	X	28.35	=	Grams (g)	X	0.035	= Ounces (oz)
Pounds (lb)	X	0.454	=	Kilograms (kg)	X	2.205	= Pounds (lb)

Force
Ounces-force (ozf; oz)	X	0.278	=	Newtons (N)	X	3.6	= Ounces-force (ozf; oz)
Pounds-force (lbf; lb)	X	4.448	=	Newtons (N)	X	0.225	= Pounds-force (lbf; lb)
Newtons (N)	X	0.1	=	Kilograms-force (kgf; kg)	X	9.81	= Newtons (N)

Pressure
Pounds-force per square inch (psi; lbf/in²; lb/in²)	X	0.070	=	Kilograms-force per square centimetre (kgf/cm²; kg/cm²)	X	14.223	= Pounds-force per square inch (psi; lbf/in²; lb/in²)
Pounds-force per square inch (psi; lbf/in²; lb/in²)	X	0.068	=	Atmospheres (atm)	X	14.696	= Pounds-force per square inch (psi; lbf/in²; lb/in²)
Pounds-force per square inch (psi; lbf/in²; lb/in²)	X	0.069	=	Bars	X	14.5	= Pounds-force per square inch (psi; lbf/in²; lb/in²)
Pounds-force per square inch (psi; lbf/in²; lb/in²)	X	6.895	=	Kilopascals (kPa)	X	0.145	= Pounds-force per square inch (psi; lbf/in²; lb/in²)
Kilopascals (kPa)	X	0.01	=	Kilograms-force per square centimetre (kgf/cm²; kg/cm²)	X	98.1	= Kilopascals (kPa)
Millibar (mbar)	X	100	=	Pascals (Pa)	X	0.01	= Millibar (mbar)
Millibar (mbar)	X	0.0145	=	Pounds-force per square inch (psi; lbf/in²; lb/in²)	X	68.947	= Millibar (mbar)
Millibar (mbar)	X	0.75	=	Millimetres of mercury (mmHg)	X	1.333	= Millibar (mbar)
Millibar (mbar)	X	0.401	=	Inches of water (inH₂O)	X	2.491	= Millibar (mbar)
Millimetres of mercury (mmHg)	X	0.535	=	Inches of water (inH₂O)	X	1.868	= Millimetres of mercury (mmHg)
Inches of water (inH₂O)	X	0.036	=	Pounds-force per square inch (psi; lbf/in²; lb/in²)	X	27.68	= Inches of water (inH₂O)

Torque (moment of force)
Pounds-force inches (lbf in; lb in)	X	1.152	=	Kilograms-force centimetre (kgf cm; kg cm)	X	0.868	= Pounds-force inches (lbf in; lb in)
Pounds-force inches (lbf in; lb in)	X	0.113	=	Newton metres (Nm)	X	8.85	= Pounds-force inches (lbf in; lb in)
Pounds-force inches (lbf in; lb in)	X	0.083	=	Pounds-force feet (lbf ft; lb ft)	X	12	= Pounds-force inches (lbf in; lb in)
Pounds-force feet (lbf ft; lb ft)	X	0.138	=	Kilograms-force metres (kgf m; kg m)	X	7.233	= Pounds-force feet (lbf ft; lb ft)
Pounds-force feet (lbf ft; lb ft)	X	1.356	=	Newton metres (Nm)	X	0.738	= Pounds-force feet (lbf ft; lb ft)
Newton metres (Nm)	X	0.102	=	Kilograms-force metres (kgf m; kg m)	X	9.804	= Newton metres (Nm)

Power
Horsepower (hp)	X	745.7	=	Watts (W)	X	0.0013	= Horsepower (hp)

Velocity (speed)
Miles per hour (miles/hr; mph)	X	1.609	=	Kilometres per hour (km/hr; kph)	X	0.621	= Miles per hour (miles/hr; mph)

Fuel consumption*
Miles per gallon, Imperial (mpg)	X	0.354	=	Kilometres per litre (km/l)	X	2.825	= Miles per gallon, Imperial (mpg)
Miles per gallon, US (mpg)	X	0.425	=	Kilometres per litre (km/l)	X	2.352	= Miles per gallon, US (mpg)

Temperature

Degrees Fahrenheit = (°C x 1.8) + 32

Degrees Celsius (Degrees Centigrade; °C) = (°F - 32) x 0.56

*It is common practice to convert from miles per gallon (mpg) to litres/100 kilometres (l/100km), where mpg (Imperial) x l/100 km = 282 and mpg (US) x l/100 km = 235

English/American terminology

Because this book has been written in England, British English component names, phrases and spellings have been used throughout. American English usage is quite often different and whereas normally no confusion should occur, a list of equivalent terminology is given below.

English	American	English	American
Air filter	Air cleaner	Number plate	License plate
Alignment (headlamp)	Aim	Output or layshaft	Countershaft
Allen screw/key	Socket screw/wrench	Panniers	Side cases
Anticlockwise	Counterclockwise	Paraffin	Kerosene
Bottom/top gear	Low/high gear	Petrol	Gasoline
Bottom/top yoke	Bottom/top triple clamp	Petrol/fuel tank	Gas tank
Bush	Bushing	Pinking	Pinging
Carburettor	Carburetor	Rear suspension unit	Rear shock absorber
Catch	Latch	Rocker cover	Valve cover
Circlip	Snap ring	Selector	Shifter
Clutch drum	Clutch housing	Self-locking pliers	Vise-grips
Dip switch	Dimmer switch	Side or parking lamp	Parking or auxiliary light
Disulphide	Disulfide	Side or prop stand	Kick stand
Dynamo	DC generator	Silencer	Muffler
Earth	Ground	Spanner	Wrench
End float	End play	Split pin	Cotter pin
Engineer's blue	Machinist's dye	Stanchion	Tube
Exhaust pipe	Header	Sulphuric	Sulfuric
Fault diagnosis	Trouble shooting	Sump	Oil pan
Float chamber	Float bowl	Swinging arm	Swingarm
Footrest	Footpeg	Tab washer	Lock washer
Fuel/petrol tap	Petcock	Top box	Trunk
Gaiter	Boot	Torch	Flashlight
Gearbox	Transmission	Two/four stroke	Two/four cycle
Gearchange	Shift	Tyre	Tire
Gudgeon pin	Wrist/piston pin	Valve collar	Valve retainer
Indicator	Turn signal	Valve collets	Valve cotters
Inlet	Intake	Vice	Vise
Input shaft or mainshaft	Mainshaft	Wheel spindle	Axle
Kickstart	Kickstarter	White spirit	Stoddard solvent
Lower leg	Slider	Windscreen	Windshield
Mudguard	Fender		

Index